GUIDE TO
Colorado Backroads & 4-Wheel Drive Trails

By **CHARLES A. WELLS**

Easy • Moderate • Difficult
Backcountry Driving Adventures

FunTreks, Inc.

Published by FunTreks, Inc.
P.O. Box 49187, Colorado Springs, CO 80949-9187
Phone:(719) 536-0722   E Mail: funtreks@pcisys.net

Copyright © 1998 by FunTreks, Inc.

Edited by Shelley Mayer

Cover design, photography, maps, and production by Charles A.Wells

First Edition

Library of Congress Catalog Card Number 98-93117
ISBN 0-9664976-0-0

Produced in the United States of America

HOW TO ORDER MORE BOOKS:

Telephone orders: Call Toll Free: 1(877) 222-7623. We accept VISA or MasterCard. Please have your card ready when you call.
Mail Orders: Send check plus name and address to:
FunTreks, Inc. P.O. Box 49187, Colorado Springs, CO 80949-9187.
Cost: $18.95 per book plus $4.00 shipping for first book and $2.00 for each additional book. (All books ship Priority Mail.) Add 60 cents tax for each book shipped to Colorado. If you live in Colorado Springs, total tax is $1.22 per book.
Guarantee: Money back if not satisfied, no questions asked.

DISCLAIMER

Travel in the Colorado backcountry is by its very nature potentially dangerous and could result in property damage, injury, or even death. The scope of this book cannot predict every possible hazard you may encounter. If you drive any of the trails in this book, you acknowledge these risks and assume full responsibility. You are the final judge as to whether a trail is safe to drive on any given day, whether your vehicle is capable of the journey, and what supplies you should carry. The information contained herein cannot replace good judgment and proper preparation on your part. The publisher and author of this book disclaim any and all liability for bodily injury, death, or property damage that could occur to you or any of your passengers.

ACKNOWLEDGMENTS

The process of writing this book has taken two years, and during that time many people have helped me by sharing their time, knowledge, and experience. I sincerely thank them all and will forever be grateful.

My wife, Beverly, has seen little of me while I've been working on this book. Without complaint, she has allowed me the freedom and time to explore this large and wonderful state of Colorado. In addition, she has been my technical advisor while I have grappled with the frustrations of keeping a complex computer system running. Most of all, she has encouraged me to continue this project even when I had self doubts.

I thank my family for their support and encouragement. To my parents, Margaret and Carl Wells, thanks for showing me how to chart my own course in life. I know the allure of four-wheeling remains a mystery to you.

To all my friends in the Colorado Four-Wheelers, I thank you for sharing your years of experience and for introducing me to the hard-core side of four-wheeling. Special thanks to Larry Leaveck, Neale Geis, Bob Niehoff, Larry Miller, Rolf Whitley, and Ron Christensen whose combined years of four-wheeling experience exceed my half century on this earth. Your patience and counsel have been invaluable.

To Linda Meyer, a four-wheeling friend and Macintosh expert, thanks for your helpful support and advice.

To my many friends at Current, Inc., where I work full-time as a print production manager, thanks for helping me convert my outdated graphic design experience to the Macintosh age. Thanks to: Jim Magill, Bill Taack, Karen Sherry, John Chlebus, Jeff Beverly, Tim Hardesty, Yudthana Pongmee, Susie Schaarschmidt, Scott Smith, Garry Dufford, Kyle Toburen, Kevin Smith, Jan Hogan, Gary Benson, Peggy Moran, Chuck Dove, Toni Skinner, Eric Goldinak, and Ron Oatney. I would also like to thank Shelley Mayer, a long time friend and colleague at Current for her painstaking effort in editing this book.

Thanks to Neil Brand, a friend in the publishing business, whose enthusiasm for this project always buoyed my spirits.

And finally, thanks to the U.S. Forest Service, the Bureau of Land Management, Tread Lightly!,® and the BlueRibbon Coalition, who helped teach me the importance of responsible land use and how we must all work together to preserve our ever-threatened backcountry.

Tread Lightly! is a registered trademark of Tread Lightly!, Inc.

Schofield Pass/Crystal River, Trail #19, rated difficult.

Contents

Trails Listed by Area

Statewide Locator Map

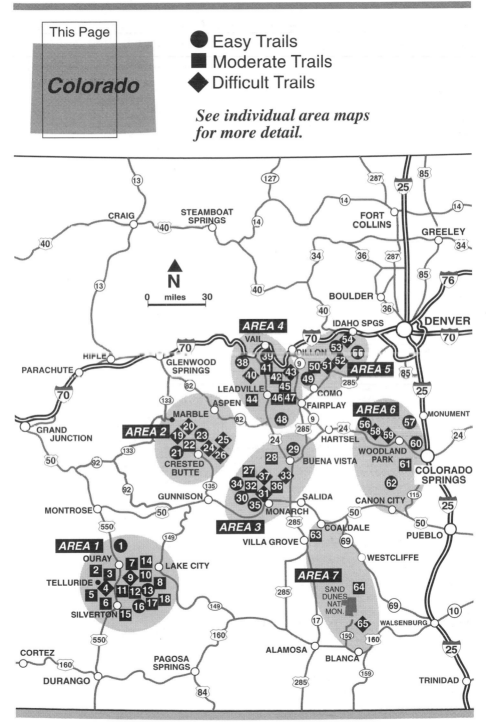

This Page

Colorado

● Easy Trails
■ Moderate Trails
◆ Difficult Trails

See individual area maps for more detail.

N
0 miles 30

CRAIG
STEAMBOAT SPRINGS
FORT COLLINS
GREELEY
PARACHUTE
RIFLE
GLENWOOD SPRINGS
BOULDER
IDAHO SPGS
DENVER
GRAND JUNCTION
MARBLE
ASPEN
LEADVILLE
VAIL
DILLON
COMO
FAIRPLAY
MONUMENT
MONTROSE
GUNNISON
CRESTED BUTTE
HARTSEL
WOODLAND PARK
COLORADO SPRINGS
BUENA VISTA
SALIDA
CANON CITY
PUEBLO
MONARCH
COALDALE
VILLA GROVE
WESTCLIFFE
OURAY
LAKE CITY
TELLURIDE
SILVERTON
SAND DUNES NAT. MON.
WALSENBURG
CORTEZ
ALAMOSA
BLANCA
PAGOSA SPRINGS
DURANGO
TRINIDAD

AREA 1
AREA 2
AREA 3
AREA 4
AREA 5
AREA 6
AREA 7

Trails Listed by Difficulty

The trails below are ranked by difficulty. Within each rating category, the first trail listed is the easiest and the last is the most difficult. For example Tincup Pass is the most difficult of the moderate trails and Lead King Basin is the easiest of the difficult trails. Although ratings are always subjective, this ranking should help in your trail selection.

Trail Ratings Defined

Trail ratings are very subjective. Descriptions attempt to describe worst case scenarios under good weather conditions, but not all situations are predictable. You must weigh your experience and confidence against the conditions of the day. Obviously not all of these conditions exist on every trail. Read each trail description carefully. The rating is based on the worst part of the trail. Remember, snow, ice, heavy rain, spring run-off, or other adverse conditions can increase the difficulty of a trail.

 ## Easy

Graded dirt road with possible short stretches of rocks, ruts, and washed out areas. Gentle grades. Water depths could reach mid hubcap. Be more careful about water depths during heavy run-off periods. Full single lane or wider with adequate room to pass most of the time. Off-camber areas minimal. Four-wheel drive recommended on most trails but some are suitable for two-wheel drive under dry conditions. Read the description carefully to be sure.

 ## Moderate

Rutted dirt or rocky road suitable for most sport utility vehicles. Four-wheel drive, low range, and high ground clearance required. Standard factory skid plates and tow hooks recommended on many trails. Rocks or holes may cause undercarriage to bottom out occasionally. Some grades fairly steep but manageable if dry. Some off-camber areas will require caution. Minimal narrow shelf roads. Water depths could reach bumper in a few situations. Be more careful about water depths during heavy run-off periods. Backing may be necessary to pass. Mud holes may be present.

 ## Difficult

Generally suitable for more aggressive stock vehicles or modified vehicles. Lifts, differential lockers, aggressive articulation, and/or winches recommended on some trails. Skid plates and tow hooks required. Body damage possible on obstacles. Grades can be steep with severe ground undulation. Off-camber areas can be extreme. Water depths extremely deep. Shelf roads extremely narrow; full-size vehicles use caution and read trail description carefully. Passing may be difficult with backing required for long distances. Brush may scrape sides of vehicle. Deep mud bogs possible.

Trails Listed Alphabetically

AUTHOR'S FAVORITE TRAILS
IN BOLD FACE TYPE

INTRODUCTION

Clear Lake, Trail #6, Moderate.

Introduction

From the first day I took my new sport utility into the Colorado back-country, I was hooked. It was more fun than I ever imagined. Why I waited so long to try this I'll never know. I guess I was a little afraid not knowing what to do or where to go. I was sure I'd damage my vehicle in some way. Years later, after hundreds of miles of backroads, I've got one small dent in my roof from hauling a Christmas tree home from the mall. I think of all the years of fun I wasted and kick myself.

Later I joined a four-wheel drive club and learned the hard-core side of wheeling. I bought a second vehicle and made a few modifications. I tackled the hardest trails in Colorado, Utah, and California, including Holy Cross, Blanca Peak, Pritchett Canyon, and the Rubicon...didn't take too many chicken routes either. Yes, I've got a dent or two, but each is a story I can tell my grandchildren.

Now that I've tried both kinds of wheeling, I can't decide which I like better. I love the luxury of my SUV, sitting back in those soft seats, the automatic transmission, air conditioning, and power windows making my life hassle free, looking out the window and watching some of the most beautiful country in the world go by. On the other hand, I'll always enjoy the thrill of driving my hard-core rig up a road so steep and rough all I see is clouds bouncing in the sky.

I'm sure of one thing, I've got a burning desire to share this love of the Colorado backcountry with you. I'll show you how to safely get to beautiful remote locations, how to select a trail that matches your vehicle's capability, and how to relax with the confidence of knowing what needs to be done. I'll share with you what I've learned from my direct experience, my many knowledgeable friends, and my sizable collection of maps, photos, personal notes, magazines, newspapers, and other books. I promise I won't sugar-coat things and get you into trouble. Let's face it, driving over a remote 12,000-foot mountain pass is a lot different from a Sunday drive across Ohio in the family station wagon. Read this book carefully and I think you too will find the confidence to venture to places you never thought possible.

HOW TO USE THIS BOOK

This book has been designed for quick and easy use. Trails are grouped by area. First use the state locator map on page 7 to determine the big picture, then turn to each area map for more detail. Each trail is shown with photos and a map. All maps are to scale and oriented with north at the top. Scale is indicated using an overall grid. Check the size of the grid at the bottom of each map. A small legend or "Mini Key" is included on each map for quick reference. Find the full map legend on page 30.

The shaded portion of the trail is described in the text. Other roads are for reference only and should be traveled at your own risk. Water crossing and bridge symbols show major stream locations. Read each map for boundary designations. Trails are described in one direction with the starting point clearly indicated. In certain cases, additional directions are given to the other end of the trail.

Trails are listed three ways for your convenience: by area on page 6, by difficulty on page 8, and alphabetically on page 10. Geometric shapes are used to indicate difficulty. A circle indicates easy, a square moderate, and a diamond difficult. Trail ratings are described in detail on page 9. Finer difficulty ratings can be determined by the order of the trails on page 8. Each trail listed is progressively more difficult than the last, although distinctions from one trail to the next may be negligible.

The text for each trail includes: general location, difficulty details, special features, approximate length and driving time, details of the drive, directions home, location of nearest services, and other maps. Other activities and historical highlights are shown for some trails.

Mileages can vary because of vehicle differences and driving habits. Readings were rounded to the nearest tenth of a mile.

The appendix of this book includes a glossary, a list of references and recommended reading, helpful addresses and phone numbers, and an index.

SELECTING THE RIGHT TRAIL FOR YOUR VEHICLE

Today's modern sport utility vehicles are amazingly well designed for off-highway travel. Modern technology is making the backcountry accessible to ever more capable stock vehicles. More and more people are buying sport utilities and setting out to discover the fun that other SUV owners are having. Sometimes, however, beginners think that once they buy a four-wheel drive vehicle, it will go anywhere. They soon learn that this is not the case. The following will help you decide which trails are right for your vehicle.

Easy: Suitable for all stock four-wheel drive sport utility vehicles with high ground clearance and low range. Some trails can be driven in two-wheel drive without low range in dry weather. A few trails, under ideal conditions, are suitable for passenger cars.

Moderate: Suitable for most stock sport utility vehicles with high ground clearance and low range. For the toughest moderate trails, factory skid plates, tow hooks, and all-terrain tires are recommended. These options are available from your dealer or local four-wheel drive shop.

Difficult: Suitable for some stock sport utility vehicles with very high ground clearance, excellent articulation, tow hooks, and a full skid plate package. All-terrain tires as a minimum, mud terrains preferred. A winch or differential lockers are recommended for the most difficult trails. Drivers who spend a great deal of time on extreme trails find it advantageous to modify their vehicles with higher ground clearance, oversized tires, and heavy duty accessories.

(These are general descriptions. Read each trail description carefully for more detail.)

IMPORTANT FACTS ABOUT COLORADO

Although similar to other Rocky Mountain states, Colorado is unique in many ways. If you are new to mountain driving, read this part carefully.

It's a big place. Colorado is a large state by eastern standards. When I first moved here from Ohio almost 20 years ago, I was surprised at how long it took to get from one place to another. When traveling to trails, check the scale of the map and determine the total number of miles to your destination. Then allow plenty of time to get there. Terrain varies considerably from one part of the state to the other, so the landscape will likely be quite different at your destination. Allow extra time for slower speeds on winding roads and washboard roads. Fortunately, the drive to the trail can be as beautiful as the trail itself. So take your time, be patient, and enjoy the ride.

When to go. The length of the four-wheel drive season in Colorado depends on the elevation of the trail. Some trails at low elevations open in late May. More trails open in June. High mountain passes typically are passable the first or second week in July; however, there are are exceptions like Pearl Pass (Trail #24) and Mosquito Pass (Trail #46) which open later. Trails in the Ouray Area (Area 1) open earlier because plows begin clearing high mountain passes very early. The best time of year to find most trails open is in August and September. September also is the peak time to enjoy the changing colors of the aspens. You may squeeze in some very late season wheeling in early October if no early winter snow has fallen. But be aware the regular Colorado hunting season begins the second week of October.

Start as early as possible in the day. Mornings are usually clear while afternoons are often cloudy with a greater chance of thunderstorms. Allow a sizable margin of daylight for your return trip to avoid being on the trail at night.

The weather. Colorado weather is often very pleasant and more moderate than people expect. Low humidity at high elevations keeps temperatures cool in the summer. In the winter, the sun shines most of the time and it stays relatively warm. There are few flies and mosquitoes except around wetlands. The downside to Colorado weather is that it is very unpredictable and can be extreme at times. Although it doesn't happen frequently, it can snow anytime during the summer, especially at higher elevations and at night when temperatures drop. Colorado can also be very windy. Pack plenty of warm clothing regardless of how hot it might be when you depart. Also, make sure you drink plenty of fluids to help you adapt to the dry thin air. Use sunscreen because you will sunburn quicker.

Changing road conditions. Colorado loves to surprise you. Watch for unexpected ice, snow, landslides, avalanches, fallen trees, washouts, deep water, and leaping deer. A clay surface road can be passable when dry but very slippery if wet.

Lightning. Thunderstorms, hail, and lightning are very common in Colorado, especially in the late afternoon. Stay below timberline if you see a storm approaching. If you get stuck above timberline, a hardtop vehicle offers more safety from lightning than being outside, but don't touch anything metal inside your vehicle. Lightning can strike from a distant storm even when it is sunny overhead.

Fires and floods. Although extremely rare, you must be aware of the possibility of forest fires and flash floods. Fires can move quickly, so watch for smoke when you are at higher points. At certain times of year, fire danger can be extremely high and the Forest Service will post fire danger warnings. During these times, campfires may be prohibited. Fines can be very steep for violators. Heavy rainstorms can cause flash floods at any time during the spring and summer. The danger is particularly acute if you are in a narrow canyon. If you have reason to believe a flash flood is imminent, do not try to outrun it in your car. Abandon your car and climb to higher ground. Most flash flood deaths occur in vehicles.

Altitude sickness. Some people experience nausea, dizziness, headaches, or weakness the first time at high altitude. This condition usually improves over time. To minimize symptoms, give yourself time to acclimate, drink plenty of fluids, decrease salt intake, reduce alcohol and caffeine, eat foods high in carbohydrates, and try not to exert yourself. If symptoms become severe, the only sure remedy is to return to a lower altitude. Consult your doctor before going to higher altitudes if you have health problems.

Hypothermia. Hypothermia is possible even in the summer. If you get caught in a sudden shower at high altitude, your body temperature can drop suddenly. Always take rain gear and extra clothing.

Don't drink the water. No matter how cool, clear, or refreshing a mountain stream or lake may appear, never drink the water. Don't let anyone convince you that high altitude water is safe. If you must drink mountain water, boil it or use iodine tablets for purification. These are available at most sporting goods stores in Colorado. Carry your own drinking water.

Mine shafts, tunnels, and old structures. Be careful around old mine buildings. Do not enter or climb on any structures. Stay away from mine shafts and tunnels. Do not let children play in these areas.

RULES OF THE ROAD

The laws of Colorado.

• Most trails require that you be licensed, street legal, and carry a valid driver's license if driving.

• Vehicles traveling uphill always have the right of way, but use common sense. If you are closer to a wide spot, move over for the other vehicle.

• Don't drink and drive.

• All vehicles including mountain bikes are prohibited in Wilderness areas.

Forest Service rules.

• Travel only on roads with signs displaying a Forest Service number, or in some forests, a small white arrow.

• Stay on the trail at all times. Don't take shortcuts at switchbacks, or drive around bad spots. Sometimes other drivers take shortcuts that you know are not responsible. Don't use their tracks as an excuse to make the same mistake. This is how illegal trails get started.

• Trails are closed for valid reasons that may not be apparent to you. Do not under any circumstances enter a closed trail.

• Forest Service roads frequently pass through private property. If a gate is unlocked, and there are no "no trespassing" signs on the gate, it is usually okay to pass through, but make sure you leave the gate the way you found it. Close gate if indicated. When following a Forest Service road across private property, stay on the trail at all times.

• Pack out your trash except in fee areas that have approved receptacles. Never throw your trash into pit toilets.

• Never drive across open meadows. Do not walk or drive on delicate tundra, pick wildflowers, or remove anything from mining or other historical sights.

• Camp within 300 feet of the road.

• Don't park your vehicle in tall grass. The intense heat from your catalytic converter may start a fire.

• Human waste should be buried 6 to 8 inches deep at least 200 feet from any water source, campsite, or trail. Keep a small shovel handy for this purpose. If possible carry a portable camping toilet.

• Consult Forest Service maps for special land use regulations.

Trail Etiquette.

• Drive slowly and use caution at all times, especially around blind curves.

• Try to be as quiet as possible. Don't play your radio loudly, gun your engine, or spin your tires. Use your horn sparingly for emergencies only. Smile and be courteous to everyone. Help create a positive image for four-wheeling.

• Always pull over to the side of the road when you are out of your vehicle or not moving. Pull over for bikers and hikers. Stop and shut off your engine for horses and pack animals.

• Avoid crossing streams if possible, but if you must cross, do it at designated crossings only.

• If someone overtakes you, pull over and let them pass.

• Control your pets at all times. Don't let them bark or chase wildlife.

Camping guidelines.

• Use developed or existing campsites whenever possible.

• Camp away from streams, lakes, hiking trails, and historical mining sites. Leave as much distance as possible between you and other campers. Respect the privacy of others.

• Use a gas stove if possible and try to avoid fires. If you must have a fire, build it inside a fire ring of rocks, preferably one that is already there. Bring your own firewood if possible. Don't cut trees or branches. Let the fire burn itself out so only ashes remain. Spread the ashes to make sure they are cold. If you must douse the fire, do it thoroughly. If you've thrown bottles or cans into the fire that have not disintegrated, pack them as trash.

• Avoid using soap if at all possible and never around lakes or streams. Heat water to clean utensils. If you must use soap to bathe, use as little as possible. Do not bathe in or near a lake or stream.

• Plan your trip carefully and prepack your food in plastic bags or reusable containers. There will be less trash to haul away.

• Inspect the area thoroughly before leaving and make sure nothing is left lying around. The goal is to leave the area the way you found it or better.

SAFETY TIPS

Wear your seat belt. You might think that because you are driving slowly, it's not necessary to wear your seat belt or use child restraints. I've learned through experience that you are much safer with a seatbelt than without. Buckle up at all times.

Keep heads, arms, and legs inside moving vehicle. Many trails are narrow. Brush, tree limbs, and rock overhangs may come very close to your vehicle. The driver must make it clear to every passenger to stay inside the vehicle at all times. Children, in particular, must not be allowed to stick their heads, arms, or legs out the windows.

Extra maps. The maps in this book will clearly direct you along the trail. However, if you get lost or decide to venture down a spur road, you'll need additional maps with more detail. At the end of each trail description, I have listed other helpful maps. I recommend you get at least one of these maps. *National Forest Service maps* are the most commonly used. A scale of 1/2 inch to a mile is adequate. More than one map may be necessary if the trail crosses forest boundaries. Forest Service maps are usually the least expensive but are not frequently updated. More expensive but worth the money are *Trails Illustrated Topo Maps*. These maps are updated every year and are made of durable waterproof plastic material. They include topographic information and the graphics are outstanding. Their only shortcoming is that they don't cover the entire state; however, they do cover most of the popular areas. Another map I strongly recommend is the *DeLorme Colorado Atlas & Gazetteer*. This is an oversized atlas that breaks down the entire state into sections. If you look hard enough you can find every trail in this book. It has a lot of detail with some topographic information but the type is small. It is a handy size because you don't have to unfold it. Although it costs as much as several of the other maps, it's an excellent investment because of its statewide coverage. All of these maps can be purchased at most larger bookstores. You can also buy Forest Service maps from your local National Forest Service office. Make sure you are buying the latest version available.

Spend a little time looking over the maps before you head out. Familiarize yourself as much as possible with the map and the area. When you get on the trail, don't be surprised to find inaccuracies on any of the maps. You can't always count on trail markers or road signs matching what is on the map. Sometimes signs have been updated but the maps have not. Many signs have been removed or vandalized.

Travel with another vehicle. Travel with other vehicles whenever possible. If you must go alone, stay on the easier, more traveled routes. Never travel alone on difficult trails. Make sure you tell someone where you are going and your return time. Leave a plan of your route if possible. Report in at preset times or after you return.

If you can't find anyone to travel with you, call ahead or write to a four-wheel drive club in the specific area of your trip and ask for help. Make sure you explain your level of experience. To locate the club nearest you, call or write the Colorado Association of 4 Wheel Drive Clubs, Inc. (See address and phone number in back of book.)

Join a four-wheel drive club. Most clubs have runs on easy as well as difficult routes but ask to make sure. Select a club most appropriate for you.

If you get lost or stuck, stay with your vehicle unless you are very close to help. Your vehicle will provide shelter and is easier to see.

Inspect your vehicle carefully. Before you start into the backcountry, make sure your vehicle is in top operating condition. If you have a mechanic do the work, make sure he is reliable and understands four-wheeling. Tell him where you plan to take your vehicle. Pay particular attention to fluids, hoses, belts, battery, brakes, steering linkage, suspension system, driveline, and anything exposed under the vehicle. Tighten anything that may be loose. Inspect your tires carefully for potential weak spots and tread wear.

Supplies and equipment to take. No single list can be all inclusive. You must be the final judge of what you need. Here's a list of basic items:

❑ Plenty of food and water. Allow enough water for drinking and extra for the vehicle. Carry water purification tablets for emergencies.

❑ Extra clothing, shoes, socks, coats, and hats even in the summer. It gets very cold at night at higher elevations.

❑ Sleeping bags in case you get stuck overnight even if you are not planning to camp.

❑ A good first aid kit including sunscreen and insect repellent.

❑ Candle, matches, and a lighter

❑ An extra set of keys and glasses.

❑ Toilet paper, paper towels, wet wipes, and trash bags.

❑ A large plastic sheet or tarp.

❑ Rain gear.

❑ Detailed maps, compass, watch, and a knife.

❑ If you plan to make a fire, carry your own firewood.

❑ Work gloves.

❑ A heavy duty tow strap.

❑ A fire extinguisher. Make sure you know where it is and can get to it easily.

❑ Jumper cables.

❑ Replacement fuses and electrical tape.

❑ Flashlight and extra batteries.

❑ A full tank of gas If you carry extra gas make sure it is in an approved container and properly stored.

❑ A good set of tools.

❑ Baling wire and duct tape.

❑ An assortment of hose clamps, nuts, bolts, and washers.

❑ A full-size spare tire. Small emergency tires arc not adequate in the backcountry.

❑ A tire pressure gauge, electric tire pump that will plug into your cigarette lighter, and a can of nonflammable tire sealant.

❑ A jack that will lift your vehicle fairly high off the ground. Take a small board to place under the jack. Carry a high lift jack if you can, especially on more difficult trails. Test your jack before you leave home.

❑ Shovel and axe. Folding shovels work great.

❑ Tire chains.

❑ CB radio and/or cellular phone.

❑ Portable toilet.

❑ If you have a winch, carry a tree strap, clevis, and snatch block.

Store these items in tote bags or large plastic containers so they can be easily loaded into your vehicle when it's time to go. Make sure you tie everything down thoroughly so it doesn't bounce around or shift.

Maintenance. Backroad travel puts your vehicle under greater stress than normal highway driving. Follow maintenance directions in your owners manual for severe driving conditions. This usually calls for changing your oil, oil filter, and air filter more frequently as well as more frequent fluid checks and lubrications. Inspect your tires carefully; they take a lot of extra abuse. After your trip, make sure you wash your vehicle. Use a high pressure spray to thoroughly clean the underside and wheel wells. Automatic car washes usually are not adequate. Do it yourself, if you want your vehicle in good shape for the next trip.

YOUR RESPONSIBILITIES AS A BACKCOUNTRY DRIVER

It is imperative that we educate ourselves on minimum impact driving techniques and diligently practice what we learn. If we don't, we will eventually lose our rights to use our remote lands. Fortunately, there are organizations whose goal is to educate the public on low impact recreational techniques. Two of the largest and most respected organizations are *Tread Lightly!, Inc.* and the *BlueRibbon Coalition.*

Tread Lightly!,® Inc. This national non-profit organization was established in 1990 to protect public and private lands by educating as many people as possible in the proper use of off-highway vehicles. It is supported by donations from corporate members including manufacturers of off-highway vehicles, environmental groups, user associations including many four-wheel drive clubs, government agencies, and people like you and me who are fighting to keep the backcountry open to enjoy. The suggestions of *Tread Lightly* are simple. Please read them, abide by them and pass them along to others.

- **T**ravel only where permitted
- **R**espect the rights of others
- **E**ducate yourself
- **A**void streams, meadows, wildlife areas, etc.
- **D**rive and travel responsibly

Join today. You'll receive many educational materials and be supporting a great cause. Your membership also includes a *Tread Lightly* bumper sticker, patch, lapel pin, quarterly newsletter, and other materials. Call or write to the address shown in appendix.

BlueRibbon Coalition. No group fights harder to keep public lands open for responsible vehicular use. Their motto is "Preserving Our Natural Resources *For* the Public Instead of *From* the Public." This organization has people in Washington constantly watching over your rights. They frequently testify at hearings on land use issues and constantly work to convince your congressmen of the importance of keeping the backcountry open. They publish the informative monthly *BlueRibbon Magazine,* which is full of interesting articles on the latest governmental actions affecting land use. It also includes educational articles and reports of fun vehicular activities that are happening all over the country. Join today. See appendix for address and phone number.

Four-wheel drive organizations. Other information specific to four-wheeling is available from the Colorado Association of 4 Wheel Drive Clubs, Inc. and the national United Four Wheel Drive Associations, Inc. Both of these organizations publish informative monthly newsletters. See appendix for addresses and phone numbers. If you are from outside Colorado, you probably have your own state four-wheel drive organization. Contact the United Four Wheel Drive Associations, Inc. for information.

BACKCOUNTRY DRIVING TECHNIQUES

The basics. It may surprise you to learn that many SUV owners have never shifted their vehicles into low range. I once encountered an SUV on the most dangerous part of Schofield Pass (Trail #19). There were four vehicles in our group going uphill. Since he was a single vehicle and we had the right of way, we assumed he would back up and let us by. When he didn't, we asked him why. When he said he didn't have enough power to back up, we looked inside and noticed that he was not in low gear. When we pointed this out he seemed a little embarrassed. Apparently it never occurred to him what that other lever was for. It is situations like this that have provided extra motivation for me to write this book. I'd like to prevent others from getting themselves in such dangerous and helpless situations. If you read this book carefully, a similar situation is unlikely to happen to you. You'll recognize dangerous trails for which you are not yet ready, and when you are ready, you will know how to drive them safely.

If you have never shifted into low, grab your owner's manual now and start practicing. Read the rest of this book, then try some of the easy trails. Gradually you'll become more proficient and eventually you'll be ready to move up in difficulty.

Low and slow. Your vehicle was designed to go over rocky and bumpy terrain but only at slow speed. Get used to driving slowly in first gear low range. This will allow you to idle over obstacles without stalling. You don't need to shift back and forth constantly. Get into a low gear and stay there as much as possible so your engine can operate at high RPM and at maximum power. If you have a standard transmission, your goal should be to use your clutch as little as possible. As you encounter resistance on an obstacle or an uphill grade, just give it a little gas. As you start downhill, allow the engine's resistance to act as a brake. If the engine alone will not stop you from accelerating, then help a little with the brake. When you need more power but not more speed, press on the gas and feather the brake a little at the same time. This takes a little practice, but you will be amazed at the control you have. This technique works equally well with automatic transmissions.

Going clutchless. Standard transmissions can be safely started in first gear low range without depressing the clutch. The starter motor has the power, when geared down, to start the engine and car moving at the same time even on a steep hill. If you stall on a steep hill, simply turn the key to get moving again. This saves tremendous wear on the clutch. You'll look like a pro as your vehicle moves smoothly forward without jerking or rolling backwards. When it's time to stop the vehicle, simply turn off the key without depressing the clutch. Try it a few times and you'll see how easily it works. I repeat, you must be in first gear **low**. This technique will not work if you are totally jammed against a major obstacle or if your vehicle has a safety device that stops you from starting in gear.

Rocks and other high points. Never attempt to straddle a rock that is large enough to strike your differentials, transfer case or other low-hanging parts of your undercarriage. Instead, drive over the highest point with your tire, which is designed to take the abuse. This will lift your undercarriage over the obstacle. As you enter a rocky area, look ahead to determine where the high points are, then make every effort to cross them with your tires. Learn the low points of your undercarriage.

Using a spotter. Sometimes there are so many rocks you get confused about which way to go. In this case, have someone get out and guide you. They should stand at a safe distance in front, watching your tires and undercarriage. With hand signals, they can direct you left or right. If you are alone, don't be embarrassed to spot for yourself by getting in and out of your vehicle several times.

Those clunking sounds. Having made every attempt to avoid dragging bottom, you'll find it's not always possible. It is inevitable that a rock will contact your undercarriage eventually. The sound can be quite unnerving the first time it happens. If you are driving slowly and have proper skid plates, damage is unlikely. Look for a different line, back up and try again. If unsuccessful, see "Crossing large rocks" below.

Crossing a log. If the log is higher than your ground clearance, you will likely become high centered. Sometimes crossing at an angle helps. If you can't make it, build a ramp by stacking rocks on each side of the log. When done, put the rocks back where you found them. It might be possible to avoid driving over the log altogether by simply pulling the log to the side of the road with a tow strap or winch.

Crossing large rocks. Sometimes a rock is too large to drive over or at such a steep angle your bumper hits the rock before your tire. The solution is the same as crossing a log. Stack rocks on each side to form a ramp. Once over the obstacle, make sure you put the rocks back where you found them.

The next driver to come along may prefer the challenge of crossing the rock in its more difficult state.

Getting high centered. You may drive over a large rock or into a rut, causing you to get lodged on the object. If this happens, don't panic. First ask your passengers to get out to see if less weight helps. Try rocking the vehicle. If this doesn't work, jack up your vehicle and place a few rocks under the tires so that when you let the jack down, you take the weight off the high point. Determine whether driving forward or reverse is best and try again. You may have to repeat this procedure several times if you are seriously high centered. Eventually you will learn what you can and cannot drive over.

Look in all directions. Unlike highway driving in which your primary need for attention is straight ahead, backcountry driving requires you to look in all directions. Objects can block your path from above, below, and from the sides. Trees fall, branches droop, and rocks slide, making the trail into an ever-changing obstacle course.

Scout ahead. If you are on an unfamiliar trail and are concerned that the trail is becoming too difficult, get out of your vehicle and walk the trail ahead of you. This gives you an opportunity to pick an easy place to turn around before you get into trouble. If you have to turn around, back up or pull ahead until you find a wide flat spot. Don't try to turn in a narrow confined area. This can damage the trail and perhaps tip over your vehicle.

Anticipate. Shift into four wheel drive or low range before it is needed. If you wait until it is needed, conditions might be too difficult, e.g., halfway up a hillside.

Blind curves. When approaching blind curves, always assume that there is a speeding vehicle coming from the opposite direction. This will prepare you for the worst. Be aware that many people drive on the wrong side of the road to stay away from the outer edge of a trail. Whenever possible, keep your windows open and your radio off so that you can hear an approaching vehicle. You can usually hear motorcycles and ATVs. Quiet SUVs are the biggest problem. Collisions do occur so be careful.

Driving uphill. Use extreme caution when attempting to climb a hill. The difficulty of hill climbing is often misjudged by the novice four-wheeler. You should have good tires, adequate power, and be shifted into four-wheel drive low. There are four factors that determine difficulty:

Length of the hill. If the hill is very long, it is less likely that momentum will carry you to the top. Short hills are easier.

Traction. A rock surface is easier to climb than dirt.

Bumpiness. If the road surface undulates to the point where all four tires do not stay on the ground at the same time, you will have great difficulty climbing even a moderately steep hill.

Steepness. This can be difficult to judge, so examine a hill carefully before you attempt it. Walk up the hill if necessary to make sure it is not steeper at the top. If you are not absolutely sure you can climb a hill, don't attempt it. Practice on smaller hills first.

If you attempt a hill, approach it straight on and stay that way all the way to the top. Do not turn sideways or try to drive across the hill. Do not use excessive speed but keep moving at a steady pace. Make sure no one is coming up from the other side. Position a spotter at the top of the hill if necessary. Do not spin your tires because this can turn you sideways to the hill. If you feel you are coming to a stop due to lack of traction, turn your steering wheel back and forth quickly. This will give you additional grip. If you stall, use your brake and restart your engine. You may also have to use your emergency brake. If you start to slide backwards even with your brake on, you may have to ease up on the brake enough to regain steering control. Don't allow your wheels to lock up. If you don't make it to the top of the hill, shift into reverse and back down slowly in a straight line. Try the hill again but only if you think you learned enough to make a difference. As you approach the top of the hill, ease off the gas so you are in control before starting down the other side.

Driving downhill. Make sure you are in four-wheel drive. Examine the hill carefully and determine the best route that will allow you to go straight down the hill. Do not turn sideways. Use the lowest gears possible, allowing the engine's compression to hold you back. Do not ride the clutch. Feather the brakes slightly if additional slowing is needed. Do not allow the wheels to lock up. This will cause loss of steering and possibly cause you to slide sideways. The natural reaction when you begin to slide is to press harder on the brakes. Try to stay off the brakes. If you continue to slide despite these efforts, turn in the direction of the slide as you would on ice or snow and accelerate slightly. This will help maintain steering control.

Parking on a steep hill. Put your vehicle in reverse gear if pointing downhill and in forward gear if pointing uphill. For automatic transmissions, shift to park. Set your emergency brake hard. For extra insurance, block your tires.

Driving side hills. Side hill situations are dangerous so try to avoid them if possible. In Colorado, this will be difficult because off-camber situations are a fact of life. No one can tell you how far your vehicle can safely lean. You must learn the limitations through practice. Remember that sport utility vehicles have a higher center of gravity and are less stable than a passenger car. However, don't get paranoid. Your vehicle will likely lean a lot more than you think. Drive slowly to avoid bouncing over. A good way to learn is to watch an experienced driver with a vehicle similar to yours. This is an advantage to traveling with a group. Once you see how far other vehicles can lean, you will become more comfortable in these situations. Use extreme caution if the road surface is slippery from loose gravel, mud, or wet clay. Turn around if necessary.

Crossing streams and water holes. You must know the high water point of your vehicle before entering any body of water. Several factors can determine this point, including the height of the air intake and the location of the computer module (newer vehicles). Water sucked into the air intake is a very serious matter. If you don't know where these items are located, check with your dealer or a good four-wheel drive shop. A low fan can throw water on the engine and cause it to stall. You may have to disconnect your fan belt. Water can be sucked into your differentials so check them regularly after crossing deep streams.

After you understand your vehicle's capabilities, you must assess the stream conditions. First determine the depth of the water. If you are with a group, let the most experienced driver cross first. Follow his line if he is successful. If you are alone, you might wait for someone else to come along. Sometimes you can use a long stick to check the depth of small streams or water holes. Check for deep holes, large obstacles, and muddy sections. If you can't determine the water depth, don't cross. A winch line or long tow strap can be used as a safety line to pull someone back if he gets into trouble, but it must be attached before entering the water. It must also be long enough for him to reach shallow water on the other side. Once in the water, drive slowly but steadily. This creates a small wake which helps form an air pocket around the engine. I've seen people put a piece of cardboard or canvas over the front of their vehicle to enhance the wake affect. This only works if you keep moving. After exiting a stream, test your brakes. You may have to ride them lightly for a short distance until they dry out.

Always cross streams at designated water crossings. Don't drive in the direction of the stream. Try to minimize disruption of the water habitat.

Mud. Don't make new mud holes or enlarge existing ones. Stay home if you have reason to believe the trail will be too wet. Some trails, however, have permanent mud holes that you must cross. Mud can build up suction around your tires and be very difficult to get through. Always check a mud hole carefully to see how deep it is. Take a stick and poke around. Check the other side. If there are no tracks coming out, don't go in. If you decide to cross, keep moving at a steady pace and if necessary, turn the steering wheel back and forth quickly for additional traction. If you get stuck, dig around the tires to break the suction and place anything hard under the tires for traction. It may be necessary to back out. If you are with a friend, and you are doubtful if you can get through without help, attach a tow strap before you enter so that you can be pulled back. But beware, sometimes the mud can be so bad, even a friend can't pull you out. Your only protection against this happening is to use your head and not go in the mud in the first place. When I've seen people stuck this badly it is usually due to a total disregard for the obvious.

If you can't get though the mud, search for an alternate route but don't widen the trail. If there is no alternate route, turn around.

Ruts. If you get stuck in a rut and have no one to pull you out, dig a small trench from the rut to the right or left at a 45 degree angle. The dirt you remove from this trench should be used to fill the rut ahead of the turning point. If both tires are in parallel ruts, make sure the trenches are parallel. Drive out following the new rut. Repair any damage after you get out.

Gullies or washouts. If you are running parallel to a washed out section of the trail, straddle it. If it becomes too large to straddle, drive down the middle. The goal is to center your vehicle so you remain as level as possible. This may require that you drive on the outer edges of your tires, so drive slowly and watch for any sharp objects. If you begin to tilt too far in one direction, turn in the direction of the tilt until you level out again. Sometimes it helps to have a spotter. To cross a gully from one side to the other, approach at a 45-degree angle and let each tire walk over indepen-dently.

Ravines. Crossing a ravine is similar to crossing a gully. Approach on an angle and let each tire go through independently. If the ravine is large with steep sides, you may not be able to cross at an angle because it could cause a rollover. If you don't cross at an angle, two things can happen. You will drag the front or rear of your vehicle, or you will high center on the edge of the ravine. If this is the case, ask yourself if you really need to cross the ravine. If you must cross, your only solution is to stack rocks to lift the vehicle at critical points.

Sand. Except for the Great Sand Dunes National Monument, Colorado has few desert areas. Sandy soil situations are mostly encountered around dry creek beds. Not all sand is a problem. Some can be quite firm and easy to drive over. Unfortunately, you can never be sure until you are in the middle of it. The trick is to keep moving so that your momentum helps carry you through. Stay in a higher gear and use a little extra power but don't use excessive power and spin your tires. If necessary, turn your steering wheel back and forth quickly to give your tires a fresh grip. Airing down your tires can also help. Experiment with different tire pressures. Some tires can go as low as 8 to 10 pounds, although use caution below 15 pounds. Make sure you have a way to air up after you get through the sand. If you do get stuck, wet the sand in front of your tires. Try rocking the vehicle. If necessary, use your floor mats under the tires .

Snow and ice. The best advice is to avoid snow and ice completely. Call ahead for trail conditions. (See appendix.) If you encounter ice or snow on a shelf road, use extreme caution. If it is drifted over and there are no tire tracks, turn around. If other vehicles have safely crossed and there is some melting to the dirt surface, it is probably all right to cross provided you feel comfortable and have proper tires. If you are not sure, get out of your vehicle and walk the route. Be careful late in the day as the road surface may be in the process of refreezing. If you encounter any place where ice is completely across the trail, turn around.

If you are starting down a slope that is snow covered or icy, go slowly until you have some idea of how slippery the surface is. Some snow can have relatively good traction. Other snow can be too slippery to walk across. If you find your vehicle sliding, steer in the direction of the slide. Pump your brakes lightly so your wheels do not lock. This will allow your wheels to turn a little which will give you some steering capability. Don't pump antilock brakes.

Use extreme caution before starting up a slippery grade. If the road surface is off-camber, you may slide off the road. If you find yourself losing traction, try turning your steering wheel back and forth quickly for a fresh grip.

If you get stuck in the snow, dig around the tire and rock your vehicle back and forth. Try shoveling some fresh dirt, gravel, or small rocks into the hole. If no other alternative, try putting your floor mats under the tires. Don't spin your tires.

Tire chains. Many of the situations described above can be eliminated with the use of tire chains, which I recommend you carry at all times. Learn how to put them on before you need them. Chains should be properly fitted to your vehicle because they can cause damage to wheel wells or steering mechanisms.

Dust and washboard roads. Dust and washboard roads are a part of Colorado travel. Vibration from these roads can be annoying. It is a problem for everybody so don't think there is something wrong with your vehicle. Experiment with different speeds to find the smoothest ride. Slowing down is usually best, but some conditions may be improved by speeding up a little. Be careful around curves where you could lose traction and slide. Check your tires to make sure they are not over inflated. Dust is less of a problem for closed SUVs. You simply roll up your windows and turn on the air conditioner or fan. The inside pressure will help keep out most dust. With an open vehicle, there is not much you can do. At slow speeds, you can fold down your windshield if you have this option. The dust will pass through rather than collect behind the windshield.

Thumbs up. Make a habit of not wrapping your thumbs inside the steering wheel when crossing over rocky terrain. If you hit a large rock, your steering wheel could spin suddenly and injure your thumbs. This is more of a problem for vehicles without power steering.

Airing down. There may be times when you need to let air out of your tires to get more traction or improve your ride, e.g., when driving through sand, going up a steep hill, or driving on washboard roads. It is usually safe to let air out of your tires until they bulge slightly, provided you are not traveling at high speed. If you let out too much air, your tires may come off the rims, or the sidewalls may become vulnerable to damage by sharp objects. Consider how or where you will reinflate. A small air pump that plugs into your cigarette lighter is handy for this purpose. Airing down on hard-core trails is essential. I've seen some wheelers with larger tires air down to as little as 3-5 lbs. A typical SUV can usually be aired down to 18 to 20 lbs. without noticeable handling difficulties at low speeds.

Winching. Next to tow points and skid plates, a winch is one of the best investments you can make. If you drive more difficult trails and you don't have a winch, travel with someone who does. I've known some hard-core wheelers who have gone for years without owning a winch but they always travel with a group. If you never intend to buy a winch, carry a high lift jack or come-along. Although these tools are slow and inconvenient, they can get you out of difficulty when there is no other way.

If you own a winch, make sure you also have these four basic winch accessories:

1. Heavy-duty work gloves.

2. A tree strap - Looks like a tow strap but is shorter. It has a loop on each end.

3. A snatch block - A pulley that opens on the side so you can slip it over your winch cable.

4. A clevis - A heavy U-shaped device with a pin that screws across one end. This enables you to connect straps together and to your vehicle. It has many other uses.

Winching tips:

• Your winch cable should be lined up straight with the pulling vehicle. If you can't pull straight, attach a snatch block to a tree to form an angle. This technique also works for pulling a fallen tree off the trail.

• If your winch cable bunches up at one end of the spool, let it go and rewind the cable later.

• Attach your winch line to the largest tree possible using your tree strap and clevis. If no tree is large enough, wrap several smaller trees. The strap should be put as low as possible on the tree.

• Keep your engine running while winching to provide maximum electrical power to the battery.

• Help the winch by driving the stuck vehicle slowly. Be in the lowest gear possible and go as slowly as possible. Don't allow slack in the winch cable. This can start a jerking motion that could break the cable.

• If there is not enough power to pull the stuck vehicle, attach a snatch block to the stuck vehicle and double the winch cable back to the starting point. This block-and-tackle technique will double your pulling power.

• Set the emergency brake on the anchor vehicle and block the wheels if necessary. In some cases, you may have to connect the anchor vehicle to another vehicle or tree.

• Throw a blanket or heavy coat over the winch cable while pulling. This will slow the end of the winch cable if it breaks and snaps back.

• Make sure there are at least 5 wraps of the winch cable left on the spool.

• Never hook the winch cable to itself. Use a tree strap and clevis. Never allow the winch cable to kink. This creates a weak spot in the cable.

• If tow points are not available on the stuck vehicle, attach the winch cable to the frame not the bumper. If you are helping a stranger, make sure he understands that you are not responsible for damage to his vehicle.

• Never straddle or stand close to the winch cable while it is under stress.

• If you are stuck alone with no place to attach your winch cable, bury your spare tire in the ground as an anchor point. When you are finished, repair any damage to the ground.

• When finished winching, don't let the end of the cable wind into the spool. It can become jammed and damage your winch. Attach the hook to some other part of your vehicle like a tow point.

OTHER ACTIVITIES

To make the trip more enjoyable for everyone, especially if children are along, plan frequent stops with a variety of activities including picnics, hiking, biking, camping, rafting, and fishing. Go to the library before your trip and learn a little history about the area or stop at museums in towns along the way. Museums like the ones in Ouray and Silverton are outstanding. Share maps with the kids and let them trace your route. Carry binoculars to look for wildlife and distant landmarks. Allow your adult passengers an opportunity to drive appropriate parts of the trail if they are so inclined. Some portions of the trail provide driving opportunities for responsible licensed teenagers. They will be eager to learn proper off-highway driving techniques and will grow up to be responsible adult backcountry drivers.

FINAL COMMENTS

I've made every effort to make this book as accurate and as easy to use as possible. If you have ideas for improvements or find any significant errors, please write to me at FunTreks, Inc., P.O. Box 49187, Colorado Springs, CO. 80949-9187. In addition, I would love to hear stories of your travels. Whether you're a novice or expert, I hope this book has made your backcountry experience safer, easier, and more fun.

Map Legend

Interstate

Paved Road*

Easy Trail*

Moderate Trail*

Difficult Trail*

Other Road*

Described in text

Hiking Trail

Boundaries, & Divides

JONES MOUNTAIN — Mountain

Lake

Map Orientation

Pass Locator

25 — Interstate

50 — U.S. Highway

35 — State & County Road

586 — Forest Service Road

Trail Closed

Trail starts here — Starting point of trail description.

Public Toilet

Gas, Service

P Parking

Picnic Area

Camping Area

Mine or Mill

Hiking Trailhead

Mountain Biking

Fishing

Water Crossing

Bridge

Falls

Cabin

Ghost Town

Scenic Point

Major Obstacle

Handicap Access

Scale indicated by grid

Scale is different for each map; check grid size at bottom of map.**

*These items repeated on each map for your convenience. See Mini Key.

**Grid size indicates distance between lines, not area in square miles.

30

THE TRAILS

Saxton Road, Trail #53, Easy

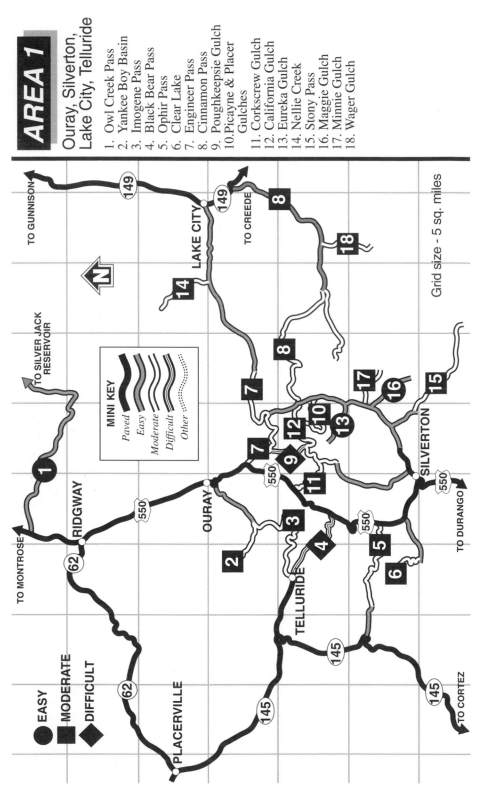

AREA 1

Ouray, Silverton, Lake City, Telluride

1. Owl Creek Pass
2. Yankee Boy Basin
3. Imogene Pass
4. Black Bear Pass
5. Ophir Pass
6. Clear Lake
7. Engineer Pass
8. Cinnamon Pass
9. Poughkeepsie Gulch
10. Picayne & Placer Gulches
11. Corkscrew Gulch
12. California Gulch
13. Eureka Gulch
14. Nellie Creek
15. Stony Pass
16. Maggie Gulch
17. Minnie Gulch
18. Wager Gulch

MINI KEY
Paved
Easy
Moderate
Difficult
Other

Grid size - 5 sq. miles

EASY
MODERATE
DIFFICULT

TO MONTROSE
TO GUNNISON
TO SILVER JACK RESERVOIR
TO CREEDE
TO DURANGO
TO CORTEZ

PLACERVILLE
RIDGWAY
OURAY
TELLURIDE
SILVERTON
LAKE CITY

Ouray, Silverton, Lake City, Telluride

A unique combination of circumstances has created perhaps the finest place in the world for off-highway driving. I'm not aware of any other place where so many high altitude backroads have been made so easily accessible to the general public. When the mining industry died in the early part of the twentieth century, so did the economy in this area. Tourism gradually grew to fill a huge void. Today, thousands of visitors enjoy a wide array of summer outdoor mountain activities including four-wheeling, camping, hiking, backpacking, mountain biking, wildflower identification, fishing, and general sightseeing from paved highways. Other places in Colorado, at these high altitudes, are closed much of the year due to winter snow pack and generally poor road conditions. But in this area, many of the higher passes are cleared of snow as early as May. During the summer, road surfaces are partially maintained, creating just the right amount of fun for sport utility vehicles. For the hard-core four wheeler, portions of some trails are left untouched. To fully enjoy your trip, learn about the history of the area. Stop at a local bookstore or visit any of several fine museums. If you have time for only one backcountry experience in Colorado, this is the place to go.

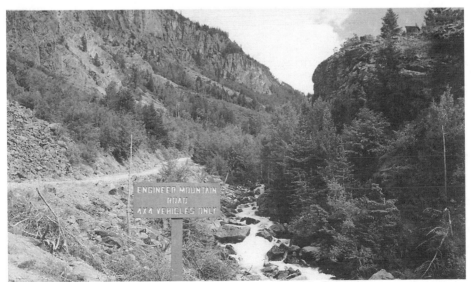

The start of Engineer Pass, perhaps the best known backroad in Colorado.

33

Silver Jack Reservoir looking south from the National Forest overlook.

Chimney Peak and Courthouse Mountain dominate the horizon at this point of the trip.

Owl Creek Pass ①

Location: North of Ouray and Ridgway. South of Montrose on US Rt. 550.

Difficulty: Easy. A gravel road with a few bumpy spots here and there but suitable for passenger cars when dry. A great alternative for those who want to view the beauty of the Ouray area but who may be uncomfortable on higher mountain roads.

Features: At the start of this trail across 550 is the Ridgway State Recreation Area with great camping, fishing, and boating. Your destination, however, will be the smaller but beautiful Silver Jack Reservoir. To get there, you cross spectacular Cimarron Ridge, a sawtooth mountain range of unusual character quite different from the other mountain ranges of the San Juans.

Time & Distance: Signs indicate that Owl Creek Pass is about 13 miles from US 550, but I measured 16 miles. The south end of the reservoir is another 6 miles beyond the pass. To completely enjoy this trip, you should allow at least half a day. You'll want to stop at various places along the way. You can easily spend a full day or more if you plan to fish, hike, or camp.

To Get There: From Grand Junction or Gunnison: Take US 50 to Montrose. About 26 miles south of Montrose on US 550, turn east on County Road 10. From Ouray: Drive north 10 miles to Ridgway on US 550. Continue another mile. Owl Creek is well marked on the right.

Trail Description: Set your odometer to zero at the start of Rd. 10. At 2.7 miles, a road to Cow Creek goes to the right. You bear left. At 4 miles County Road 8 goes to the left, which takes you back out to 550. Go right, which will also be marked as Rd. 8. At 7.9 miles you enter the Uncompahgre National Forest. The road is now marked as F.S. 858. At 8.8 miles, Vista Point turns off to the right. Stop here a moment for some great pictures.

After that, you will pass through a dense aspen forest before reaching Owl Creek Pass at 15.6 miles. A small parking area to the left has a minimal toilet facility. Less than 0.5 miles after Owl Creek Pass, follow the signs left to Silver Jack Reservoir. At 22.1 continue straight following signs over a one-lane bridge. After crossing the bridge, turn left at the next intersection which indicates Cimarron is 22 miles. After a mile or so of smooth road, an access road to a fishing area goes left. There is a small parking area for fishermen. Wide paths around the lake are designed for handicap access.

If you continue north on 858, there is a Forest Service overlook to the left. I'd recommend a stop here. There are some great views, a modern toilet, and access to picturesque hiking trails. Continuing on the main road will take you to the large Silver Jack Campground with many paved sites suitable for RVs and camping trailers. There are several smaller campgrounds beyond this one.

Return Trip: Depending on your final destination, you can continue north to Cimarron or return the way you came. Be aware that the return trip to Cimarron includes one area that is prone to washouts. Cimarron is located on US 50 west of Gunnison. This direction will also take you to the Black Canyon of the Gunnison and the Curecante National Recreation Area, the better known tourist attractions in the area.

Services: Full services in Ridgeway, Ouray, and Montrose.

Other Activities: Besides fishing, hiking, and camping, there are several side roads in the area that are fun to explore. Many of these side roads lead to posted hiking trails.

Maps: Uncompahgre National Forest, Trails Illustrated Silverton, Ouray #141, Colorado Atlas and Gazetteer.

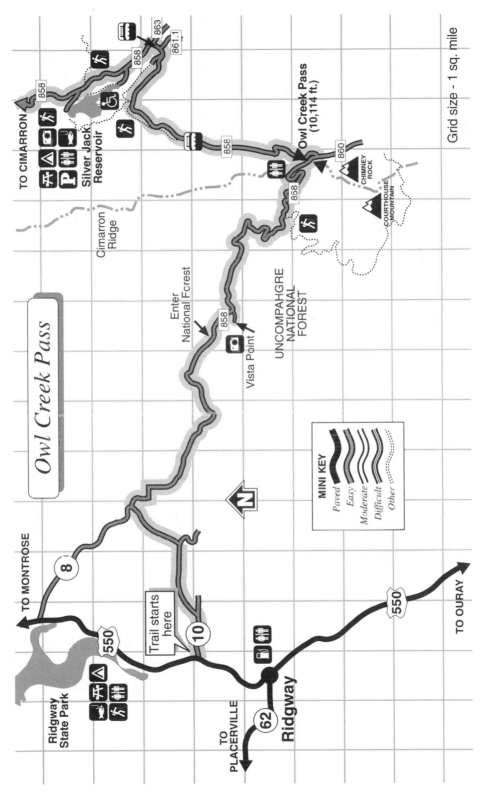

Owl Creek Pass

Grid size - 1 sq. mile

TO CIMARRON

858

Silver Jack Reservoir

858

861.1

863

Cimarron Ridge

Enter National Forest

858

Vista Point

UNCOMPAHGRE NATIONAL FOREST

858

Owl Creek Pass (10,114 ft.)

860

CHIMNEY ROCK

COURTHOUSE MOUNTAIN

N

MINI KEY

Paved
Easy
Moderate
Difficult
Other

TO MONTROSE

8

Trail starts here

10

550

Ridgway State Park

Ridgway

62

TO PLACERVILLE

550

TO OURAY

Approaching Yankee Boy Basin.

Camp Bird Road is an easy drive but use caution around numerous blind curves.

Yankee Boy Basin

2

Location: South of Ouray off US 550.

Difficulty: Moderate. This rating is based on just a few rocky sections above the Imogene turnoff. Generally, however, this trail is easy. There is a section above the public toilet that is moderate to difficult depending on how far up you go; however, this section is usually closed.

Features: One of the most popular destinations in the Ouray area due to its close proximity to town, rich history, and colorful wildflower display. At the height of spring color, amateur and professional photographers flock to this area. On your way, you will pass by some of the most popular landmarks in the area, including the Camp Bird Mine and the Sneffels Townsite. Yankee Boy Basin is private land closed to public camping and fires. Please respect the land so that the owners of this property will continue to allow you to drive through. Never stray off the road. And above all, don't pick the wildflowers. It may seem like there are plenty, but over the years their numbers have noticeably diminished. If this continues, the area may be closed.

Time & Distance: From US 550 the trip is only about 8 miles one way Allow several hours for maximum enjoyment.

To Get There: Head south from Ouray on US 550. Less than a half mile from the south end of town, turn right on Camp Bird Road marked as County Road 361.

Trail Description: Set your odometer to zero as you turn off 550 on Camp Bird Road. This road is an easy gravel road with some car traffic. Don't let the sight of passenger cars, however, cause you to become complacent. Blind curves and high cliffs require your utmost attention. You will pass by Weehawken Hiking Trail more than a half mile on the right after the Canyon Creek bridge. Across from the hiking trail is a two-story boarding house of the Thistledown Mine. If you look up the slope on the left, other mine buildings can be seen.

At about 5 miles you come to Camp Bird, a massive area of tailings. After this mine, the road narrows to one lane and cuts across the steepest part of the canyon. At one point, rock hangs over the road. At 5.9 miles you encounter the turn off for Imogene Pass on the left. Continue straight for Yankee Boy Basin. You immediately come to the remains of the Sneffels Townsite. The Torpedo Eclipse Mill is on the right and the Ruby Trust Mine is on the left. Next is the Atlas Mill on the hillside to the left.

At 6.6 miles bear to the right. Going straight would take you up the difficult and narrow Governor Basin Road. From here to the public toilet the road gets a little rougher, but just enough to make it fun. Just short of 8 miles, you reach a parking area and public toilet identified as a Biological Waste Conversion Station. Usually the road is closed here and you have to hike beyond this point. If open, and you decide to drive on, it gets progressively more difficult. The Yankee Boy Mine is on the right after the public toilet.

Return Trip: This is not a loop trail. You return the way you came. However, if you are looking for more adventure, you can explore the lower section of the Imogene Pass Road (Trail #3).

Services: Full services in Ouray.

Other Activities: This is a beautiful area to hike and explore. The Blue Lake Trail at the end of Yankee Boy Basin climbs above Wrights Lake toward Mt. Sneffels. Many find hiking more enjoyable by learning more about the history of the area. Also, identifying wildflowers is very popular.

Historical Highlights: The main feature of this road is the Camp Bird Mine. In its heyday, this mine had advanced creature comforts including hot and cold running water, electric lights, and steam heat. It was discovered in 1896 by Tom Walsh, who felt that the 400 miners who worked there should be treated to a decent lifestyle. He required only eight hours of work per day rather than the standard 12 hours. His humanitarian approach brought big rewards as he made over 4 million dollars by 1900. He sold the mine in 1902 for 5.2 million dollars. The mine continued to operate until 1911 and made over 26 million dollars. The road up to Camp Bird was built by the legendary Otto Mears in 1891 after others had tried and failed.

Maps: Uncompahgre National Forest, Trails Illustrated Silverton, Ouray #141, Colorado Atlas and Gazetteer. Local stores also sell small pocket-size guides," BACK ROADS of the San Juans," that are very handy and have a lot of detailed information. They are published by Backcountry Travelers, Inc. of Durango, CO.

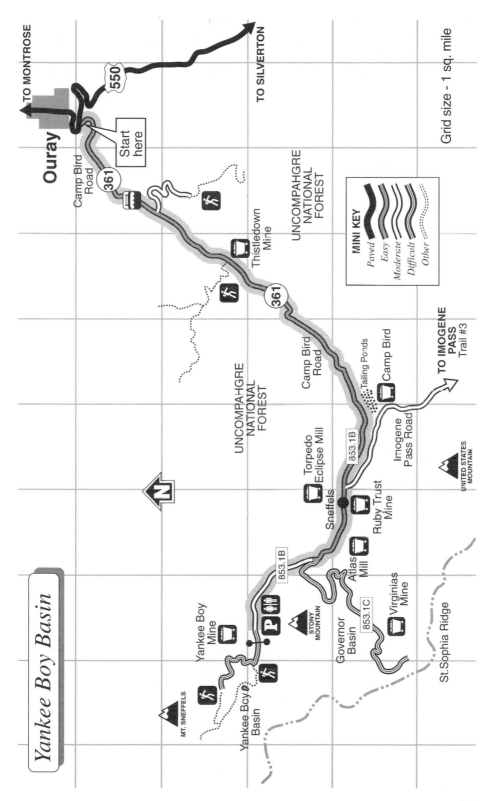

Yankee Boy Basin

MINI KEY
Paved
Easy
Moderate
Difficult
Other

Grid size - 1 sq. mile

TO MONTROSE

Ouray

550

361

Start here

Camp Bird Road

TO SILVERTON

UNCOMPAHGRE NATIONAL FOREST

361

Thistledown Mine

Camp Bird Road

UNCOMPAHGRE NATIONAL FOREST

N

Tailing Ponds

Camp Bird

TO IMOGENE PASS Trail #3

Torpedo Eclipse Mill

853.1B

Sneffels

Imogene Pass Road

Ruby Trust Mine

UNITED STATES MOUNTAIN

853.1B

Atlas Mill

Yankee Boy Mine

P

STONY MOUNTAIN

853.1C

Governor Basin

Virginias Mine

MT. SNEFFELS

Yankee Boy Basin

St. Sophia Ridge

41

Stream crossing below Richmond Basin. Still plenty of snow left on July 17th.

Tomboy Road is relatively smooth but is narrow and steep. Portions of the road have been reinforced to help combat erosion.

Imogene Pass

Location: Between Telluride and Ouray.

Difficulty: Moderate. The road surface from Telluride up to the Tomboy Townsite is relatively smooth, but this section of the trail can't be rated easy because it is steep and narrow. In places, the road has been crudely reinforced to combat erosion. Above the townsite, high clearance four-wheel drive and low range are definitely required. The descent of the upper north side is steeper and rougher than the south side and is therefore easier traveled going downhill. The lower north side descent is more pastoral but with several stream crossings. Overall, this trail is rated at the high end of moderate. Some off-highway driving experience is recommended.

Features: Imogene Pass is the second highest pass in Colorado at 13,114 ft. and is one of the most thrilling passes to cross in Colorado. This trail would be impassable most of the summer if not routinely cleared of snow. Many mines border the route. The remains of the Tomboy Mine Townsite cover the floor of the Savage Basin on the south side. Prior to the mine closure in 1927, there were dozens of structures here including dwellings and a public school. Located at the summit is the deteriorated Lineman's Shack. Imagine living here alone all winter to maintain the power lines which served Camp Bird on the other side of the mountain.

Time & Distance: The complete trip from Telluride to Ouray is approximately 18 miles. You should plan several hours or more to fully enjoy the trip.

To Get There: It is recommended that you travel this trail from Telluride to Ouray. Experienced travelers usually make this the second leg of a loop starting in Ouray and reaching Telluride via Ophir Pass. In the town of Telluride, find Oak Street on the north side of town. It does not intersect with Colorado (Main Street) so it must be accessed from Aspen or Fir Streets. (See map detail on next page.) Tomboy Road goes to the right at the very end of Oak after Gregory. Tomboy Road, at the start, looks more like someone's driveway but quickly turns into a well defined trail.

Trail Description: Set your odometer to zero at the start of Tomboy Road. The first half mile skirts a hillside residential area as you pass by the Jud Wiebe Hiking Trail on the left. As you begin to climb the walls of this steep canyon, the road gets a little rougher. You pass by several points that look across the valley to the switchbacks of the notorious Black Bear Road (Trail #4) and Bridal Veil Falls. Avoid the early temptation to take photos because this view improves as you proceed. You continue to twist and wind up the canyon with each turn of the trail bringing ever more breathtaking views. At the 4.5 mile point, you approach the Tomboy Townsite. Don't be surprised to find a passenger car reaching this point. I passed a stock two-wheel drive car heading downhill with a small emergency tire in use, a chilling reminder that this is no place for such vehicles. In addition, it points out the need to carry a full-size spare tire.

As you pass through the townsite, the need for high-clearance four-wheel drive becomes apparent. Often snow remains above this area. With the exception of a few muddy spots, road traction remains good even in the wettest weather. Just short of 7 miles, you reach the summit and the Lineman's Shack described earlier. Temperatures are very brisk at this elevation, even on the warmest summer day. As you descend the next several miles, you encounter the steepest and roughest part of the trail. You may scrape bottom occasionally, but if you take your time and select your route carefully, you should have no problems. You might find it helpful to get out of your vehicle to inspect the trail on some of the tougher sections.

After several miles, it begins to flatten out, but water crossings of Imogene Creek are frequent. Then at 9.7 you reach a small bridge over Richmond Creek. Turn left after the bridge and continue downhill. This area is wonderfully photogenic and a great place to camp. There are still several miles of rocky trail through the trees before you reach Camp Bird Road at 12.2 miles. Going left, at this point, takes you to Yankee Boy Basin (Trail #2). Going right takes you back to Ouray.

Return Trip: If you wish to return to Telluride, take US 550 to Ophir Pass (Trail #5) which connects to Rt.145 into Telluride. Or to return via paved highway, take 550 north to Ridgway, 62 southwest to Placerville, and 145 southeast to Telluride.

Services: Full services in Ouray and Telluride.

Other Activities: Telluride is a fantastic town to visit in the summer, offering many hiking trails and numerous other activities. Stop at the Visitors Center on the west end of town for helpful information. It is open all year.

Maps: Uncompahgre National Forest, Trails Illustrated Silverton, Ouray #141, Colorado Atlas and Gazetteer.

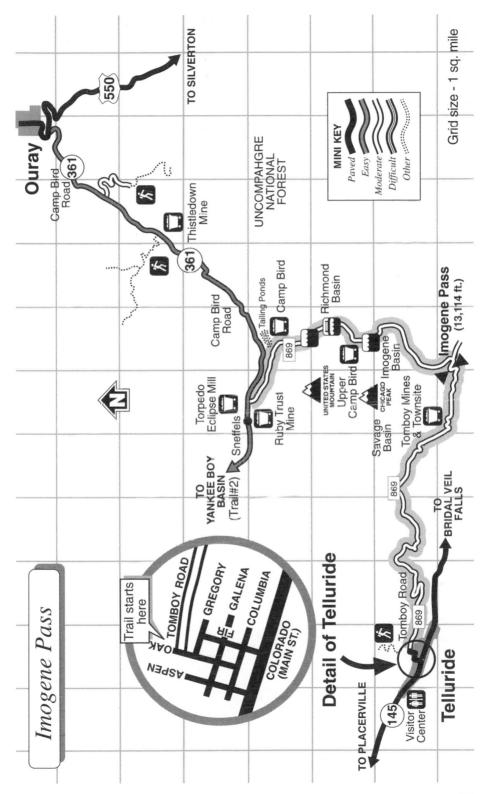

Imogene Pass

MINI KEY
Paved
Easy
Moderate
Difficult
Other

Grid size - 1 sq. mile

Ouray

550

TO SILVERTON

361

Camp Bird Road

Thistledown Mine

361

Camp Bird Road

UNCOMPAHGRE NATIONAL FOREST

Tailing Ponds

Camp Bird

869

Richmond Basin

Torpedo Eclipse Mill

Sneffels

Ruby Trust Mine

UNITED STATES MOUNTAIN

Upper Camp Bird

CHICAGO PEAK

Imogene Basin

Savage Basin

Tomboy Mines & Townsite

Imogene Pass (13,114 ft.)

TO YANKEE BOY BASIN (Trail #2)

N

869

TO BRIDAL VEIL FALLS

Detail of Telluride

Trail starts here

TOMBOY ROAD

GREGORY

GALENA

COLUMBIA

ASPEN

OAK

COLORADO (MAIN ST.)

TO PLACERVILLE

Tomboy Road

869

Telluride

145

Visitor Center

45

View of Black Bear from Imogene.

Looking down on Bridal Veil Falls.

The start of the descent above Telluride.

The tightest switchback. Backing required.

Black Bear Pass

Location: South of Ouray between Red Mountain Pass and Telluride.

Difficulty: Difficult. This rating is based on the difficulty of the switchbacks that descend into Telluride more than on the roughness of the road. It is extremely dangerous and for experienced drivers only.

Features: To drive this trail in its entirety, you must start at the Ouray end. The switchbacks at the Telluride end are one-way. You can turn around any-time until you start to descend the switchbacks which are extremely tight and narrow. To make the turns, backing up is required for even the shortest wheel base vehicles. From the switchbacks, however, there are incredible views of Bridal Veil Falls and Telluride below. This road is closed November through May 1st.

Time & Distance: It is about 12 miles from the start at US 550 to the edge of Telluride. Allow 2 to 3 hours.

To Get There: Head south from Ouray on US 550 for about 13 miles. One tenth mile after the summit of Red Mountain Pass, turn right. Black Bear Road is marked. After you start down the trail, there is a Forest Service marker 823.

Trail Description: Set your odometer to zero as you turn right off 550. The road starts climbing quickly, so shift immediately into four-wheel drive low. At 1 mile, take the right fork. Subsequent forks eventually come back to the main trail. There are a few steep, narrow, rocky sections as you quickly climb above timberline. Views of the highway below are impressive. At 2.3 miles it begins to level out as you cross a flatter, more barren area. Watch for heavy equipment at all times because this area is still an active mining area.

At 2.9 choose a harder route to the right or an easier one to the left. The main trail, to the left, then becomes less defined but it is fairly easy to pick your way to the top. As you approach the ridge line at approximately 3.2 miles, bear more to the left. If you find yourself driving parallel to the ridge line to the right, you have probably gone too far. Several places look like the right way but they are not. You may have to get out of your vehicle and look over the ridge to be sure you are going the right way. After you cross the ridge, the road turns to the right as it starts down. The entire valley opens up into view and is quite impressive. After crossing this valley at the

47

5 mile point, go straight not left. You should soon be able to see Telluride in the distance.

The trail starts getting tougher as you descend more rapidly. You will have different choices to make depending on the level of difficulty you prefer. Ingram Creek will be on your left. Some of the switchbacks begin to get a little tight, providing an opportunity to practice your turns before the more difficult ones that follow. At 6.5 you encounter the steepest and roughest part of the trail. Also the rock is a little loose and unnerving. You will pass by Ingram Falls on the left. The road flattens out briefly as it passes directly through some mine buildings that are now no more than piles of lumber. You cross Ingram Creek before reaching the tightest switchback on the trail. At this point, passengers may prefer to get out and watch or to help spot. Swing as wide as possible, being careful not to go too high up the rock wall on the left. It is best to point yourself downhill somewhat to avoid getting too off-camber. It is safer to back up several times to make the turn, rather than trying to swing wide to avoid backing up. It is very difficult to keep all four wheels on the ground, and you may rock a little as I did. This sensation is not for the faint of heart. If all goes well, you will eventually find yourself pointing in the opposite direction ready for the next switchback. Each switchback gets progressively easier and soon you reach a wide section where two-way traffic begins. This is the highest point you can reach if driving up from the bottom so cars may be parked here. A gate to the Bridal Veil Falls Power House is also here. From this point, the road is much easier with several splits which all lead to the bottom. You will pass by the historic Pandora Mill before reaching pavement. Telluride follows at about 11.7 miles.

Return Trip: To get back to Ouray on a paved road: Take Rt. 145 to Placerville, 62 to Ridgway, and 550 to Ouray. This is a relaxing and scenic 50 mile ride. You can also return via Imogene Pass (Trail #3) or Ophir Pass (Trail #5).

Services: Full services in Ouray and Telluride.

Other Activities: Telluride has more activities in the summer than in the winter. There are hiking and mountain biking trails in every direction. Stop in at the Visitors Center at the west end of town for a complete list and activities. The center is open all year long.

Maps: Uncompahgre National Forest, Trails Illustrated Silverton, Ouray #141, Colorado Atlas and Gazetteer.

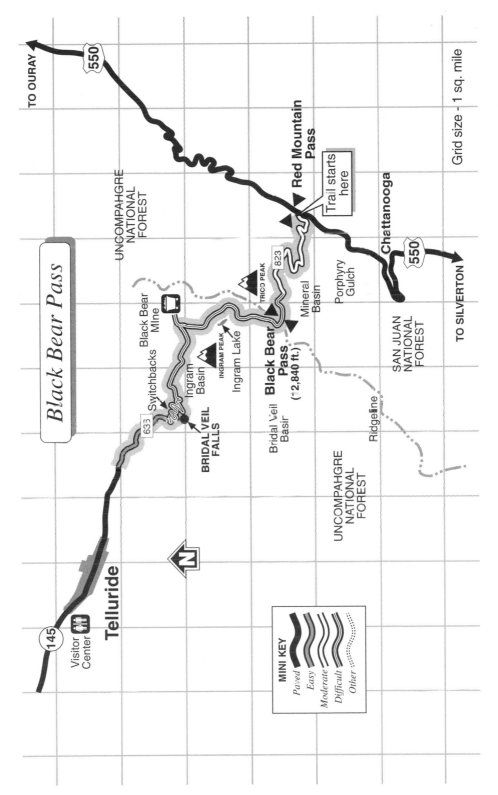

Black Bear Pass

TO OURAY

550

Grid size - 1 sq. mile

UNCOMPAHGRE NATIONAL FOREST

Red Mountain Pass

Trail starts here

Chattanooga

550

Porphyry Gulch

Mineral Basin

SAN JUAN NATIONAL FOREST

TO SILVERTON

823

TRICO PEAK

Black Bear Mine

Switchbacks

635

Ingram Basin

INGRAM PEAK

Ingram Lake

Black Bear Pass (12,840 ft.)

BRIDAL VEIL FALLS

Bridal Veil Basin

Ridgeline

UNCOMPAHGRE NATIONAL FOREST

N

Telluride

145

Visitor Center

MINI KEY
Paved
Easy
Moderate
Difficult
Other

Descending the west side of Ophir Pass is easy except for a couple of narrow rocky sections.

The summit of Ophir Pass on July 17.

Side trip to Alta Lakes.

Ophir Pass 5

Location: Between Silverton and Telluride.

Difficulty: Moderate. This rating is based on a few narrow rocky sections on the upper west side of Ophir Pass. Most of the trail is easy.

Features: This is perhaps the most popular way to reach Telluride from Silverton and Ouray over a high mountain backroad. Because it is well maintained, it is frequented by many first-time backcountry travelers.

Time & Distance: The trip is about 10 miles from Route 550 to 145. Allow a couple of hours one way.

To Get There: Head north from Silverton on US 550 for about 4 miles. Watch for County Rd. 8 on the west side of the road.

Trail Description: Set your odometer to zero as you turn west onto Rd. 8. You head down into a small valley crossing Mineral Creek and immediately begin climbing up the other side. In a short distance, F.S. 820 goes to the right. This road will take you to a hiking trail up to Columbine Lake. There are a number of other side roads in the area to explore for those looking for additional adventure or secluded camping. (Difficulty ratings unknown.) To get to Ophir Pass, stay on well defined County Rd. 8. It gets a little narrower and steeper in places before reaching Ophir Pass in about 4 miles. This is a very popular place to stop because of the views in both directions. Use caution when pulling over to the side of the road. Watch for loose sharp rock that can cut through the sidewalls of your tires. This rock is called "talus" or "scree" and is caused by constant freezing and thawing above timberline.

As you start down the other side, there are spectacular views of the valley below. The road gets steeper and narrower for a couple of miles. There are several narrow sections of loose rock where it is difficult to pass. Watch for vehicles coming uphill and wait if necessary. Remember they have the right-of-way. After coming down off this rocky section, you pass through a section of tall aspen trees, which makes this trip particularly dramatic in the fall. Also, there are several shallow stream crossings that add to the enjoyment of the trip. Watch for a series of beaver ponds on the left before reaching what is left of the town of Ophir, now no more than a residential community. This area is mostly private property, so stay on the main road and respect the rights of others.

From this point the road is very well graded until you reach highway 145 at about the 10 mile point. Going left on 145 takes you to Lizard Head Pass. Turn right to get to Telluride. This way will take you past Alta Lakes Road in about 2 miles. If you have time, this is a nice side trip. Turn right and head up the hill about 4 miles. You will pass the ghost town of Alta before reaching a series of small lakes with camping and fishing. There is a small outhouse at the lakes. Take insect repellent.

Return Trip: From Telluride, the shortest high mountain pass road back to Ouray is Imogene (Trail #3). If you want to get back by paved road: Take 145 northwest into Placerville, 62 northeast to Ridgway, and 550 south to Ouray.

Services: Full services in Silverton and Telluride.

Other Activities: Hiking, mountain biking, camping, and fishing remain the most popular summertime pastimes. Stop at the Visitors Center in Telluride for a complete list of all their summertime activities.

Historical Highlights: Built in 1891, Ophir Pass was originally a toll road between Silverton and Telluride. The town of Ophir once provided supplies to hundreds of mines in the area. Later, the town moved two miles west to be closer to the railroad.

Maps: Uncompahgre National Forest, Trails Illustrated Silverton, Ouray #141, Colorado Atlas and Gazetteer.

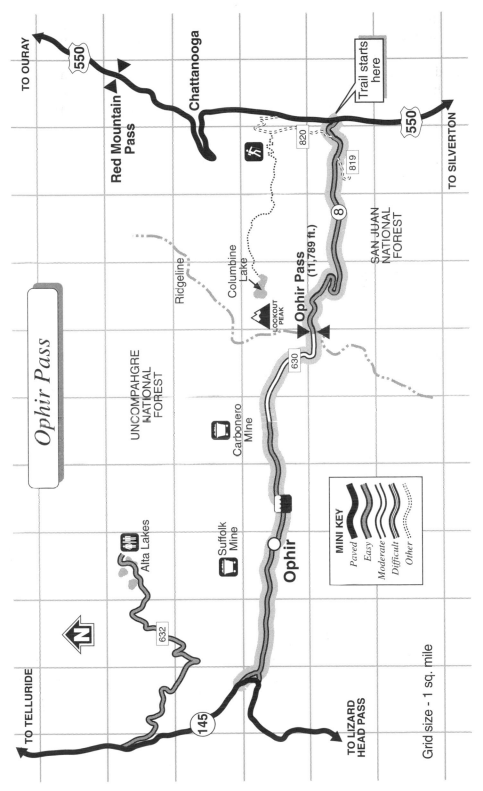

Ophir Pass

TO OURAY

550

Red Mountain Pass

Chattanooga

Trail starts here

820

819

8

SAN JUAN NATIONAL FOREST

550

TO SILVERTON

Ridgeline

Columbine Lake

LOOKOUT PEAK

Ophir Pass (11,789 ft.)

630

UNCOMPAHGRE NATIONAL FOREST

Carbonero Mine

Suffolk Mine

Ophir

Alta Lakes

632

MINI KEY

Paved
Easy
Moderate
Difficult
Other

N

TO TELLURIDE

145

TO LIZARD HEAD PASS

Grid size - 1 sq. mile

The switchbacks at the top are narrow and steep but the views are spectacular.

A family prepares to fish Clear Lake on a cool crisp afternoon in late July.

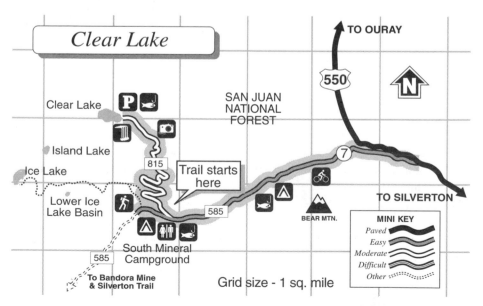

Clear Lake

TO OURAY

550

N

Clear Lake

SAN JUAN
NATIONAL
FOREST

Island Lake

Ice Lake

815

Trail starts
here

7

Lower Ice
Lake Basin

585

South Mineral
Campground

585

To Bandora Mine
& Silverton Trail

BEAR MTN.

TO SILVERTON

Grid size - 1 sq. mile

MINI KEY

Paved
Easy
Moderate
Difficult
Other

Location: West of Silverton.

Difficulty: Moderate. Steep and narrow at the top. Just one or two rocky sections. Otherwise, the road surface is easy most of the way.

Features: Close to the South Mineral Campground. A very popular camping, hiking, and fishing area. Camping is allowed at various places along the South Fork of Mineral Creek which parallels County Road 7.

Time & Distance: It is 4.3 miles to the campground on a very good road. The drive up to the lake is another 4.5 miles and takes less than an hour.

To Get There: Head north from Silverton on US 550 about 2.5 miles. Turn left on County Road 7. It is well marked.

Trail Description: Follow County Road 7 west for 3.7 miles. The trail to Clear Lake is marked as F.S. 815 and goes up the hill to the right. There are numerous places to camp and fish along County Road 7. This area is suitable for larger RVs and motorhomes. The four-wheel drive portion begins at 815. This road is a constant series of switchbacks that climbs through dense forest quickly ascending above timberline. The switchbacks get narrow and steep at the top, but the road is fairly smooth except for a couple of rocky sections. There is a nice waterfall on the left as you near the lake. The lake can't be seen until you reach the top. There is one water crossing just before the lake that is the hardest part of the trail.

Return Trip: Go back the way you came.

Services: In Silverton and Ouray. There is a decent public toilet at the South Mineral Campground.

Other Activities: Silverton is a must-see town. Residents here take real pride in their community. It has a rich mining history with many great stores and restaurants. Visit the museum or take a ride to Durango on the famous "Denver and Rio Grande Narrow Gauge Railroad".

Maps: Uncompahgre National Forest, San Juan National Forest, Trails Illustrated Silverton, Ouray #141, Colorado Atlas and Gazetteer.

This stretch is within the first mile.   You must hike down to see Whitmore Falls.

My Grand Cherokee had no trouble getting to the summit on this cool, damp day.

Engineer Pass

Location: Between Ouray and Lake City.

Difficulty: Moderate. The lower section is quite rocky; however, with a little care, it can be easily negotiated by any high clearance four-wheel drive vehicle. The upper section is a little easier, but several narrow rocky sections at the top can cause anxiety for nervous drivers.

Features: This trail, combined with Cinnamon Pass (Trail #8), constitutes the famous Alpine Loop. It is an exhilarating trip for drivers of all experience levels. There are many mines and points of historical interest along the entire trail.

Time & Distance: It is about 27 miles from US 550 to Lake City. Much of the trip is slow going so allow half a day one way. If you are driving the entire Alpine Loop, you will need the rest of the day for the return trip.

To Get There: Head south from Ouray on US 550 for 3.7 miles. Watch for a tight curve to the left at an overlook. The start of Engineer Pass is a wide road to the left after that point. It is well marked.

Trail Description: Set your odometer to zero as you turn off 550. The road quickly gets rough. If you have never been on a road like this, it can be a little disconcerting at first. Remember to place your tires on the high points of the rocks and go slowly. Short of one mile, you cross through the steep walled canyon pictured on the opposite page. There are just a few places to pass, so watch for oncoming cars. Technically, you have the right-of-way, but pull over first if it is easier. The Uncompahgre River is on the right. At 1.6 miles you pass the well preserved Mickey Breene Mine. At 2.4 you reach the turnoff for Poughkeepsie Gulch (Trail #9) on the right. The main trail switchbacks to the left. Poughkeepsie is extremely difficult and impassable when wet.

At 4.1 miles you pass the Des Ouray Mine. Not much is left here but a small tin building and a boiler. The turnoff for Mineral Point and the San Juan Chief Mill is at 5.1 miles. This is an interesting area to explore but very difficult. Stay out of this area when wet to avoid damaging the trail. At 5.8 miles there is a nice overlook of the San Juan Chief Mill and Mineral Point. Also here is a modern pit toilet. The road continues across an open area as you climb above timberline and at 7.1 miles you reach an intersection. Right takes you back down the mountain on an easier stretch to

Animas Forks and eventually Silverton. This way also takes you down to Cinnamon Pass Road (Trail #8). Turn left to continue up Engineer. The road climbs quickly and starts getting rougher again. It gets narrow in a few places especially just before "Oh Point." This is a nice place to stop on a clear day. You circle around the side of the mountain and reach Engineer Pass at 9.7 miles. The downhill side is much easier. You pass by the Frank Hough Mine, the Palmetto Gulch Powerhouse, the Palmetto Gulch Mill and a modern ski system hut. At 13.1 you pass Rose's Cabin. It is back off the road on the left and difficult to find. This was once a stagecoach stop with a 22-room hotel. Little remains today. There is good camping in this area and a forest service toilet just ahead. Henson Creek, on the right, is very popular for fishing. The large structure on the left at 14.3 miles is the Empire Chief Mine.

At this point the road is now suitable for cars. Whitmore Falls, at 17 miles, can't be seen without hiking down a very steep trail. Short of 19 miles, you reach Capital City. Not much is here but a road that goes off to the left. It turns into a four-wheel drive trail and is a very popular hiking area. Continuing on the main road takes you past another rest stop and Nellie Creek (Trail #14). Continuing on the main road takes you through a beautiful rocky canyon on its way down to Lake City at 27 miles. Turn right at the stop sign and go two blocks to 149.

Return Trip: For Gunnison, turn left at 149. To complete the second part of the Alpine Loop, Cinnamon Pass (Trail #8), turn right at 149.

Services: Full services in Ouray, Lake City, and Silverton.

Other Activities: You might want to spend a little time in Lake City. It is a quiet little town with many log cabins and old Victorian churches. South of Lake City is the beautiful Lake San Cristobal, popular for fishing, boating, and camping. There are also rental cabins available in the area.

Historical Highlights: From the rest stop at timberline, you look down on the Mineral Point area. Most people mistake the scattered remains of the San Juan Chief Mill directly below for Mineral Point. However, Mineral Point is actually located beyond a swampy area one quarter mile south. It is barely distinguishable in a small grove of trees. Mineral Point was settled in 1873 and was a respite for travelers on their way to Ouray. It once had a store, several restaurants and saloons and the highest post office in the nation.

Maps: Uncompahgre National Forest, Trails Illustrated Silverton, Ouray #141, Colorado Atlas and Gazetteer.

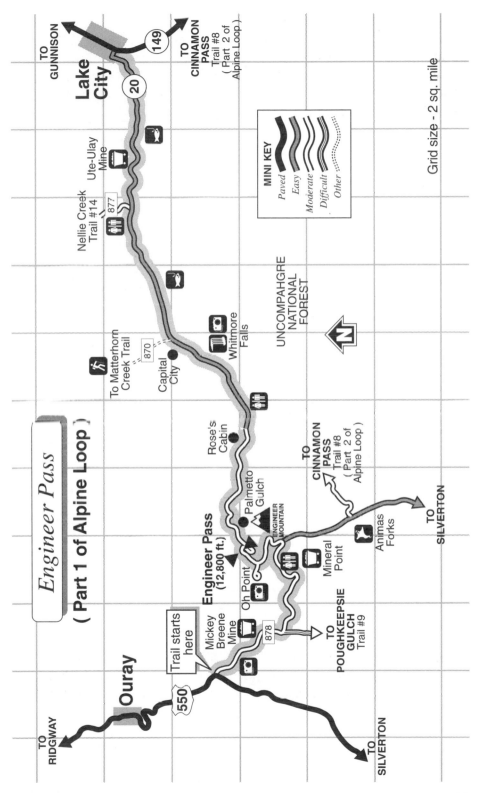

Engineer Pass
(Part 1 of Alpine Loop)

TO
RIDGWAY

Ouray

550

TO
SILVERTON

Trail starts here

Mickey Breene Mine

Engineer Pass
(12,800 ft.)

Oh Point

878

TO
POUGHKEEPSIE
GULCH
Trail #9

Mineral
Point

ENGINEER MOUNTAIN

Palmetto
Gulch

Rose's Cabin

Animas
Forks

TO
SILVERTON

TO
CINNAMON
PASS
Trail #8
(Part 2 of
Alpine Loop)

UNCOMPAHGRE
NATIONAL
FOREST

N

Capital
City

To Matterhorn
Creek Trail

870

Whitmore
Falls

877

Nellie Creek
Trail #14

Ute-Ulay
Mine

Lake
City

20

149

TO
GUNNISON

TO
CINNAMON
PASS
Trail #8
(Part 2 of Alpine Loop)

MINI KEY
Paved
Easy
Moderate
Difficult
Other

Grid size - 2 sq. mile

Beautiful views and smooth going greet you at the summit.

Looking down the east side from near the summit.

This is the most difficult section for an optional side trip up to American Basin.

Cinnamon Pass 8

Location: Between Lake City and Silverton. The trail can be driven in either direction but is described here starting in Lake City.

Difficulty: Moderate. Most of this trail is easy with the exception of a few spots.

Features: This trail combined with Engineer Pass (Trail #7), constitutes the famous Alpine Loop. This half of the trip passes Lake San Cristobal. After crossing the easier Cinnamon Pass, you drop down into a beautiful valley exposing the ghost town of Animas Forks and California Gulch.

Time & Distance: From Lake City to Animas Forks is almost 28 miles. Allow about 2 to 3 hours plus stopping time. It is about 13 miles and another half hour from Animas Forks to Silverton on much better road.

To Get There: Lake City can be reached via Engineer Pass as described in Trail #7 or via Route 149 from Gunnison.

Trail Description: Set your odometer to zero in Lake City at the bridge over Henson Creek and head south on 149. At 2.3 miles turn right on County Road 30. You reach Lake San Cristobal at 3.5 miles. There is a small parking area on the left at the north end of the lake. You are in the area of the Slumgullion Slide, a massive landslide that formed the lake centuries ago. At approximately 6.3 miles the pavement ends. At 9.1 Williams Creek Campground and hiking trail are on the right. Wager Gulch (Trail #18), County Road 36 is at 11.3 miles. On the right at 12.5 miles is another public toilet and access to fishing at Bent Creek. The Millcreek Campground is at 13.1 miles. County Road 35 goes to the left at 14.4 miles. This road passes the remains of the town of Sherman and leads to some nice hiking trails.

To continue on to Cinnamon Pass, go right at Rd. 35. At this point the road is marked as Rt. 3, but I could not find this designation on any map. Rt. 3 gradually climbs and becomes a high shelf road but remains in good condition. At 18.5 you reach Burrows Park with more hiking trails and a public toilet. American Basin goes to the left at 22.1 miles. If you have time, this is a pleasant side trip, only slightly more difficult than Cinnamon Pass. Bear right on the main road to continue on to Cinnamon Pass. At about 25.6 miles you reach the summit of Cinnamon Pass at 12,640 ft. From here, it is another 2 miles down to the ghost town of Animas Forks. Just before Animas Forks you drop down a steep, narrow, bumpy section before you intersect a larger road running north and south. This road was not marked when I was there, but it is indicated as 586 on my Trails Illustrated map. There is another public toilet near Animas Forks.

Return Trip: If you have already driven Engineer Pass, you will probably want to turn left and head into Silverton. You will be on F.S. 586 which eventually turns into paved road 110. Turning right takes you back up to Engineer Pass and Ouray.

Services: Full services in Lake City and Silverton.

Other Activities: Lake City and the surrounding Lake San Cristobal are popular tourist attractions. With side trips to Wager Gulch, County Road 35 at Sherman, and American Basin, you could easily spend a whole day in this area. Hiking trails and fishing opportunities are everywhere.

Historical Highlights: If you approach Animas Forks from the south, you will see giant stone foundations on the hillside. This is all that remains of the Gold Prince Mill, once the largest mill in Colorado. It was the first large mill constructed of steel in 1904 and was dismantled only 10 years later. Most of the building materials were reused for the great Sunnyside Mill at Eureka (Trail #13). Animas Forks was reborn in 1904 when the Silverton Northern Railroad terminated here. At one time, 400 people lived in Animas Forks, which had a post office, school, and jail.

Maps: Uncompahgre National Forest, Trails Illustrated Silverton, Ouray #141, Colorado Atlas and Gazetteer.

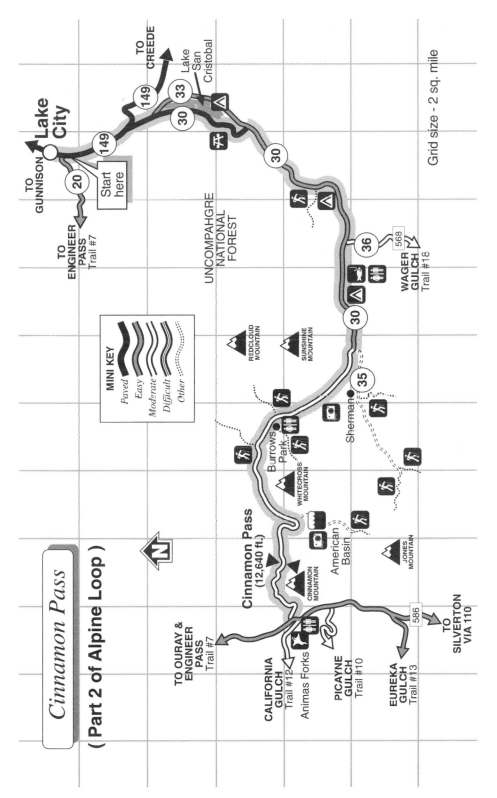

Cinnamon Pass

(Part 2 of Alpine Loop)

MINI KEY
Paved
Easy
Moderate
Difficult
Other

N

TO GUNNISON

Lake City

TO CREEDE

Start here

20

149

149

30

33

30

Lake San Cristobal

30

TO ENGINEER PASS
Trail #7

UNCOMPAHGRE NATIONAL FOREST

30

36

568

WAGER GULCH
Trail #18

35

REDCLOUD MOUNTAIN

SUNSHINE MOUNTAIN

Burrows Park

WHITECROSS MOUNTAIN

Sherman

Cinnamon Pass
(12,640 ft.)

CINNAMON MOUNTAIN

American Basin

JONES MOUNTAIN

TO OURAY & ENGINEER PASS
Trail #7

CALIFORNIA GULCH
Trail #12

Animas Forks

PICAYNE GULCH
Trail #10

EUREKA GULCH
Trail #13

586

TO SILVERTON
VIA 110

Grid size - 2 sq. mile

63

Poughkeepsie Gulch from Engineer.   Some of the difficult upper section.

Looking down Poughkeepsie Gulch from California Pass. Como Lake is to the left.

Poughkeepsie Gulch

Location: South of Ouray. Trail is a side road off Engineer Pass road.

Difficulty: Difficult. The lower half is easier than the upper half which is more often used for hiking than four wheeling. If you attempt the upper portion you will need a winch or lockers. Avoid this trail under wet conditions. It is not plowed so it can be driven for only a short time during the summer.

Features: Because of the difficulty of this trail, it is not well traveled. It has a stark beauty and remote quality unlike any other trail in the area. By the time you reach Como Lake at the top, you might think you've just crossed a lunar landscape. Mines on this trail include the Old Lout and Poughkeepsie.

Time & Distance: By itself, this trail is only 4.2 miles in length and would take less than an hour if no problems were encountered. Since this trail is best traveled with a friend or a group, allow extra time because someone in the group is likely to need help. Add a half hour for the Engineer Pass section and a couple more hours to get back down from the top.

To Get There: Head south from Ouray on US 550 for 3.7 miles. Turn left and start up the road to Engineer Pass. Travel 2.5 miles to Poughkeepsie on the right. It is well marked.

Trail Description: Set your odometer to zero at the start. The trail drops down to the right and heads into the trees. There may be large mud holes in this area depending on how much rain has fallen. Some are very deep. I once encountered a new Grand Cherokee stuck in a hole with water over the tires right at the beginning of the trail. A mother allowed her teenage son to drive and he thought it would be cool to dive into one of these holes. Unfortunately, he got stuck and several inches of muddy water seeped in through the door cracks. Use good judgment when entering any body of water. If necessary, check the water depth with a stick.

At 0.1 miles, bear right at a small dilapidated bridge. After that, you cross a stream and start up a hill. The trail cuts through an area of fallen timber at 0.3 miles. At 2.1 miles the trail becomes loose talus with moguls making it difficult to get traction. This section of the trail is much easier coming down. At 2.5 you ascend above timberline about 11,000 feet. There is a confusing section at 2.6 miles. The main trail appears to go straight. You want to swing right and go up a different canyon. Just short of 3 miles, things begin to get a little tricky as the trail becomes less defined. You have to choose the best trail for your vehicle. When faced with a choice of going up a flatter muddy section or a steeper rocky section, I chose the rocky section because of better traction and because less damage is done to the trail. Depending on which route you take, you should reach Lake Como at about 3.7 miles. From here, the trail goes to the left with several choices to make along the way. You may want to walk ahead to inspect blind portions of the trail to avoid having to turn around. The trail ends at about 4.3 miles where it joins California Gulch (Trail #12).

Return Trip: You have several choices for the return trip. The fastest and easiest way is to go west over Hurricane Pass which drops down to Gladstone and Route 110 into Silverton. Before Gladstone, you come to a turn for Corkscrew Gulch (See Trail #11.) This turn is marked as County Road 11 and takes you back to 550 and Ouray. The other way is to head east from Poughkeepsie over California Pass. This way takes you to the ghost town of Animas Forks and ultimately Silverton.

Services: Full services in Ouray and Silverton.

Other Activities: Hiking, backpacking, and camping are the dominate activities in Poughkeepsie Gulch. There are several excellent hiking trails which branch off from the main vehicle trail that lead to several mines in the area.

Historical Highlights: A mile or so from the start of Poughkeepsie there is a dump by the road. There is a hiking trail here that leads up to the Old Lout Mine. This mine was started in 1876 and produced over $400,000 in silver before it closed in the silver panic of 1893. The Poughkeepsie Mine, active at the same time as Old Lout, is further up the road on the other side of the creek.

Maps: Uncompahgre National Forest, Trails Illustrated Silverton, Ouray #141, Colorado Atlas and Gazetteer.

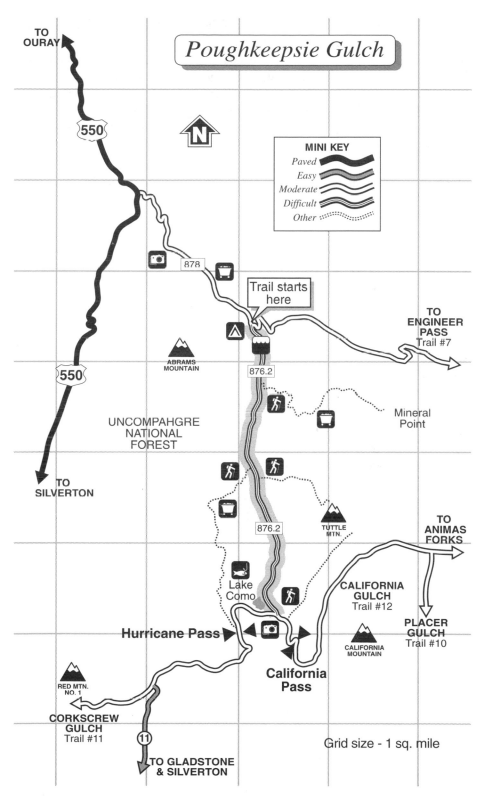

Poughkeepsie Gulch

TO OURAY

550

550

TO SILVERTON

MINI KEY
Paved
Easy
Moderate
Difficult
Other

N

878

Trail starts here

ABRAMS MOUNTAIN

UNCOMPAHGRE NATIONAL FOREST

876.2

876.2

TO ENGINEER PASS
Trail #7

Mineral Point

TUTTLE MTN.

Lake Como

Hurricane Pass

California Pass

TO ANIMAS FORKS

CALIFORNIA GULCH
Trail #12

CALIFORNIA MOUNTAIN

PLACER GULCH
Trail #10

RED MTN. NO. 1

CORKSCREW GULCH
Trail #11

11

TO GLADSTONE & SILVERTON

Grid size - 1 sq. mile

67

Crossing the ridgeline between Placer and Picayne on a foggy, wet day.

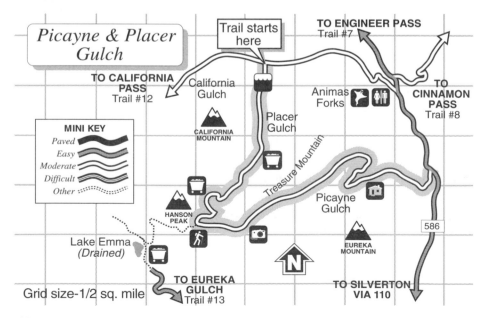

This photogenic setting can be seen as you near the lower section of Picayne Gulch.

Picayne & Placer Gulch

Trail starts here

TO ENGINEER PASS
Trail #7

TO CALIFORNIA PASS
Trail #12

California Gulch

Animas Forks

TO CINNAMON PASS
Trail #8

MINI KEY
Paved
Easy
Moderate
Difficult
Other

CALIFORNIA MOUNTAIN

Placer Gulch

Treasure Mountain

Picayne Gulch

HANSON PEAK

586

Lake Emma
(Drained)

EUREKA MOUNTAIN

N

Grid size-1/2 sq. mile

TO EUREKA GULCH
Trail #13

TO SILVERTON VIA 110

Picayne & Placer Gulch 10

Location: Southeast of Ouray and north of Silverton.

Difficulty: Moderate. Fairly narrow and steep in places with several rocky water crossings.

Features: Two of the lesser traveled trails in the area. Placer is very stark and desolate, a contrast to the forested beauty of Picayne.

Time & Distance: The two trails combined are about 6.5 miles in length and should take between 1 and 2 hours.

To Get There: Follow 110 and the Alpine Loop signs northeast out of Silverton about 13 miles to Animas Forks. Bear left past Animas Forks to California Gulch and head west for about one mile. Placer Gulch is on the left. If you run the trail in the other direction, Picayne Gulch intersects F.S. Rd. 586 about two miles south of Animas Forks.

Trail Description: Set your odometer to zero at the start of Placer Gulch. You immediately encounter a small stream crossing. Verify the water depth before crossing. You pass through a long desolate valley, portions of which are being reclaimed, so stay on the trail. At 1.8 miles, after passing several mines, you bear left and begin to climb a series of narrow switchbacks out of the valley. At 2.5 miles it begins to level off as you reach the ridgeline. West of this point, in the adjacent valley, is the Sunnyside Mine at the end of Eureka Gulch (Trail #13). You cross a long flat area across Treasure Mountain before beginning the descent down Picayne Gulch. At 5.4 miles you pass the wooden structure shown on the opposite page. After that use caution because the road becomes very narrow and steep. Driving down this section is much easier than going up. You reach F.S. 586 at 6.5 miles.

Return Trip: Turn right on F.S. 586 to go back to Silverton.

Services: Full services in Silverton.

Maps: Uncompahgre National Forest, Trails Illustrated Silverton, Ouray #141, Colorado Atlas and Gazetteer.

The start of Corkscrew is to the right. Going left takes you down to Gladstone.

The trail weaves its way between Red Mountain No.1 and Red Mountain No.2.

Looking down at Corkscrew while descending from Hurricane Pass.

Corkscrew Gulch 11

Location: North of Silverton and Gladstone. South of Ouray.

Difficulty: Moderate. The road surface is not extremely rough. The moderate rating is based on the narrowness and steepness of the trail. The lower section can be more difficult if wet because it is cut through slippery yellow clay. For this reason it is easier to travel in a downhill direction as described here.

Features: This trail cuts through the heart of old mining country as it winds between Red Mountain No. 1 and No. 2. There is active logging taking place on the lower section. You may encounter large trucks along the way. Located in Corkscrew Gulch on the lower part of the trail are the foundational remains of the Corkscrew Turntable. (See Historical Highlights.)

Time & Distance: About 5 miles in length. Allow a minimum of one hour in good weather.

To Get There: This trail is described in the easier downhill direction. The easiest way to reach the start of the trail is to head north from Silverton to Gladstone on Rt. 110. From Gladstone head north on County Road 11 to the start of the trail marked as 886. You will also reach the start of this trail after you complete California Gulch (Trail #12) or Poughkeepsie Gulch (Trail #9). Completion of these trails will bring you across Hurricane Pass. As you descend from Hurricane Pass, you see the view of Corkscrew pictured at bottom of opposite page. If you are interested in driving the trail in the opposite direction, follow 550 south about 6 or 7 miles out of Ouray. Turn at what appears to be a large dam on the left. This is actually an area of tailings under reclamation and, when seen from above, is just a large grassy area. This trail is very confusing traveling uphill because of the many poorly marked side roads.

Trail Description: Set your odometer to zero at the start. Corkscrew goes up the hill to the west and was well marked when I took the top picture on the opposite page. The road climbs steeply and becomes a narrow shelf road. There are quite a few blind curves so you may be surprised by an oncoming vehicle. Make a mental note of wide spots to pass. At 1.3 miles take the right fork downhill. You descend rapidly with some spectacular views of the Red Mountains. The talus road surface demands that you go slowly. At 2.2 miles it flattens out and you bear right as you enter the trees. There is a creek crossing at 2.1 miles. After that, you enter an area of active logging so watch for trucks. Bear to the left at 3.4 miles. The road surface becomes yellow clay in this area and can be very slippery if wet. You should have no trouble if you are careful. At 3.9 a road goes to the right. You go straight. As you continue to descend steeply, you eventually see an odd-looking area off to the left. It looks like a field surrounded by viaducts. This is a tailings area being reclaimed. You pass through a couple of wider areas in the trees where cars may be parked. Follow the main part of the road out to 550.

Return Trip: Turn right on 550 for Ouray or left for Silverton.

Services: Full services in Silverton and Ouray.

Other Activities: There are a few hiking trails off the lower section of Corkscrew, but the primary activity in this area is four-wheeling.

Historical Highlights: If you look across Corkscrew Gulch from the lower part of the trail, you should be able to see what remains of the Corkscrew covered turntable built by civil engineer C. W. Gibbs, who was employed by the Silverton Railway. The gulch was too tight for trains to turn around at this point. The direction of the entire train could be reversed by turning each car around individually with gravity doing most of the work. The turntable is immediately south of the town of Ironton, built in 1883 as a supply town for the mines in the area. In 1890 the population of Ironton was over 300. Structures at that time included an electric plant, a post office, two churches, a fire department and many houses. There were still people living here until 1960. Little remains today.

Maps: Uncompahgre National Forest, Trails Illustrated Silverton, Ouray #141, Colorado Atlas and Gazetteer.

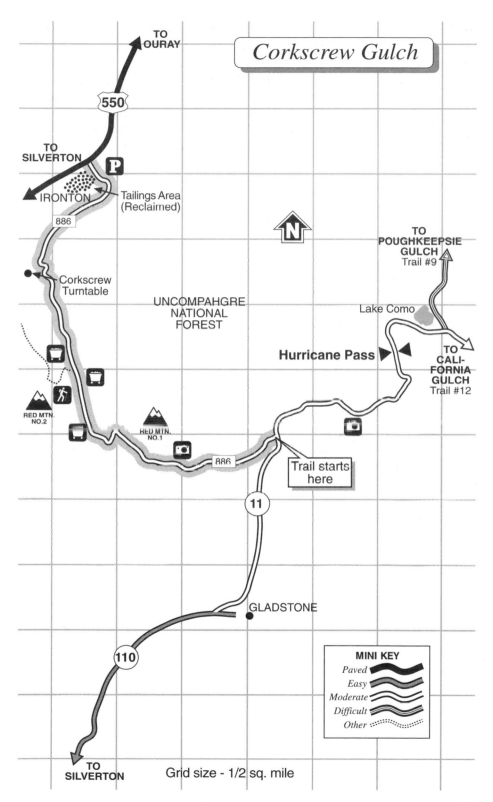

Corkscrew Gulch

TO OURAY

550

TO SILVERTON

IRONTON

P

Tailings Area (Reclaimed)

886

N

TO POUGHKEEPSIE GULCH
Trail #9

Corkscrew Turntable

UNCOMPAHGRE NATIONAL FOREST

Lake Como

Hurricane Pass

TO CALI-FORNIA GULCH
Trail #12

RED MTN. NO.2

RED MTN. NO.1

886

Trail starts here

11

GLADSTONE

110

TO SILVERTON

Grid size - 1/2 sq. mile

MINI KEY

Paved
Easy
Moderate
Difficult
Other

The summit of California Pass. The road to the right leads to Hurricane Pass.

Looking down from Cinnamon Pass to California Gulch. Animas Forks is on the left.

California Gulch 12

Location: Midway between Ouray and Silverton at Animas Forks.

Difficulty: Moderate. The only challenging part of this trail is the climb up and over California Pass. Snow accumulates on the east side of the pass and can be present well into late summer. When I went through this area in early July, from a distance there appeared to be no road at all. However, as I got closer, I could see deep trenches cut through the snow by the plows. The road itself was clear, although a little muddy from the melting snow.

Features: At the start of the trail is the town of Animas Forks, a nice place to get a close-up look at a well-preserved ghost town. Please don't go into the buildings or take any souvenirs. There is a decent public toilet near the townsite. The trail has several mines along the way, including a large well-preserved one within the first mile. Just below the summit of California Pass, on the east side, are the remains of the Mountain Queen Mine. This mine has a 400 ft. deep shaft which connects to a quarter mile long tunnel going back to lower California Gulch.

Time & Distance: From Animas Forks to California Pass is 4 miles. Add another mile to Hurricane Pass. It is 6.6 miles to the start of Corkscrew (Trail #11). The entire trip can take an hour or more depending upon conditions. Allow additional time to get back down out of the mountains.

To Get There: Assuming you drive in the direction described here, you will start at Animas Forks, which is about 13 miles northeast of Silverton. Take 110 and follow the signs for the Alpine Loop. You can also get to Animas Forks via Cinnamon Pass (Trail #8) from Lake City or by heading south from Engineer Pass (Trail # 7) from Ouray.

Trail Description: Set your odometer to zero at the start of the trail just north of Animas Forks. Head west on a bumpy but fairly easy road. A wide valley opens up and you come to a large mine on the right. At about one mile, Placer Gulch (Trail #10) goes to the left. You begin to approach California Pass at about 3 miles. If snow is present, the road may appear impassible from a distance, but as you get closer, the plowed road comes into view. In early summer, you will likely be driving through deep trenches of snow which are more like tunnels. You reach the summit of the pass at about 4 miles. There is a large area to pull over and park although it is not flat. (See picture on opposite page.) From here views are spectacular in all directions. To the east you can see the vast valley through which you have just come. To the west is a shelf road over to Hurricane Pass. Just below the summit, the trail to Poughkeepsie Gulch (Trail #9) goes north. This area is extremely difficult. If snow is present, it should not be driven by anyone. Also, looking west, you can see Lake Como, a deep blue color. Before you start down from the summit, check to make sure no one is coming up. There are few places to pass, and you will have to back up. After crossing a long shelf road, you reach Hurricane Pass just short of 5 miles.

Return Trip: Experts can return via Poughkeepsie Gulch if conditions are clear. This may occur only one or two weeks all year or perhaps not at all. Most people, however, return via Corkscrew Gulch (Trail #11), which is about 1.7 miles below Hurricane Pass. The easiest route is County Road 11, which goes to the left at the intersection of Corkscrew. This takes you down an easy road to Gladstone. From there 110 takes you into to Silverton.

Services: Full services in Silverton or Ouray.

Other Activities: There are few hiking trails in the area until you get to the top of Poughkeepsie Gulch. Otherwise, this trail is primarily for sightseeing. When I started down this trail, I felt like I was the first one to come this way in a long time. This feeling quickly vanished, however, when I encountered a full tour Jeep coming down from California Pass.

Maps: Uncompahgre National Forest, Trails Illustrated Silverton, Ouray #141, Colorado Atlas and Gazetteer.

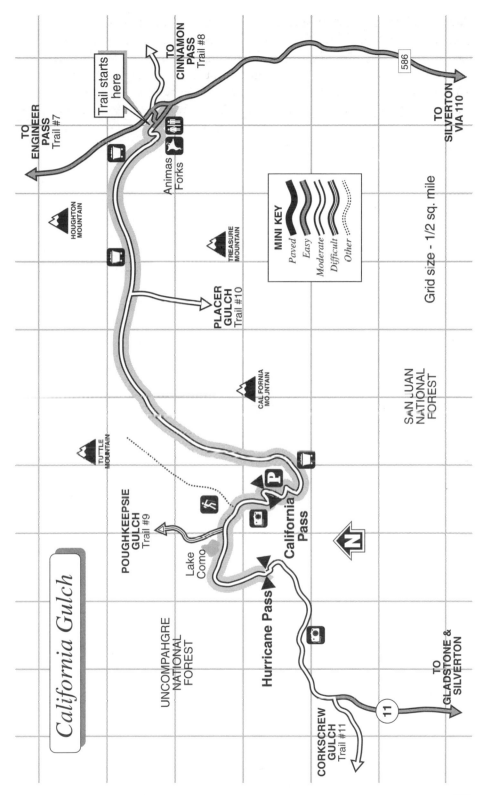

California Gulch

TO ENGINEER PASS Trail #7

TO CINNAMON PASS Trail #8

Trail starts here

Animas Forks

HOUGHTON MOUNTAIN

TREASURE MOUNTAIN

586

TO SILVERTON VIA 110

PLACER GULCH Trail #10

CALIFORNIA MOUNTAIN

MINI KEY
Paved
Easy
Moderate
Difficult
Other

Grid size - 1/2 sq. mile

SAN JUAN NATIONAL FOREST

TUTTLE MOUNTAIN

POUGHKEEPSIE GULCH Trail #9

Lake Como

P

California Pass

N

UNCOMPAHGRE NATIONAL FOREST

Hurricane Pass

11

TO GLADSTONE & SILVERTON

CORKSCREW GULCH Trail #11

This waterfall is about halfway up the trail.

The Sunnyside Mine is just ahead.

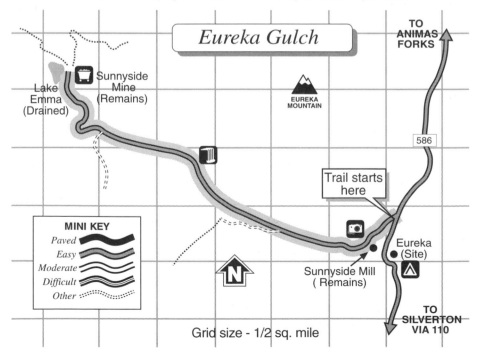

Eureka Gulch

TO
ANIMAS
FORKS

Sunnyside
Mine
(Remains)

Lake
Emma
(Drained)

EUREKA
MOUNTAIN

586

Trail starts
here

Eureka
(Site)

Sunnyside Mill
(Remains)

MINI KEY

Paved
Easy
Moderate
Difficult
Other

N

TO
SILVERTON
VIA 110

Grid size - 1/2 sq. mile

Eureka Gulch

Location: Northeast of Silverton and south of Animas Forks.

Difficulty: Easy. The road is wide and graded. The most difficult part is a steep climb at the beginning.

Features: This trail has more historical significance than beauty. It ends at the famed Sunnyside Mine. Unfortunately, only foundations remain today.

Time & Distance: 3.6 miles one way. Takes about an hour with return trip.

To Get There: Go northeast from Silverton on Highway 110 for about 10 miles. Follow signs to the Alpine Loop. Turn left just past the townsite of Eureka, now just a wide barren valley with a large concrete foundation up on the hillside. The road climbs steeply up the hillside in a reverse direction to F.S. 586.

Trail Description: Follow a wide steep road as it heads west up Eureka Gulch. You may see heavy equipment that is being used to reclaim the area. At 2.2 miles you pass the waterfall pictured on the opposite page. At 2.5 miles there are several gates. The uphill road goes to the Sunnyside Mine site and should be open. At 3 miles bear right. At 3.6 miles the road ends at the Sunnyside Mine site and the drained Emma Lake at 12,300 feet.

Return Trip: Return the way you came.

Services: Full services in Silverton.

Historical Highlights: There is so little left in the area, it is hard to imagine what a bustling town and mining community this once was. The town of Eureka was located at the great Sunnyside Mill. Its foundation remains on the hillside. Eureka was established in 1875 and had an active post office until 1942. The Sunnyside Mine produced over $50 million in ore by 1948. A tragedy occurred in 1978, when tunnels under Lake Emma were cut too close to the bottom of the lake causing it to drain unexpectedly at Gladstone. Fortunately, no one was in the mine at the time. It took over two years to repair the damage.

Maps: Uncompahgre National Forest, Trails Illustrated Silverton, Ouray #141, Colorado Atlas and Gazetteer.

A beautiful waterfall nestled in the trees.

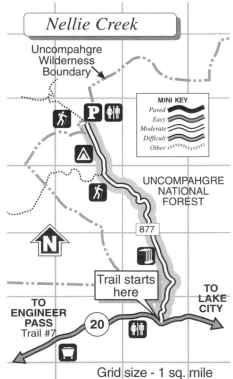

This water crossing can get deeper.

A fun roller coaster ride in places.

Nellie Creek

Uncompahgre
Wilderness
Boundary

MINI KEY
Paved
Easy
Moderate
Difficult
Other

UNCOMPAHGRE
NATIONAL
FOREST

877

N

Trail starts
here

TO
LAKE
CITY

TO
ENGINEER
PASS
Trail #7

20

Grid size - 1 sq. mile

Nellie Creek

14

Location: West of Lake City.

Difficulty: Moderate. There are just a few narrow, bumpy places and some water crossings at the beginning. The last half of the trail is fairly easy.

Features: One of my favorite short trails. A wonderful variety of beautiful terrain. At the end is the popular Uncompahgre Hiking Trail that leads to a vast network of other trails into the Uncompahgre Wilderness.

Time & Distance: 4.1 miles one way. You can do the round trip in less than an hour but you will likely want to spend more time.

To Get There: As part of the Alpine Loop, follow County Road 20 directly west of Lake City about 5 miles. If you are coming down from Engineer Pass (Trail #7), the trail is on the left.

Trail Description: There is a large brown and white sign marking the beginning of the trail. As you start down the trail, it is marked as F.S. Road 877. Set your odometer to zero at the start. Shift into low gear immediately because the toughest part of the trail is at the beginning. The road is fairly narrow and you begin to climb quickly. At 0.8 miles on the left, watch for the waterfall pictured on the opposite page. It is back in the trees and easy to miss. This is a great place to stop and take some pictures. At 1.9 miles, there is the first of a series of water crossings. Most of the time the water is fairly shallow; however, during spring run-off it may be deeper. A smaller dead-end trail goes to the right at 2.3 miles. You reach a flatter open area at 3.3 miles. Many people find this a great place to camp. As you continue, the forest changes from aspen to pine, and at 4.1 miles you reach a large parking area for the Uncompahgre Hiking Trail. When I was there, a public restroom was under construction by the parking lot.

Return Trip: Go east 5 miles on County Rd. 20 to Lake City or take the much longer route west over Engineer Pass back to Ouray.

Services: Full services in Lake City.

Maps: Uncompahgre National Forest, Trails Illustrated Silverton, Ouray #141, Colorado Atlas and Gazetteer.

Starting down the east side.

This SUV crosses Pole Creek with ease.

Photographer prepares to catch the morning light from near the summit looking east.

Stony Pass

15

Location: Northeast of Silverton.

Difficulty: Moderate. This trail has an interesting variety of terrain including steep, narrow rocky sections, stream crossings, and muddy areas. The Pole Creek stream crossing can be too deep to cross during spring run-off.

Features: This trail crosses the continental divide and skirts the Weminuche Wilderness. It is one of the longest uninterrupted climbs in the state. It passes through an area rich in mining history. At one point, you cross under an aerial tramway with a bucket suspended over the road. Many of these buckets still contain ore. One might think the mines were shut down only yesterday.

Time & Distance: This trail eventually connects to County Road 149 into Creede, which is over 60 miles from Rt 110 at Howardsville. The high mountain portion or the first 13 miles is described here. You should allow at least 3 hours to go this distance and return.

To Get There: From 550 at Silverton, drive east through town and bear right on paved road 110. A left turn would take you in the wrong direction to Gladstone. After 5 miles, turn right at Howardsville on County Road 4.

Trail Description: Set your odometer to zero at Howardsville. Head south on County Rd. 4, following signs to Stony Pass. The road is marked dead end but you will turn before that occurs. At 0.2 miles bear right and follow Cunningham Creek. You pass several mine buildings and one that appears to be converted into a residence. At 1.7 miles, turn left up the hill then make an immediate right on County Rd. 3. It should be marked to Creede and Stony Pass. As the road gets steeper, you pass under a suspended tram bucket. You turn back into the woods at 2.5 miles and cross a small stream. Go straight at 3.3 and bear left at 3.6 miles. You make several more stream crossings as the road gets steeper. It gets rockier but begins to flatten out as you approach the summit at 5.9 miles. A sign marks the summit at an elevation of 12,650 ft. When I stopped here, I noticed quite a few marmots scurrying about. These are furry little creatures that make a distinctive high pitch sound, that has earned for them the nickname "Whistle Pigs."

The east side descent is more gradual but there are minor rough spots occasionally. There are several places where the soil looks like wet cement. You reach Pole Creek at about the 12 mile point. During the spring this creek can get very deep so if you are not sure of the water depth, check before crossing. Turn around here if you don't think it is safe to cross. If you continue, expect muddier conditions. After the creek the road is marked as F.S. 520. Within a mile you come to a decision point. A sign indicates that Creede is 47 miles straight ahead, Bear Town is 4 miles to the right, and Kite Lake is 6 miles to the right. If you decide to explore any of these routes, make sure you are with a friend or have a winch. You are a long way from a service station. The road to Creede is a 4-wheel drive road for another 10 miles before it reaches the popular Rio Grande Reservoir. Here you will find several Forest Service campgrounds and an improved gravel road.

Return Trip: I recommend you reverse your direction to return to Silverton. If you continue to the Rio Grande Reservoir, you will eventually reach Road 149. From there head north to Lake City or continue east to Creede. I did not scout this portion of the trail, so you are on your own if you proceed.

Services: Full services at Silverton.

Other Activities: There are quite a few hiking trails in this area offering the serious backpacker plenty of challenge. They connect to a network of trails, some heading north and some heading into the Weminuche Wilderness area.

Historical Highlights: Stony Pass was once a major supply route between Del Norte and Silverton. In 1882, the Denver and Rio Grande narrow gauge railroad was completed into Silverton and Stony Pass was abandoned. In recent years the road has been improved primarily for tourist use.

Maps: Uncompahgre National Forest, Trails Illustrated Silverton, Ouray #141, Colorado Atlas and Gazetteer.

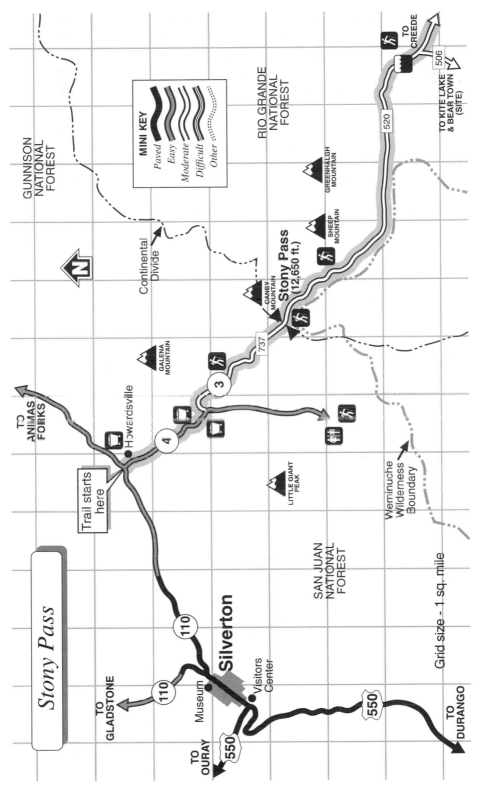

Stony Pass

MINI KEY

Paved
Easy
Moderate
Difficult
Other

N

GUNNISON NATIONAL FOREST

RIO GRANDE NATIONAL FOREST

Continental Divide

TO CREEDE

506

520

TO KITE LAKE & BEAR TOWN (SITE)

GREENHALGH MOUNTAIN

SHEEP MOUNTAIN

Stony Pass (12,650 ft.)

CANBY MOUNTAIN

737

GALENA MOUNTAIN

3

4

Howerdsville

TO ANIMAS FORKS

Trail starts here

LITTLE GIANT PEAK

Weminuche Wilderness Boundary

SAN JUAN NATIONAL FOREST

Grid size - 1 sq. mile

110

Silverton

Museum

Visitors Center

110

TO GLADSTONE

550

TO OURAY

550

TO DURANGO

The road gets a little narrow through this section, but the view is worth the trip.

Make sure you stay on the road here.

Maggie Gulch 16

Location: Northeast of Silverton.

Difficulty: Easy. A little narrow and steep in a few places but the road surface is fairly smooth until it reaches the top of the mountain.

Features: A couple of unique features stand out on this short trip. One section is dominated by remarkable talus slopes hundreds of feet high. Later you cross a narrow ledge which showcases an interesting waterfall.

Time & Distance: The road remains easy for the first 3 miles. You can continue farther but conditions gradually worsen. Allow about an hour to go up and back.

To Get There: From 550 at Silverton, drive east through town and bear right on paved road 110. Go 6.8 miles and watch for signs to the Middleton public toilet on the right. The trail departs from this point.

Trail Description: Set your odometer to zero at the start. Follow the left fork at the beginning of the trail. The road is cut through reddish soil and switchbacks up through the trees. The scenery changes abruptly at 0.8 miles as you come out of the trees into an open valley. To the left are giant slopes of talus which should not be disturbed in any way. Although a remote possibility, slopes like these have been known to give way and carry the careless driver down the mountainside. At 1.3 miles you encounter the shelf road pictured on the opposite page. The view here is quite nice, but don't be distracted. You pass through a slightly rockier section before it begins to flatten out into a beautiful valley. In the summer wildflowers are abundant in this area. You can drive much farther but the road worsens and hiking may be more appropriate. There are several hiking trails at the top that tie into trails coming over from Stony Pass. Turn around at your own discretion.

Return Trip: Return the way you came.

Services: Full services in Silverton.

Maps: Uncompahgre National Forest, Trails Illustrated Silverton, Ouray #141, Colorado Atlas and Gazetteer.

These two small cabins are very well preserved. Do not enter or climb on them.

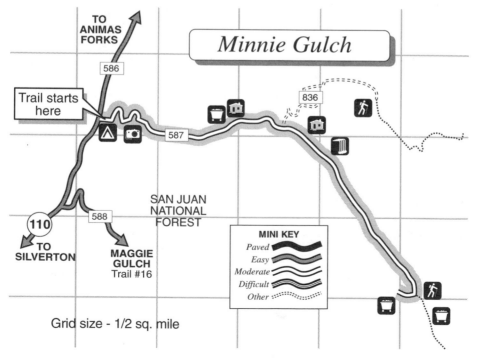

TO ANIMAS FORKS

586

Minnie Gulch

Trail starts here

836

587

110

TO SILVERTON

588

MAGGIE GULCH Trail #16

SAN JUAN NATIONAL FOREST

MINI KEY
Paved
Easy
Moderate
Difficult
Other

Grid size - 1/2 sq. mile

Minnie Gulch

Location: Northeast of Silverton.

Difficulty: Moderate. This rating is based on just a couple of moderately difficult spots. Most of the trail is easy.

Features: This short trail climbs rapidly up a beautiful valley. There are mines along the way with several well-preserved cabins. There are a few primitive camping spots nestled in the trees at the beginning of the trail.

Time & Distance: About 3 miles one way. Allow about an hour to go up and back.

To Get There: From 550 at Silverton, drive east through town and bear right on paved road 110. Go about 7.4 miles and watch for the trail on the right. This trail is F.S. Road 587 but I found no markings.

Trail Description: Set your odometer to zero at the start. You first pass through a wooded section that has become an unofficial camping area. A well graded road then begins to climb. Part of the the trail is cut through some fairly unstable soil, so watch for rocks that may have fallen onto the road. This is also a popular area for ATVs, so proceed with caution. At 1.1 miles you pass a large foundation of an old mining mill. Just around the corner are two cabins. The most interesting one is on the right in the trees. Please do not enter or take any souvenirs. These cabins are private property. At 1.5 take the fork to the right. At 1.7 miles there are two tiny cabins on the left. They are in such good condition that, at first, you wonder if they are occupied. Again, do not enter or climb on these artifacts. There is a waterfall at 2.3, followed by a deep ditch that you should cross carefully. After 2.5 miles the road begins to deteriorate, so proceed until conditions warrant turning around. The upper section is a great place to hike.

Return Trip: Return the way you came.

Services: Full services in Silverton.

Maps: Uncompahgre National Forest, Trails Illustrated Silverton, Ouray #141, Colorado Atlas and Gazetteer.

The remains of Carson, one of the best preserved ghost towns in Colorado.

Wager Gulch from high above Carson.

Wager Gulch

TO LAKE CITY

TO CINNAMON PASS

30

36

Trail starts here

Forest Boundary

MINI KEY
Paved
Easy
Moderate
Difficult
Other

568

GUNNISON NATIONAL FOREST

Continental Divide

Carson

Heart Lake Rd.

BENT PEAK

518

Grid size - 1/2 sq. mile

Wager Gulch 18

Location: Southwest of Lake City.

Difficulty: Moderate. This rating applies to the section below Carson. Above Carson the trail is more difficult.

Features: Most people drive this trail to see the well-preserved ghost town of Carson. Historians claim this town is really Bachelor Cabins, which serviced the Bachelor Mine, and that the original town of Carson is up the hill farther.

Time & Distance: It is less than 4 miles to the town of Carson. You should allow about 1.5 hours plus stopping time. Add additional time if you continue past the town.

To Get There: Head south on 149 from Lake City following signs for the Alpine Loop. After a couple of miles, turn right on County Rd. 30 and continue another 9 miles to Wager Gulch on the left marked as County Rd. 36.

Trail Description: Set your odometer to zero at the start. The first 0.3 miles passes through private property. After that you go through some pretty ugly logging country before reaching the Gunnison National Forest at 1.5 miles. Here the road is marked as F.S. 568. At 2.8 miles it begins to level off as you enter a wide valley. Take the left fork at 3.5 miles to the ghost town of Carson. The road to the right takes you farther up the mountain; however, you can still see Carson off to the left. It is a total of 5 miles to the top of the ridge which is the Continental Divide. It gets more difficult as you go higher, but with some care, I was able to reach the top in my stock Grand Cherokee without scraping bottom. There are several trails down the other side but they are remote and difficult.

Return Trip: Most people turn around and head back down the mountain. Serious four-wheelers, however, may continue on to the far reaches of the backcountry. It is possible to connect with Stony Pass and Silverton.

Services: Full services in Lake City.

Maps: Uncompahgre National Forest, Trails Illustrated Silverton, Ouray #141, Colorado Atlas and Gazetteer.

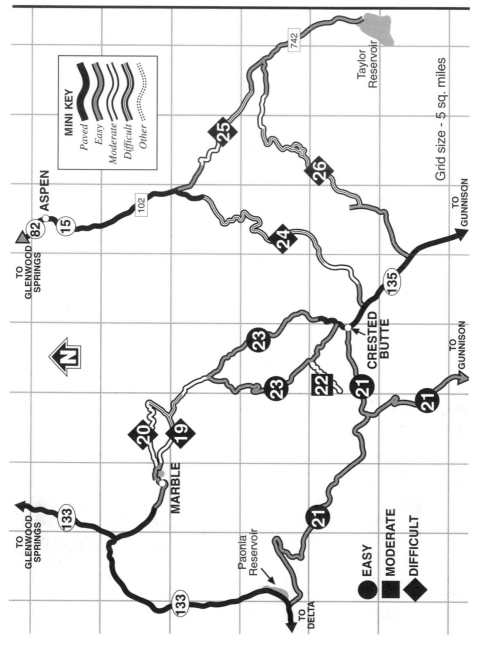

AREA 2

Crested Butte, Aspen, Marble

19. Schofield Pass,
    Crystal River
20. Lead King Basin
21. Kebler & Ohio Pass
22. Gunsight Pass
23. Slate & Gothic Road
24. Pearl Pass
25. Taylor Pass
26. Italian Creek Road

MINI KEY

Paved
Easy
Moderate
Difficult
Other

ASPEN

TO GLENWOOD SPRINGS

82

15

102

742

Taylor Reservoir

25

26

24

N

23

23

22

21

135

CRESTED BUTTE

21

20

19

MARBLE

TO GLENWOOD SPRINGS

133

133

Paonia Reservoir

21

TO DELTA

TO GUNNISON

TO GUNNISON

Grid size - 5 sq. miles

EASY

MODERATE

DIFFICULT

AREA 2
Crested Butte, Aspen, Marble

Crested Butte and Aspen are internationally known for winter activities. Summer visitors, however, will tell you much of the beauty is buried under winter snows. Only in summer can this area be explored and appreciated to its fullest extent. Surrounded by four wilderness areas, including the fabulous Maroon Bells-Snowmass Wilderness, this area dishes out a massive dose of unspoiled beauty. When a wilderness is created, it is not unusual for the best four-wheel drive trails nearby to be lost. Here, however, many wilderness boundaries were graciously made contiguous with existing vehicular trails. This is as close as one can get to driving through a wilderness. Fortunately, beloved trails like Schofield Pass through Crystal River Canyon and Pearl Pass were of such renowned importance, that they have been preserved for all to enjoy. As you travel through these pristine lands, make sure the land is left exactly the way you found it. Better yet, do something to make it a better place. For example, carry out one piece of trash that someone else has left behind.

Schofield Pass Road as it begins to descend down the Crystal River Canyon.

Looking up at the Devil's Punch Bowl from the bridge below.

Narrowest part of the ledge around the Devil's Punch Bowl; a difficult place to back up.

The much photographed powerhouse on the Crystal River.

Schofield Pass, Crystal River 19

Location: Between Crested Butte and Marble.

Difficulty: Difficult. The upper portion of this trail is extremely narrow with loose rock that can cause a vehicle to move sideways unexpectedly. Passing is difficult, especially through the Devil's Punch Bowl. You may have to back up quite a distance to find a place wide enough to pass. Full-size vehicles are not recommended. Do not attempt if snow or ice are present because avalanches are possible. Many serious accidents have occurred on this trail primarily because it tempts inexperienced tourists who come to visit the powerhouse on the easier lower section. At the bottom, large signs indicate when you are entering the difficult section. *(Note: On July 9, 1970, the worst offroad accident in Colorado history occurred when nine tourists died when a full-size vehicle plummeted off the ledge at the Devil's Punch Bowl.)*

Features: Starting from the Crested Butte side, this trail drops steeply through a narrow valley called the Devil's Punch Bowl, which is part of Crystal River Canyon. The challenge, beauty, and unique character of this trail make it one of my favorites. In addition to several outstanding waterfalls and stream crossings, you pass by the much photographed powerhouse mill. The less adventurous can reach the powerhouse and the town of Crystal from Marble without having to cross the difficult upper section.

Time & Distance: The complete trip from the top of Schofield Pass to the town of Marble is about 10 miles. Allow at least two hours one way. Add more time for busy weekends and holidays. Add another half hour to reach Schofield Pass from Crested Butte. To fully enjoy the trip, plan to spend a full day going from Crested Butte to Marble and back.

To Get There: This trail is described here going downhill starting from the top of Schofield Pass, which can be reached by passenger car from the town of Crested Butte via Rd. 317. Follow signs north of town to the Mt. Crested Butte Ski Area and continue on past the town of Gothic. You can also reach Schofield Pass via Slate Road 519. Either way is quite beautiful and is described in Trail #23. If you are interested in traveling only the lower, easier part of the trail from the Marble side, Marble can be reached heading south on Route 82 and 133 from Glenwood Springs.

Trail Description: Set your odometer to zero at the top of Schofield Pass.

Leaving Schofield Pass heading north, bear right on 317 at the first fork. The road narrows a little as it drops downhill. This section is very slippery if wet and can be difficult coming back up. After crossing a small stream, you enter a wide flat valley with a beautiful scenic backdrop. Cars may be parked off to the right for a hiking trail. After about 2 miles, you may want to shift into low gear as you begin to descend a rocky steep section. You cross a small wooden bridge at 2.3. Stop here to inspect a beautiful waterfall on the right. After this point, the trail continues to deteriorate as it crosses back and forth across the south fork of the Crystal River. The largest stream crossing is at 2.7 miles just before you start the descent into the Devil's Punch Bowl. Allow time for brakes and tires to dry before descending and wait for anyone coming up. There are only a couple of places wide enough to pass. Watch for these places as you descend because you may have to back up to them later. Remember, vehicles coming up have the right of way.

There is one very narrow rocky section pictured on page 94. At this point, it is best to have someone out of the vehicle spotting for you. Passengers may want to get out and walk anyway. After this section you cross another bridge. The road gets a little easier from this point, but is still extremely narrow as it twists along the steep canyon wall. At 4.6 miles, Lead King Basin (Trail # 20) goes to the right. Bear to the left for the town of Crystal and the powerhouse, both encountered in the next mile. The next 4 miles are much easier as the trail winds through spectacular scenery along the wider part of the Crystal River. Towards the end of the trail, you pass Lizard Lake and climb a short hill into a residential area. At about 9 miles, the other end of Lead King Basin (315) goes to the right. Bear to the left for Marble. Beaver Lake, just before Marble, is a great place to stop for lunch. There is a modern pit toilet located beside the lake.

Return Trip: You have several choices for the return trip. You can continue through Marble to Route 133 which takes you north to Redstone and Glenwood Springs or south to Hotchkiss and Delta. You may wish to return the way you came. If so, you can vary the return trip by taking a northerly option through Lead King Basin (Trail # 20).

Services: Full services in Crested Butte. Gas and limited services in Marble.

Other Activities: Fishing at Beaver Lake and the lower part of the Crystal River. A marvelous place to hike. Some find this a challenging area to mountain bike. Marble is a nice little town to look around.

Maps: White River National Forest, Trails Illustrated Maroon Bells, Redstone, Marble #128, Colorado Atlas and Gazetteer.

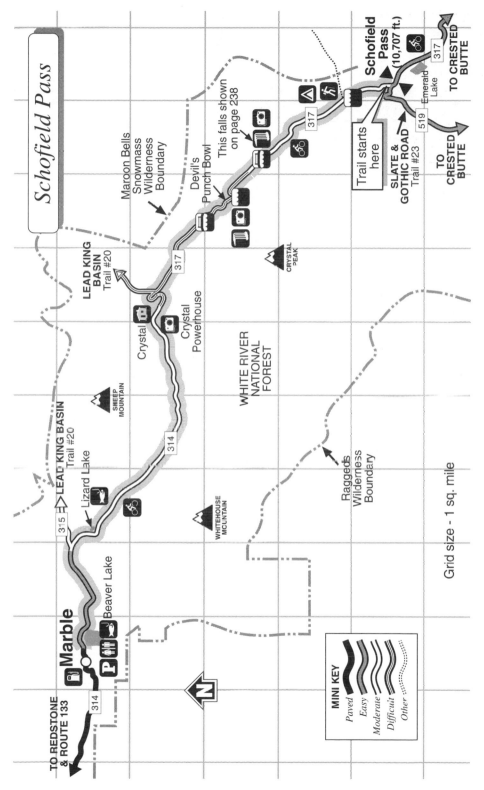

Schofield Pass

Schofield Pass (10,707 ft.)

317
TO CRESTED BUTTE

Trail starts here

SLATE & GOTHIC ROAD Trail #23

519

Emerald Lake

TO CRESTED BUTTE

Maroon Bells Snowmass Wilderness Boundary

Devil's Punch Bowl

This falls shown on page 238

317

CRYSTAL PEAK

LEAD KING BASIN Trail #20

317

Crystal

Crystal Powerhouse

WHITE RIVER NATIONAL FOREST

Raggeds Wilderness Boundary

SHEEP MOUNTAIN

314

LEAD KING BASIN Trail #20

Lizard Lake

315

Beaver Lake

WHITEHOUSE MOUNTAIN

Marble

314

TO REDSTONE & ROUTE 133

N

MINI KEY
Paved
Easy
Moderate
Difficult
Other

Grid size - 1 sq. mile

North fork of the Crystal River.

The more difficult eastern end of the trail.

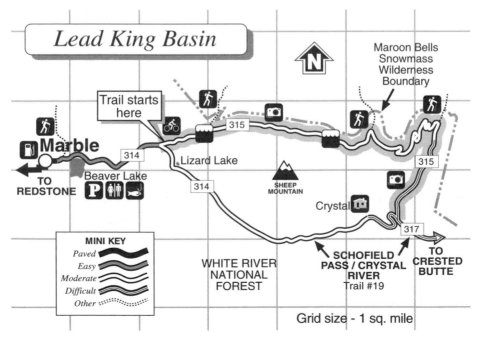

Lead King Basin

Maroon Bells Snowmass Wilderness Boundary

Trail starts here

315

Marble

314

Lizard Lake

TO REDSTONE

Beaver Lake

314

315

SHEEP MOUNTAIN

Crystal

317

MINI KEY
Paved
Easy
Moderate
Difficult
Other

SCHOFIELD PASS / CRYSTAL RIVER
Trail #19

WHITE RIVER NATIONAL FOREST

TO CRESTED BUTTE

Grid size - 1 sq. mile

Lead King Basin  20

Location: East of Marble.

Difficulty: Difficult. Moderate for the first 6.5 miles when approached from the west side as described here. The last 1.5 miles are difficult.

Features: The scenery is absolutely spectacular at almost every point along the way. Several hiking trails connect to the nearby wilderness.

Time & Distance: Lead King Basin is about 8 miles by itself and takes a couple of hours. Add another hour to return to Marble via the Schofield Pass (Trail #19) along the Crystal River.

To Get There: To get to Marble via paved roads, follow routes 82, 133, and 314 from Glenwood Springs. About a mile west of Marble, turn left and follow signs to Lead King Basin marked as 315. To get to Marble from Crested Butte, follow directions for the Schofield Pass trail.

Trail Description: Set your odometer to zero where 314 and 315 split. There is a stream crossing at 0.7 miles and a place to park if you intend to hike or mountain bike. After that you begin to climb an increasingly steep dirt road with moguls, twists, and turns. It is really quite fun if the road is dry but use caution if wet. Just past 2 miles the road splits. Bear to the left following signs for 315. Around 3.5 miles you reach the top and start down. At 3.9 bear to the right. The views of the valley below on this side of the mountain are wonderful. The road is quite narrow in places. You may have to back up if someone is coming uphill so make a mental note of wide spots as you descend. You cross a small stream a couple of times and at 6.5 miles you reach the popular Geneva Lake North Fork Trailhead on the left. The trail gets more difficult from this point. Although passable for some stock vehicles, excellent driving skills are needed to proceed. At 8 miles the trail intersects the Schofield Pass trail.

Return Trip: Turn right and follow the Schofield Pass trail back into Marble. Left will take you to Crested Butte over very difficult terrain.

Services: Gas and limited services in Marble.

Maps: White River National Forest, Trails Illustrated Maroon Bells, Redstone, Marble #128, Colorado Atlas and Gazetteer.

Smooth going on Kebler Pass road.

Looking down from near the top of Ohio Pass.

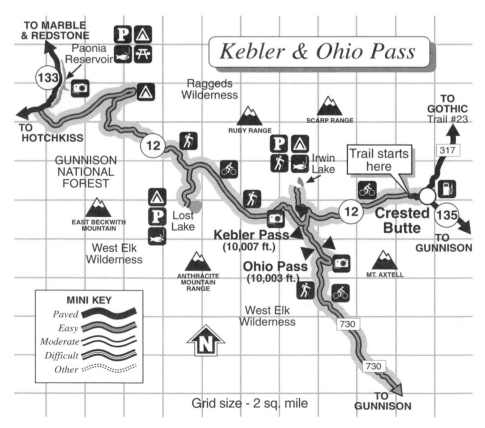

Kebler & Ohio Pass

TO MARBLE & REDSTONE

Paonia Reservoir

133

TO HOTCHKISS

Raggeds Wilderness

SCARP RANGE

RUBY RANGE

12

GUNNISON NATIONAL FOREST

Irwin Lake

Trail starts here

TO GOTHIC
Trail #23

317

EAST BECKWITH MOUNTAIN

Lost Lake

West Elk Wilderness

Kebler Pass
(10,007 ft.)

12

Crested Butte

135

TO GUNNISON

ANTHRACITE MOUNTAIN RANGE

Ohio Pass
(10,003 ft.)

MT. AXTELL

West Elk Wilderness

730

MINI KEY
Paved
Easy
Moderate
Difficult
Other

N

730

Grid size - 2 sq. mile

TO GUNNISON

Kebler & Ohio Pass ㉑

Location: Immediately west of Crested Butte

Difficulty: Easy. Both trails are extremely smooth wide gravel roads. Kebler is wide enough for motorhomes and boat trailers. Ohio is not.

Features: The scenery on both trails is outstanding. Great hiking, camping and fishing at Irwin Lake, Lost Lake, and Paonia State Recreation Area.

Time & Distance: Kebler Pass road from Rt.135 in Crested Butte to 133 at Paonia Reservoir is about 35 miles. Allow about 1.5 hours driving time. The unpaved portion of Ohio Pass road heading south from Kebler is about 8 miles and takes about a half hour. After the pavement begins, it is another 18 miles to Gunnison.

To Get There: To get to the start of Kebler Pass road as shown here, head west on Whiterock Avenue off 135 in Crested Butte. Whiterock becomes County Road 12. If you are coming from Gunnison, you may want to reach Kebler heading north on Ohio Pass road 730 which turns left off of 135 about 3.5 miles north of Gunnison.

Trail Description: Set your odometer to zero when the pavement ends coming out of Crested Butte on Whiterock Avenue. Bear left at a gated road at 0.5 miles. At 5.2 miles Irwin Lake road goes to the right. All side trips to the lakes are well worth the time. At 5.6 miles Ohio Pass forks to the left. The nicest part of Ohio Pass is the unpaved portion which is the first 8 miles south. Continuing on Kebler from where Ohio turns off, Kebler Pass is just 0.2 miles farther. As you begin the gentle descent down the other side of Kebler Pass, the road actually gets wider for quite a distance. The main road is obvious all the way to Rt.133 from this point. The balance of the trip is lengthy but very beautiful. If you are boating, Paonia Reservoir, at 34 miles, should be your final destination. Otherwise, Lost Lake, which turns off at 14.7 miles, offers fishing and camping.

Return Trip: Most people return the way they came.

Services: Full services in Crested Butte.

Maps: Gunnison National Forest, Trails Illustrated Kebler Pass, Paonia Reservoir #133, Colorado Atlas and Gazetteer.

Go around this unsafe bridge at the start.

The road switchbacks up the mountain side.

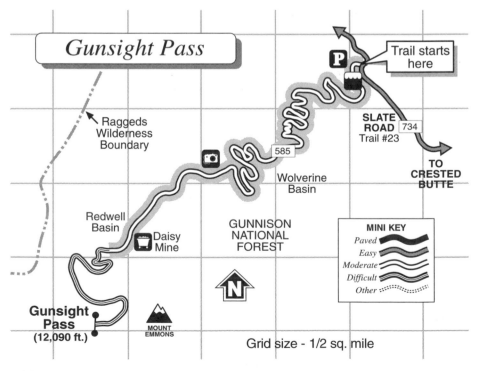

Gunsight Pass

Raggeds
Wilderness
Boundary

Trail starts
here

SLATE
ROAD 734
Trail #23

585

TO
CRESTED
BUTTE

Wolverine
Basin

Redwell
Basin

Daisy
Mine

GUNNISON
NATIONAL
FOREST

MINI KEY
Paved
Easy
Moderate
Difficult
Other

N

Gunsight
Pass
(12,090 ft.)

MOUNT
EMMONS

Grid size - 1/2 sq. mile

Gunsight Pass

Location: Northwest of Crested Butte.

Difficulty: Moderate. This rating is due to the steep narrow switchbacks and the initial water crossing. The road surface is fairly easy to the Daisy Mine. Beyond this point is not recommended. Do not attempt if snow, ice, or high water are present.

Features: A very short trip but a dramatically beautiful climb. Several unique characteristics make this road popular for parasailing. In late summer wild raspberries grow by the side of the road.

Time & Distance: The sign at the bottom says Gunsight Pass is 5 miles. I measured 5 miles to the Daisy Mine. The round trip to the mine can be done in an hour but you will probably want to take more time to admire the views.

To Get There: About a mile north of Crested Butte on 135, turn left on Slate Road 734. Bear right after Nicholson Lake. The turnoff for Gunsight Pass is on the left at 4 miles. Watch for the bridge pictured on the opposite page.

Trail Description: Set your odometer to zero as you turn off Slate Road. The first part of the trail including the water crossing is actually the roughest part. Do not cross the bridge. Examine the depth of the water carefully for the shallowest part. I found places to the left of the bridge no deeper than a foot in late summer. At 0.5 miles bear right. A gate follows at 0.7. Make sure you close it after you pass through. There are no other road splits until after the Daisy Mine. The road switchbacks up the mountain side rapidly and is a little narrow in places. Take your time and watch for other vehicles as you proceed. The remains of the Daisy Mine are on the left at about 5 miles. Just beyond the mine is a good place to turn around. The road is difficult and unstable beyond this point.

Return Trip: Return the way you came.

Services: Full services in Crested Butte.

Maps: Gunnison National Forest, Trails Illustrated Kebler Pass, Paonia Reservoir #133, Colorado Atlas and Gazetteer.

Upper portion of Slate Road approaching Paradise Divide.

Looking down from Paradise Divide to Paradise Basin.

Emerald Lake. Snow can sometimes block road below the lake in late summer.

Slate & Gothic Road ㉓

Location: Immediately north of Crested Butte.

Difficulty: Easy. Gothic Road is the easier of the two roads with passenger cars frequently seen at the top of Schofield Pass although an area just below Emerald Lake is often blocked with snow even in late summer. Slate Road is a little narrower and bumpier, especially the upper portion.

Features: The pictures shown on the opposite page represent only a small part of the varied scenery that you will experience on this loop trail. Gothic Road is more popular with tourists while local residents will tell you Slate Road offers slightly more challenge and is therefore the more interesting of the two roads. F.S. Road 811 is located between Gothic and Slate Roads and is an easy, beautiful alternative drive.

Time & Distance: From the intersection of 135 and Slate Road, the entire loop is about 30 miles. You should allow a minimum of 2 hours but will likely spend closer to half a day if you stop at many of the interesting places along the way.

To Get There: Take Rt.135 north out of Crested Butte about a mile and turn left on Slate Road 734. If you want to drive the loop in the opposite direction described here, follow signs to the Mt. Crested Butte ski area and continue on to Gothic.

Trail Description: Set your odometer to zero when you turn off 135 at Slate Road. This road starts as a nice, easy, wide gravel road and follows the course of the Slate River. Although maps show this area as part of the Gunnison National Forest, most of the surrounding land is private property so please respect the rights of property owners. After a couple of miles, you pass private Nicholson Lake. Just after the lake, bear to the right. At 3.5 miles the Gunsight Pass road (Trail # 22) is on the left. Shortly after, you pass a sign for Oh-Be-Joyful Pass. This was once a challenging four-wheel drive road. However, when part of the forest was declared a wilderness area, most of the trail is now a hiking trail and off limits to all types of vehicles, including mountain bikes. You can still drive far enough to reach several nice unofficial camping spots. About 7.1 miles, you pass the Daisy Pass road to the left. It too becomes a hiking trail at the Raggeds Wilderness boundary. After passing through the nearly invisible town of Pittsburg, the road switchbacks sharply up the hill to the right at 8.8 miles. As you climb, the road becomes much narrower but is still fairly smooth as it climbs towards the Paradise Divide. At 10.6 miles, Rd. 811 meets Slate Road. Road 811 is a beautiful, easy return route to Mt. Crested Butte. Paradise Divide, at the crest of the hill, can be identified by a small picturesque lake on the left and a sign indicating that you are at 11,250 feet. This is a great spot to stop and admire the beautiful sights in every direction. After the lake, bear to the right and start down. From this point the road gets a little rougher with a few small water crossings. You can see the road twisting into the distance as it crosses Paradise Basin. There is a gate at the top as you start down. If conditions are not safe, it will be closed.

The road now becomes 519. Bear right at 13.7 miles and pass through an area frequented by campers. In another 0.6 miles you intersect with Gothic Road 317. Turning left takes you to Marble over difficult trail #19. Turn right and you immediately get to Schofield Pass, a good spot for a photo. There is also a challenging hiking and mountain biking trail that descends east from Schofield Pass almost down to the town of Gothic. Gothic Road is a little narrow above Emerald Lake but widens significantly as you descend. An area just below Emerald Lake is prone to avalanches and the road can be blocked by snow even in late summer. Some years it may not open at all. Gothic Road has no confusing side roads, so just enjoy the views as you continue. There are many places to camp along this road, including Gothic Forest Service Campground a few miles below Emerald Lake. There should be a pit toilet in the campground. Just past the campground is the Avery Picnic Area.

After that you pass through the town of Gothic. Make sure you abide by the very slow speed limit as local police often hang out here. As you get closer to Crested Butte, the ski area will appear clearly in front of you. Most people see it only in the winter, but it is also very impressive in the summer. The development around the ski area dominates the small town of Crested Butte below. Just below the ski area, you return to the starting point.

Other Activities: Beyond the roadside camping areas lie the Maroon Bells-Snowmass Wilderness and the Raggeds Wilderness offering some of the most incredible hiking and backpacking anywhere. Mountain biking is very popular on the main roads in addition to the Trail Riders Trail that descends from Schofield Pass. This trail skirts the edge of the wilderness.

Services: Full services in Crested Butte and Mt. Crested Butte.

Maps: Gunnison and White River National Forests, Colorado Atlas and Gazetteer. Three Trails Illustrated Maps are required to cover the whole route: #128, #131, and #133.

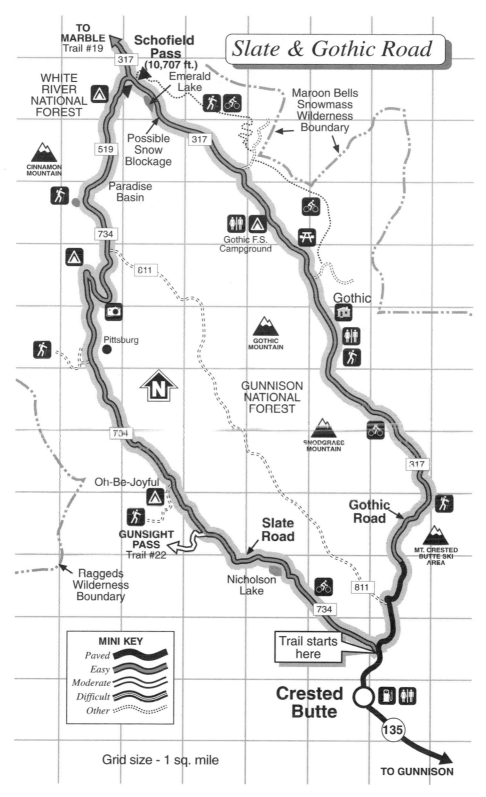

Slate & Gothic Road

TO MARBLE Trail #19

Schofield Pass (10,707 ft.)

317

WHITE RIVER NATIONAL FOREST

Emerald Lake

317

Maroon Bells Snowmass Wilderness Boundary

519

Possible Snow Blockage

CINNAMON MOUNTAIN

Paradise Basin

734

811

Gothic F.S. Campground

Gothic

Pittsburg

GOTHIC MOUNTAIN

GUNNISON NATIONAL FOREST

734

SNODGRASS MOUNTAIN

317

Oh-Be-Joyful

GUNSIGHT PASS Trail #22

Raggeds Wilderness Boundary

Slate Road

Gothic Road

Nicholson Lake

MT. CRESTED BUTTE SKI AREA

811

734

Trail starts here

MINI KEY

Paved
Easy
Moderate
Difficult
Other

Crested Butte

135

Grid size - 1 sq. mile

TO GUNNISON

Looking north from the summit. Pearl in foreground, Montezuma Basin in background.

This section, just below the summit on the north side, was still blocked in late August.

Location: Between Crested Butte and Aspen.

Difficulty: Difficult. Many boulder fields, steep climbs, water crossings, and narrow shelves. These conditions are magnified by snow and ice that are present well into late summer at higher elevations. During years of heavy snowpack, the summit can be blocked for the entire year. (See photo on opposite page.) Always travel with another vehicle or group of vehicles whenever attempting to drive the entire trail and check with local authorities to see if the trail is open.

Features: Located between two of the most famous recreational areas in the state, this very long and exhausting trail offers an unmatched variety of different landscapes from rolling hillsides to challenging rock ledges. High elevation sections of the trail follow the border of the Maroon Bells-Snowmass Wilderness and pass through some of the most remote and strikingly beautiful areas of Colorado.

Time & Distance: About 22 miles from Route 135 in Crested Butte to Castle Creek Road on the Aspen side. The south side of Pearl Pass is about 16 miles compared to 6 miles on the north side. Due to the ruggedness of the trail, you should allow 3 to 5 hours for the complete trip. Allow adequate time to turn around and head back because the trail is often blocked at the top.

To Get There: From Crested Butte, drive south 2 miles on paved road 135 and follow signs left to the country club. This is Brush Creek Road 738. From Aspen, head south on Castle Creek Road 102 about 13 miles and turn right at the sign to Pearl Pass.

Trail Description: Set your odometer to zero as you turn off 135. Past the country club the road becomes a gentle country drive as it winds around the south side of Mount Crested Butte across private ranch land. At 5.6 miles West Brush Creek Trail 738.2A goes to the left. There should be a sign here indicating Pearl Pass to the right. You pass through a beautiful little valley before coming to a double stream crossing at 6.2 miles. You may want to shift into low range at this point. Bear to the right and cross the creek. At the next fork, bear left as a lesser road goes right. You'll twist through the aspens on undulating terrain. After that you cross through an open valley which is nice for camping. At 8.6 miles there is another stream crossing, a little deeper than the others. East Brush Creek Trail 738.2B splits to the right at 8.8 miles. You bear left. The next several miles become more difficult as you wind in and out of the trees climbing large moguls and diving through deep mud holes. At 11.8 miles there is a flat spot to park for the Twin Lakes Hiking Trail to the left. Signs indicate Pearl Pass is 5 miles to the right. Additional stream crossings follow.

The trail is now quite difficult as you begin to rapidly climb a shelf road out of the valley. Many tough rocky sections follow. Take time with tire placement and you should get through just fine. There is also a lot of loose rock making it difficult to keep tires from spinning unless you are equipped with differential lockers. There is a long narrow shelf road just before the summit that is often blocked with snow. If it is blocked here, you must turn back. If not, you reach the summit at about 16.1 miles. There is not much room to park on the summit.

Descending the summit on the north side you will most likely encounter the snow blocked section pictured on page 108. Sometimes you can get around this section if you are going downhill and the blockage is not too wide. We had a large group of experienced four-wheelers and managed to get around the blockage.

After this section, you pass through a long, wide boulder field, followed by a fairly tough obstacle at about 18.5. The scenery through here is breathtaking. The Montezuma Basin Trail (not described) goes to the left at about 19.1 miles. Another water crossing at 20.8 passes by a footbridge. When you reach the paved portion of Castle Creek Road 102, turn left for Aspen. You'll see Express Creek Road 15C on the right after 2.5 miles.

Return Trip: From the end of the trail, drive north on Castle Creek Road 102 about 13 miles to Aspen or turn right on Express Creek Road 15C to head over Taylor Pass (Trail #25).

Services: Full services in Aspen and Crested Butte.

Other Activities: This trail is very popular for serious mountain bikers and hikers. In the winter cross-country skiing is very popular.

Maps: White River and Gunnison National Forests, Trails Illustrated, Aspen, Independence Pass #127 and Crested Butte, Pearl Pass #131, Colorado Atlas and Gazetteer.

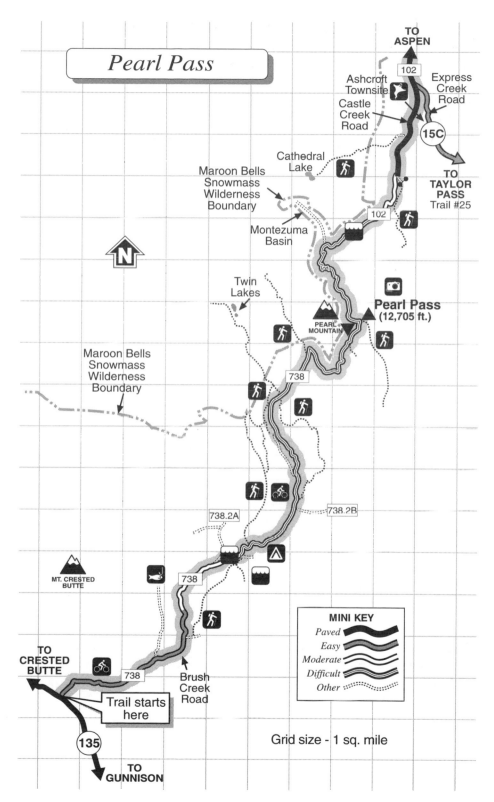

Pearl Pass

TO
ASPEN

102

Ashcroft
Townsite

Express
Creek
Road

Castle
Creek
Road

15C

Cathedral
Lake

TO
TAYLOR
PASS
Trail #25

Maroon Bells
Snowmass
Wilderness
Boundary

102

Montezuma
Basin

N

Twin
Lakes

Pearl Pass
(12,705 ft.)

PEARL
MOUNTAIN

Maroon Bells
Snowmass
Wilderness
Boundary

738

738.2A

738.2B

MT. CRESTED
BUTTE

738

738

TO
CRESTED
BUTTE

738

Brush
Creek
Road

Trail starts
here

135

TO
GUNNISON

MINI KEY

Paved

Easy

Moderate

Difficult

Other

Grid size - 1 sq. mile

The difficult southeast side includes a long stretch of boulder fields as shown here.

The northwest side is fairly smooth.

Broken levee turns trail into stream.

Taylor Pass

Location: Northeast of Crested Butte between Aspen and Taylor Reservoir.

Difficulty: Difficult. This rating applies primarily to the upper southeast side of Taylor Pass. There are several miles of boulder-strewn trails and one section where the trail may be flooded by a nearby stream. In the spring, the water can be fairly deep. The balance of the trail is moderate to easy.

Features: Taylor Pass has great views looking down on Taylor Lake, a popular fishing spot. The ghost town of Ashcroft is located at the start of the trail. Portions of Taylor Pass are adjacent to the Collegiate Peaks Wilderness.

Time & Distance: It is about 9 miles from the start of this trail to Taylor River Road 742. The tough section between Taylor Lake and Taylor River Road takes most of the time. You should allow two or three hours depending upon the ground clearance of your vehicle.

To Get There: From Crested Butte, you reach the start of Taylor Pass after completing Pearl Pass (Trail #24). Just watch for Express Creek Road on the right, marked as 15C. From Aspen, the route to Taylor Pass is fairly easy. Head south from Aspen on Castle Creek Road about 11 miles and turn left on Express Creek Road. From the Taylor Reservoir area, head north about 17 miles on F.S. Road 742. Watch for signs to Taylor Pass on the right after the Dorchester Campground. Create a great loop trail by combining Pearl, Taylor, and Italian. If you drive all three passes, allow more than one day.

Trail Description: Set your odometer to zero as you enter Express Creek Road. Although a little rocky, this road is fairly easy. It passes through groves of aspen trees which make this a colorful trail to drive in the fall. From the start it is about 4.8 miles to the top of Taylor Pass. There are several switchbacks as the road narrows and becomes a shelf road. You find a large parking area at the pass with several side roads. To avoid difficult terrain, return the way you came. To continue the route described here, make a quick jog to the right then back to the left. Conditions become more difficult as you pass around the east side of the lake. At 5.5 miles, there is a sign for the Taylor Pass Divide Road 761.1A to the right. This road goes around the other side of the lake. Continue straight. The trail branches off in several directions, providing choices of boulder fields. Select a path and continue downhill until the trail becomes a single lane again. At about 7.4 miles, you enter an area where the trail drops steeply down into a narrow rocky stream. Make an immediate right turn after you drop down. A levee here should direct the stream to the left, however, it may be washed out. If this is the case, water may flow down the trail as shown on page 112. This is especially true during the spring when high water is more likely. The trail remains narrow after the stream section for about another 1.5 miles. You reach Taylor River Road 742 at about 9 miles. Turn left and follow this wide dirt road south past the Dorchester Forest Service Campground. Italian Creek Road 759 (Trail #26) goes to the right at 5.8 miles.

Return Trip: There are several choices from this point. To head back to Crested Butte, take either Italian Creek Road 759 or Rocky Brook Road 748 just several miles farther. It is an easy two-wheel drive road but is longer than Italian Creek Road. Continue straight if your destination is Taylor Reservoir.

Services: Full services in Aspen and Crested Butte.

Other Activities: Stop and visit the ghost town of Ashcroft at the start of the trail on the Aspen side. The northwest side of Taylor Pass is a very popular mountain biking area in the summer and cross-country ski area in the winter. There are many places to fish in the area.

Historical Highlights: Before Independence Pass was opened in 1881, Taylor Pass was the main route to get supplies to Aspen from the east. At that time, Ashcroft was a bustling mining town and stage stop for passengers and supplies coming in from Buena Vista. By the late 1880s, railroads into Aspen eliminated the need for Taylor Pass.

Maps: White River and Gunnison National Forests, Trails Illustrated, Aspen, Independence Pass #127 and Crested Butte, Pearl Pass #131, Colorado Atlas and Gazetteer.

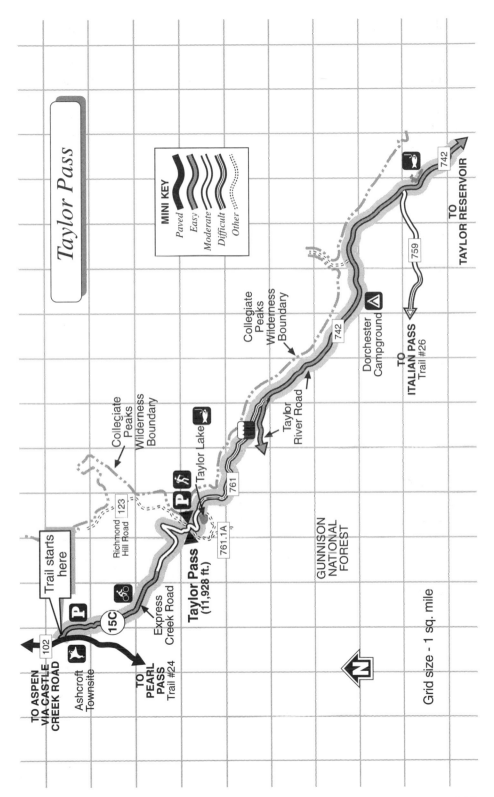

Taylor Pass

MINI KEY
Paved
Easy
Moderate
Difficult
Other

TO ASPEN
VIA CASTLE
CREEK ROAD 102

Ashcroft
Townsite

Trail starts
here

P

15C

Express
Creek Road

TO
PEARL PASS
Trail #24

Richmond
Hill Road 123

Taylor Pass
(11,928 ft.)

761.1A

P

Taylor Lake

761

Collegiate Peaks
Wilderness Boundary

Collegiate Peaks
Wilderness Boundary

742

Taylor
River Road

Dorchester
Campground

759

TO
ITALIAN PASS
Trail #26

GUNNISON
NATIONAL
FOREST

742

TO
TAYLOR RESERVOIR

N

Grid size - 1 sq. mile

115

The first part of the trail is just a relaxing drive through beautiful countryside like this.

The right fork after the Reno Divide takes you across this unstable looking talus ledge.

Location: Between Crested Butte and Taylor Park.

Difficulty: Difficult. This rating is based on the higher elevation portion of the trail. The approach from the east starts as a relaxing drive and gradually gets more difficult. After crossing the Reno Divide as described here, the trail splits into two different but difficult sections. Cement Creek Road on the western side is an easy county road.

Features: Italian Creek Road is not as well known as Pearl Pass and Taylor Pass. However, it offers some unique challenges to the hard-core four-wheeler, primarily in the form of boulder fields and bogs. It is part of a great loop trail when combined with Pearl and Taylor.

Time & Distance: Italian Creek Road is about 17 miles in length. Add another 9 miles for Cement Creek Road. Allow 3 to 4 hours for the entire distance from Taylor Park to Route 135 on the Crested Butte side.

To Get There: The trail is described here from the Taylor Park side as part of a clockwise three-part loop including Pearl Pass (Trail #24) and Taylor Pass (Trail #25). The starting point, as shown here, is encountered after completing Taylor Pass north to south. You can also reach this point by taking 742 north from Taylor Reservoir. If you are starting from the Crested Butte side, head south about 7 miles from Crested Butte on Route 135 to Cement Creek Road 740 on the left. Follow Cement Creek Road 9 miles to Italian Creek Road 759 on the right.

Trail Description: Set your odometer to zero as you turn off Taylor River Road 742. The first part of the trail is quite easy as it follows Italian Creek Road 759 through a popular camping and fishing area. After several miles a sign indicates four-wheel drive required and it begins to get more difficult. At 6.5 miles make a right turn following signs to Cement Creek. Turn left at 7.1. The road swings to the right at 7.2 miles and you drop down into Italian Creek. At 7.5 you make a hard left away from some old buildings. This stretch is steep in places and can get muddy. At 8.5 bear to the right. Bear to the right again at 9 miles and follow a gravel road. At 10.2 a sign indicates Reno Divide 759 to the left. Since our group was looking for maximum challenge, we took the fork to the right. I have not driven the left fork but understand it drops down a steep clay-surfaced road that is very slippery when wet. It then passes through an area of mud bogs. The right fork, on the other hand, is the high road and offers its own set of challenges. At 10.7 miles, there is an off-camber section of about 25 degrees followed immediately by the rocky ledge shown on page 116. One takes pause before starting across the ledge because it has the appearance of being ready to collapse at any moment. One member of our group did take a little body damage as he squeezed through several tight rocky sections. From this ledge, I could see the other road below and it looked a lot easier. I breathed a sigh of relief after getting off the ledge as we started to descend quickly through tight brush on a dirt surface.

Just as we neared the end of the trail, we encountered a large challenging mud hole. It was difficult because there was a steep bank on the other side followed by a tight left turn. Those in the group with lockers struggled successfully to get over the bank on the higher left side. However, one member of our group, in a stock vehicle, found it necessary to use speed to throw his vehicle through the shallower right side of the bog. Somehow, after flying across the bog, he managed to make a left turn without rolling over. I would not recommend this technique. There were no trees in the area for winching. (Note: I was not able to get pictures of this spot because our group had driven Pearl, Taylor, and Italian all in one day and night fell before we finished Italian. Next time, I would take two days and camp overnight along the way.)

At 13.4 miles we rejoined the lower branch of the trail and passed through a gate after turning right. From this point, we shifted into two-wheel drive and headed straight downhill on a long twisting road through the forest. At 17.1 miles Italian runs into Cement Creek Road 740. Turn left to reach 135 at 26.6 miles.

Return Trip: Crested Butte is 7 miles to the right on 135. If you had driven the trip in the other direction, Italian would end at Taylor River Road 742. From that point you would turn left for Taylor Pass and right for Taylor Reservoir.

Services: Full services in Crested Butte.

Other Activities: Both sides of this trail offer easy access for all vehicles and provide a wide variety of fishing, camping, hiking, and mountain biking. There is a Forest Service Campground on Cement Creek Road about 3.5 miles east of 135.

Maps: Gunnison National Forest, Trails Illustrated Crested Butte, Pearl Pass #131, Colorado Atlas and Gazetteer.

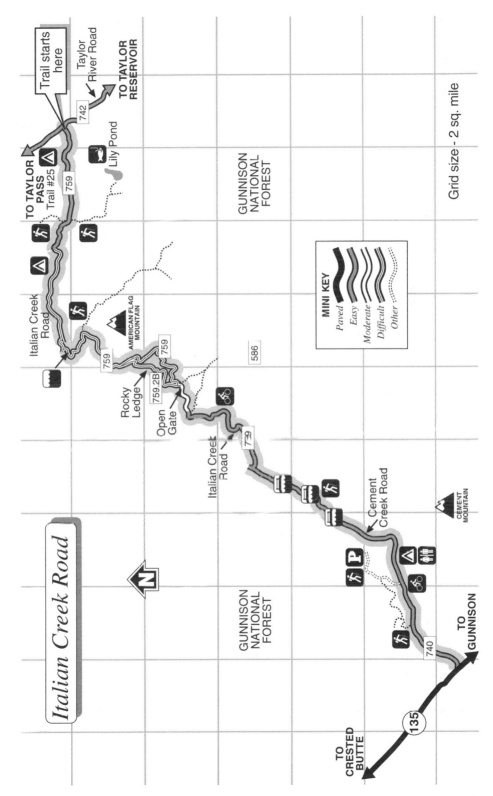

Italian Creek Road

Trail starts here

Taylor River Road

TO TAYLOR RESERVOIR

742

TO TAYLOR PASS
Trail #25

759

Lily Pond

Italian Creek Road

759

AMERICAN FLAG MOUNTAIN

Rocky Ledge

759.2B

Open Gate

759

586

GUNNISON NATIONAL FOREST

Italian Creek Road

79

Cement Creek Road

CEMENT MOUNTAIN

MINI KEY
Paved
Easy
Moderate
Difficult
Other

GUNNISON NATIONAL FOREST

N

P

TO GUNNISON

740

135

TO CRESTED BUTTE

Grid size - 2 sq. mile

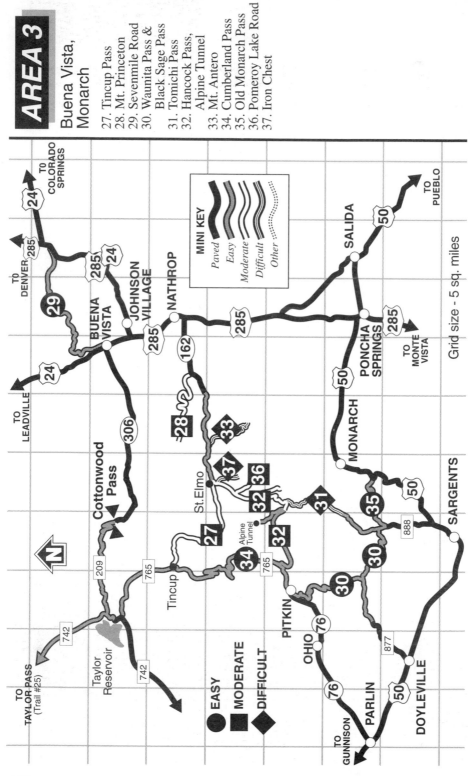

AREA 3

Buena Vista, Monarch

27. Tincup Pass
28. Mt. Princeton
29. Sevenmile Road
30. Waunita Pass &
    Black Sage Pass
31. Tomichi Pass
32. Hancock Pass,
    Alpine Tunnel
33. Mt. Antero
34. Cumberland Pass
35. Old Monarch Pass
36. Pomeroy Lake Road
37. Iron Chest

MINI KEY
Paved
Easy
Moderate
Difficult
Other

Grid size - 5 sq. miles

● EASY
■ MODERATE
◆ DIFFICULT

120

Buena Vista, Monarch

The Buena Vista area is one of the most popular four-wheeling areas in Colorado because it offers a wide variety of beautiful trails within a two-hour drive of Denver and Colorado Springs. Colorado residents have discovered that summer seems to last a little longer in this part of the state. Winter snows often miss the lower elevations, making it possible to drive some backroads even in the winter. Obviously, this does not apply to the higher elevation mountain passes which must wait for Mother Nature to melt sometimes heavy winter snowpack. Like Areas 1 and 2, Buena Vista is proud of its rich mining history and the vast network of backroads that has resulted. The central corridor to many of the trails is Route 162 which heads west from Nathrop just south of Buena Vista. This stretch of road offers several forest service campgrounds and great fishing along Chalk Creek. After a long day of wheeling, you can stop and soak in the steaming waters of the Mt. Princeton Hot Springs. Visit the historic Alpine Tunnel and the barely occupied towns of St. Elmo and Tincup. Just slightly larger is the wonderful little town of Pitkin, where you can gas up and step back in time with a stop at the general store in the center of town.

Road 839 leading to the Alpine Tunnel follows the route of the original railroad.(Trail #32).

Entering the town of Tincup from the south on Route 765.

It gets rockier towards the top.

Mirror Lake with Tincup Pass in the background.

Starting down the east side of Tincup Pass. This section is dangerous if snow covered.

122

Location: Between Tincup and St. Elmo, southwest of Buena Vista and southeast of Taylor Reservoir.

Difficulty: Moderate. Tincup Pass is moderately difficult under dry conditions. It is more difficult if attempted while snow is present which can be well into July. Another factor that can increase difficulty is the water level in Mirror Lake. During spring run-off, the water rises high enough to cover the trail around the southeast edge of the lake.

Features: Relics of once booming mining towns, Tincup and St. Elmo are two places you should stop and see. Once on the trail, Mirror Lake is the dominant feature. This great fishing lake is nestled in a beautiful valley framed by the Sawatch Mountains with Tincup Pass in the distance. Camping and picnicking at the water's edge make it a great place to spend an afternoon or quiet weekend. Nearby Timberline Hiking Trail connects to a network of trails leading to the Cottonwood Pass area. The east side of Tincup Pass has many primitive camping spots for those looking to escape the crowds.

Time & Distance: The entire trail from Tincup to St. Elmo is about 13 miles. Allow two or three hours for maximum enjoyment. You may wish to combine this trail with Hancock Pass (Trail #32) and Cumberland Pass (Trail # 34) to form a loop trail that is 54 miles in length. Allow a full day for this trip.

To Get There: This trail is described from west to east starting in the town of Tincup, which can be reached from Buena Vista via Cottonwood Pass 306 and 209 to Taylor Reservoir. From there, head southeast on 742 and 765 to Tincup. If you drive Hancock and Cumberland as a loop, you will find Tincup about 8 miles north of Cumberland Pass.

Trail Description: From the center of Tincup at a small church with white steeple, head east on Rt. 267 towards Mirror Lake. Just before you reach Mirror Lake at about 3 miles, you pass the Timberline Hiking Trail and some modern pit toilets. Just a little farther is Mirror Lake with a Forest Service campground and a parking area for fishing. There is another pit toilet in the campground, but it is more primitive. Set your odometer to zero at the campgrounds.

To reach Tincup Pass, follow the trail to the left of Mirror Lake. In

123

spring the water level of the lake can flood the trail, but it is still passable by driving through the water along the edge of the lake. Bear left as far as possible along the shore line. You may feel more comfortable if you watch someone else go through first. After this section, you cross a small stream and the trail heads up the mountain to the left. The trail is rocky but very passable. At 2 miles, Old Tincup Pass Trail goes to the left. This is a difficult hard-core trail. At 2.3 you reach a rutted area that can be very muddy after a rain. You can usually get around this area by bearing to the right. Just remember to stay on the trail. After this section, you climb quickly over some fairly rocky terrain. If you are not accustomed to driving under these conditions, you may feel more comfortable with a spotter guiding you. Tincup pass is 3.5 miles above the campground.

As you start down the other side of the pass, watch for a short narrow shelf section that can be covered with snow as late as July. If so, you may have to turn around. If clear, cross this section and follow wider switchbacks down the mountain. You'll notice a lot of nice primitive camping spots on this side of the mountain. The trail follows the north fork of Chalk Creek all the way down to St. Elmo, which is about 6 miles from the pass. When you get into St. Elmo, cross a small wooden bridge and turn left.

Return Trip: From St. Elmo, take 162 east back to Nathrop and Rt. 285. Turn left on 285 to Buena Vista.

Services: Full services in Buena Vista and Johnson Village. Nathrop has a small gas station and store.

Other Activities: There are many places to fish, hike, and camp between Nathrop and St. Elmo, including several Forest Service campgrounds. The Colorado Trail also crosses this route about 7 miles from Nathrop. Don't forget to visit the Mt. Princeton Hot Springs.

Historical Highlights: During the silver boom of the 1880s, Tincup was the largest producer of silver in the region. Population was once as high as 6,000 residents.

Maps: San Isabel National Forest, Gunnison National Forest, Trails Illustrated Salida, St Elmo #130, Colorado Atlas & Gazetteer.

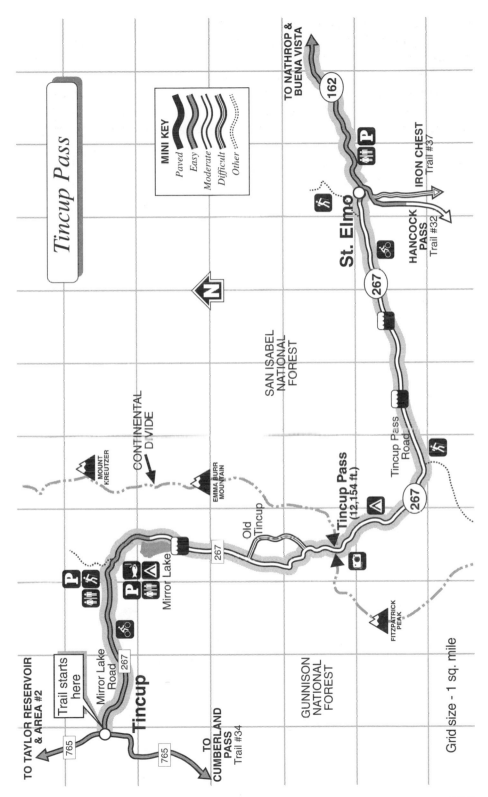

Tincup Pass

MINI KEY
- Paved
- Easy
- Moderate
- Difficult
- Other

TO NATHROP & BUENA VISTA

162

IRON CHEST
Trail #37

HANCOCK PASS
Trail #32

St. Elmo

267

N

SAN ISABEL NATIONAL FOREST

CONTINENTAL DIVIDE

MOUNT KREUTZER

EMMA BURR MOUNTAIN

Old Tincup

267

Tincup Pass
(12,154 ft.)

Tincup Pass Road

267

Mirror Lake

267

P

Mirror Lake Road

Tincup

Trail starts here

765

TO TAYLOR RESERVOIR & AREA #2

765

TO CUMBERLAND PASS
Trail #34

FITZPATRICK PEAK

GUNNISON NATIONAL FOREST

Grid size - 1 sq. mile

Note top of trail on Mt. Princeton above sign. Swiss-style cabin at end of the trail.

Snow tends to accumulate on this part of the trail about a half mile from the top.

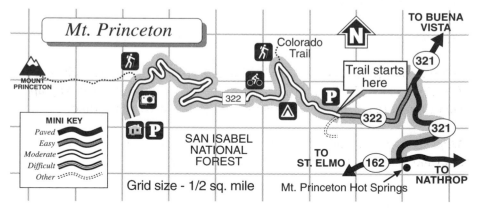

Mt. Princeton

TO BUENA VISTA

Colorado Trail

N

321

Trail starts here

322

322

321

P

MOUNT PRINCETON

MINI KEY
Paved
Easy
Moderate
Difficult
Other

SAN ISABEL
NATIONAL
FOREST

TO
ST. ELMO

162

Mt. Princeton Hot Springs

TO
NATHROP

Grid size - 1/2 sq. mile

Mt. Princeton

Location: Southwest of Buena Vista. Directly west of Nathrop.

Difficulty: Moderate. Most of the road is easy except for several steep bumpy sections. The last mile is a narrow shelf road. Low range is required at higher elevations. You may see passenger cars on the lower part of trail.

Features: A popular tourist road because of its easy access. A relatively short drive to some outstanding views.

Time & Distance: About 5.5 miles from the entrance to the end of the trail, which is just above 12,000 ft. Allow about 2 hours for the round trip depending upon how far up you go.

To Get There: Head west on 162 from Nathrop 4.7 miles to the Mt. Princeton Hot Springs. Turn right and head up the hill on paved road 321 until you reach 322 in about 1.5 miles. Turn left and follow 322 to the entrance.

Trail Description: Set your odometer to zero at the Mt.Princeton entrance. Drive through a parking area and continue on a narrower road still marked as 322. Be careful passing. You have the right of way but use commonsense. Stay in four-wheel drive even though there are just a few places where you need it. You will lose power as you climb, so shift into low range when needed. The road becomes a narrow shelf the last half mile. If you feel uncomfortable, stop here and hike the rest of the way. There is also a hiking trail at this point that goes to the summit. At the top is a Swiss-style cabin and a small parking area to turn around.

Return Trip: From the entrance, return the way you came or stay on 321 all the way into Buena Vista.

Services: Full services in Buena Vista. Gas is available in Nathrop.

Other Activities: Hiking, mountain biking, camping, and horseback riding. The ColoradoTrail follows part of this road and branches off part way up. Don't forget to try the Mt. Princeton Hot Springs if you have time.

Maps: San Isabel National Forest, Trails Illustrated Salida, St. Elmo, Shavano Peak #130, Colorado Atlas and Gazetteer.

The Collegiate Peaks form a dramatic backdrop for the entire area.

Poorly marked roads go in all directions making it easy to get lost.

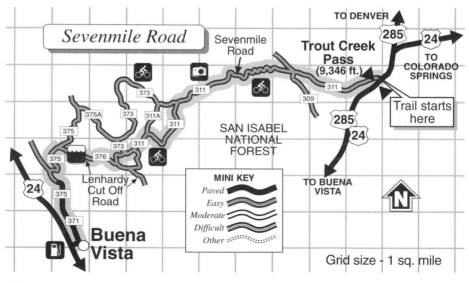

Sevenmile Road

Sevenmile Road

Trout Creek Pass
(9,346 ft.)

TO DENVER

TO COLORADO SPRINGS

Trail starts here

TO BUENA VISTA

SAN ISABEL NATIONAL FOREST

Lenhardy Cut Off Road

Buena Vista

373
311
375A
373
311A
375
311
373
311
375
376
371
309
311

MINI KEY
Paved
Easy
Moderate
Difficult
Other

285 24
285 24
24

N

Grid size - 1 sq. mile

Sevenmile Road ㉙

Location: Between Trout Creek Pass and Buena Vista.

Difficulty: Easy. Difficulty is increased during heavy runoff periods.

Features: A great place to relax and spend a day exploring gentle roads through beautiful countryside. You can camp just about anywhere.

Time & Distance: It is about 16 miles if you follow the road straight through from 285 to Buena Vista. This trip takes an hour or two, but allow more time to explore the huge network of trails in the area.

To Get There: Exit route 285 at Trout Creek Pass, which is about a mile south of the intersection of 24 and 285. Turn west at County Road 311.

Trail Description: Set your odometer to zero when you turn off 285 onto 311. After you turn, there is a small parking area set back from the road. This wide dirt road bends to the left and gradually descends. After about 2.7 miles continue straight past County Road 309. The road starts climbing and gets a little rougher. F.S. Road 373 goes right at 6.8 miles. Bear left staying on 311. After a small stream crossing shift into four-wheel drive as you climb a short steep hill. The views through this area are great. At 9.0 bear to the left again. Bear right at 9.6, left at 10.1, then right at 10.4. This puts you on the Lenhardy Cutoff Road 376 heading west. Follow a sandy creek bed for a short distance before you enter a confusing area with roads going in all directions. Follow the widest road which swings to the right a little. There is a fairly good stream to cross at 11.4. At 12.5 miles you run into a larger road marked as 375. Turn left on 375, and it winds down the hill for another mile to yet a larger road still marked as 375. Turn left again and follow this road as it parallels the Arkansas River. The road becomes paved as it heads into Buena Vista and becomes 371 by the time you hit Main Street in 2.5 miles. Turn right on Main to reach Rt. 24.

Return Trip: Follow 24 south to 285 and turn left back to Trout Creek Pass.

Services: Full services in Buena Vista and Johnson Village.

Maps: San Isabel National Forest, Trails Illustrated Buena Vista, Collegiate Peaks #129, Colorado Atlas and Gazetteer.

Looking down from Waunita Pass.

A reminder that you are on open range land.

Waunita, Black Sage Passes

Pitkin 765

TO
CUMBERLAND
PASS
Trail #34

763

Waunita Pass
(10,303 ft.)

N

76

TO PARLIN
& ROUTE 50

GUNNISON
NATIONAL
FOREST

MINI KEY
Paved
Easy
Moderate
Difficult
Other

GUNNISON
NATIONAL
FOREST

763

Waunita
Hot Springs

TO
TOMICHI PASS
Trail #31

887

888

Trail starts
here

TO
DOYLEVILLE
& ROUTE 50

887

237

TO
OLD
MONARCH
PASS
Trail #35

Black Sage Pass
(9,745 ft.)

887

888

Grid size - 1 sq. mile

TO
SARGENTS
& ROUTE 50

Waunita & Black Sage Pass ㉚

Location: South of Pitkin, southwest of Monarch.

Difficulty: Easy. Smooth road all the way.

Features: Just a beautiful stressless scenic drive. Will not require four-wheel drive when dry. Spend some time in the great little town of Pitkin.

Time & Distance: One way is about 18 miles. Allow 1 or 2 hours.

To Get There: From eastern Colorado, take 50 west over Monarch Pass and turn right on F.S. 888 about a mile before Sargents. Follow 888 north about 6 miles to 887. Turn left at the sign for Black Sage Pass. A more interesting way to get there is to take Old Monarch Pass (Trail #35) west from 50 and turn right at 888. The turn for Black Sage is about 1.4 miles north on 888.

Trail Description: Set your odometer to zero at the start of 887. As you head west, you cross a picturesque valley before starting to climb. In the summer and fall you can smell the pungent aroma of black sage. You reach Black Sage Pass at 3.6 miles and start descending to another wide valley on the other side. This is open range so watch for cattle on the road. At 6.8 miles you come to an intersection. Turn left and continue on 887. You immediately intersect with 763. Turn right and head north. The buildings you see to the left are the private Waunita Hot Springs Ranch. The road narrows and begins to climb through the forest towards Waunita Pass at about 13 miles. As you start down the other side, views begin to open up, and at 13.9 there is a curve with a nice overlook. From here you can see the town of Pitkin and Cumberland Pass to the north. The road you're on becomes First Street as you enter Pitkin at 16.5 miles. Turn right on State and left on Second before reaching paved road 76.

Return Trip: From Pitkin, take Cumberland Pass Road 765 (Trail #34) north to Taylor Reservoir and Cottonwood Pass Road 209/306 east to Buena Vista. To Gunnison, take 76 west to Parlin and 50 west to Gunnison.

Services: There is gas and a general store in Pitkin and Sargents.

Maps: Gunnison National Forest, Colorado Atlas and Gazetteer. This trail is not completely covered by the Trails Illustrated maps but #130 and #132 cover most of it.

The north side of Tomichi Pass as seen from Hancock Pass. Attempt only if clear of snow.

The south side approach to the summit is wider and easier than the north side.

The north side as it nears the summit.

Tomichi cemetery.

132

Location: Southwest of Buena Vista between St. Elmo and Sargents.

Difficulty: Difficult. This rating is based on the narrowness of the trail rather than the road surface. The north side is very narrow and passing is extremely difficult. You may have to back up a considerable distance. There are no hard-core obstacles, but several sections will pose some manageable challenge for stock vehicles. The lower north side has a rocky section that is always flooded but is not deep. This trail should not be attempted by anyone if snow is still present. Your best chance of avoiding snow is in August and early September.

Features: This is a challenging and difficult trail but it can be driven by stock high-clearance vehicles with low-range gearing. It is an opportunity for an aggressive and experienced sport utility owner to get a taste of hard-core four-wheeling without the worry of major body damage. The high elevation sections of this trail are stark and remote, providing a true backcountry experience.

Time & Distance: It is about 12 miles from the intersection of Old Monarch Pass and White Pine Road 888 to the intersection of Tomichi and Hancock (Trail #32). Allow 2 to 3 hours under dry conditions. Add more time to get out of the area.

To Get There: From eastern Colorado take U.S. 50 west over Monarch Pass and turn right on F.S. 888 about a mile before Sargents. Follow 888 north about 4.5 miles to the point where Old Monarch Pass Road 237 (Trail #35) intersects 888. You can reach this same point by taking Old Monarch Pass west from 50.

Trail Description: Set your odometer to zero where Old Monarch Pass 237 intersects with White Pine Road 888. Head north on 888. At 1.5 miles, Black Sage Pass goes to the left. Continue straight on 888. You pass Snowblind Campground at 3.2 miles. At 4.9 you pass through an area of mine tailings. There are several side trails in this area. You soon come to the small town of White Pine. Once a booming mining town, it is now just a summer retreat for a few hardy folks.

After White Pine the road begins to narrow and becomes more rocky as you pass by a number of private cabins. At 7.2 miles there is a metal sign with holes punched in it that indicates Tomichi Pass to the right. This is a good place to shift into low gear as you head up the hill to the right. Again there are various side roads along the way for those looking for more adventure. There is a small water crossing at 7.5 miles before reaching the Tomichi townsite, which was totally destroyed by an avalanche in 1899. All that remains is a small but interesting little graveyard. A sign indicates four-wheel drive required beyond this point. Bear to the left and head downhill through the trees. From here the trail twists up and down through the forest and is a great deal of fun. It is fairly narrow and crosses shallow water several times as it climbs aggressively towards the summit. The trail becomes more of a shelf road above timberline but is not too difficult. The summit is reached at 10.6 miles. There is a small place to pull over.

At the summit you must assess whether you really want to go down the other side. It is quite an intimidating sight. Do not start down if anyone is coming up or if there is any snow on the trail. The trail is wide enough for a full-size vehicle but just barely. Take your time and you should be fine. After the ledge portion of the trail there is a plank bridge that crosses a bog. Have someone spot your tires if you find it difficult to follow the planks. You pass a mine before coming to a section of the trail that is always flooded. There is rock under the water which provides good traction. At about 11.7 miles you intersect with Hancock (Trail # 32).

Return Trip: The easiest way out is to continue straight on 888 when you reach Hancock trail. You run into the easy Alpine Tunnel Road 839 in 0.6 miles. Turn right for the tunnel and left to reach Cumberland Pass Road 765 (Trail #34). The more difficult way out is to turn right when you reach Hancock trail, which takes you up over Hancock Pass and back down to St. Elmo.

Services: Gas in Sargents and Pitkin. Full services in Buena Vista.

Other Activities: You can hike to the top of Tomichi via the Canyon Creek/ Horseshoe Creek Trail that departs across the road from the Snowblind Campground. This campground has over 20 Forest Service campsites and is typically not very crowded.

Historical Highlights: It is hard to believe that during the boom years of mining in the 1880s White Pine had a population of 3,000. The town of Tomichi, now just a graveyard, had a population of 1,500. Most of the ore was hauled out of the area over the lower Black Sage Pass road.

Maps: Gunnison National Forest, Trails Illustrated Salida, St. Elmo #130, Colorado Atlas and Gazetteer.

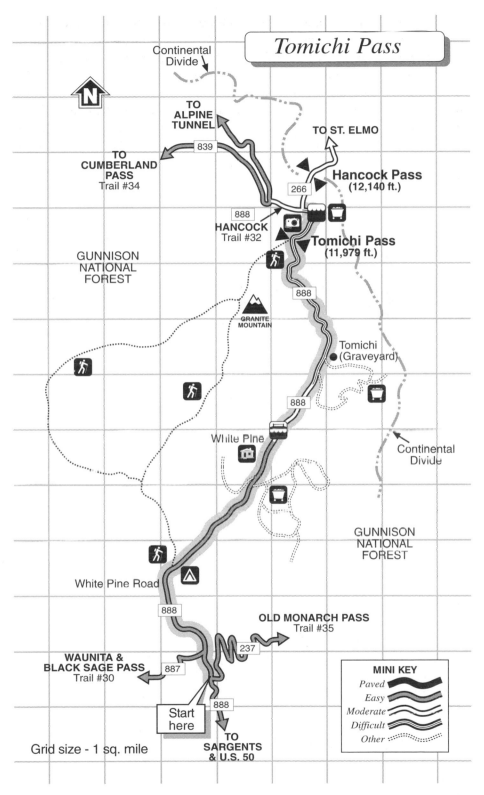

Tomichi Pass

Continental Divide

N

TO ALPINE TUNNEL

839

TO CUMBERLAND PASS
Trail #34

TO ST. ELMO

266

Hancock Pass
(12,140 ft.)

888

HANCOCK
Trail #32

Tomichi Pass
(11,979 ft.)

GUNNISON NATIONAL FOREST

GRANITE MOUNTAIN

888

Tomichi (Graveyard)

888

Continental Divide

White Pine

888

GUNNISON NATIONAL FOREST

White Pine Road

888

OLD MONARCH PASS
Trail #35

237

WAUNITA & BLACK SAGE PASS
Trail #30

887

Start here

888

TO SARGENTS & U.S. 50

Grid size - 1 sq. mile

MINI KEY
Paved
Easy
Moderate
Difficult
Other

Brittle Silver Basin, the south side of Hancock Pass as seen from Tomichi Pass.

Climbing the north side is rough in spots but manageable. Don't attempt if snow covered.

The town of St. Elmo. Stop in and say hello but don't look for a gas station.

136

Hancock Pass, Alpine Tun.

Location: Southwest of Buena Vista and south of St. Elmo.

Difficulty: Moderate. There are several fairly rocky sections but this trail is passable for stock high-clearance vehicles with low-range gearing. Skid plates are helpful. The drive should not be attempted if snow is on the trail. Alpine Tunnel Road 839 is an easy graded dirt road.

Features: This trail offers just the right amount of challenge for high-clearance sport utility vehicles. There are outstanding views on the upper section. Two side trips are recommended. The first is to Hancock Lake, which requires passing through a fairly rocky section. The second is to the Alpine Tunnel over a well maintained and easy ledge road. This road has signs along the way to explain the history of the area.

Time & Distance: It is about 9.5 miles from St. Elmo to the end of Hancock where it runs into 839. The side trip to Hancock Lake adds 2.8 miles and the round trip to the Alpine Tunnel adds another 4.5 miles. Allow half a day including the side trips. Remember to add more time after you are done for your return trip. If you combine Cumberland Pass (Trail #34) and Tincup Pass (Trail #27), allow a full day.

To Get There: From 285 turn west on Rt. 162 near Nathrop. St. Elmo is about 15 miles west on Rt. 162.

Trail Description: Turn left on Chaffee County Road 295 just before St. Elmo. Before you start up the trail, you may want to see St. Elmo, just around the corner to the right. Set your odometer to zero as you start up 295. At the beginning the road is fairly straight because you are following the original railroad bed that once led to the north side of the Alpine Tunnel. This is apparent at 2.7 miles where there is a detour around an old deteriorated railroad bridge. After the detour there are signs to the Mary Murphy Mine to the left. Continue straight and at 5.4 miles you come to the historic remains of the old town of Hancock. Please obey all signs and respect the property.

Immediately as you leave Hancock take the left fork marked as 295.2. Just after that you come to a clearing after passing through some big trees marked with orange arrows. As you enter the clearing, look to your right and you will see trail 299 which leads to Hancock Pass. Before heading up to the pass, however, I recommend you continue straight on 295.2 to

Hancock Lake for some great wheeling and beautiful scenery. As you continue on 295.2 there is another fork at 6.5 miles. Bear left. From this point, the trail gets a little rockier. You should find it just enough challenge to be fun. The lake is another 0.6 miles ahead. You have to walk to the lake to see it. After visiting the lake, return to the clearing and turn left on 299. The road continues to be rocky and at about the 10 mile point, you start climbing above timberline. You cross a short section of shelf road before the road swings left and reaches Hancock Pass.

As you start down the other side, the road is steep and bumpy but not as rocky. At 11.6 miles, you reach the intersection of Hancock and Tomichi (Trail # 31). Continue straight on what is now Rt. 888. It winds through the trees for 0.6 miles before coming out on gravel road 839, which follows the old railroad bed to the Alpine Tunnel, about 2.3 miles to the right. Be sure to take this side trip. There are some spectacular views and some interesting history. After visiting the Alpine Tunnel, turn around and follow 839 about 10 miles all the way down the valley until you intersect with Cumberland Pass Road 765.

Return Trip: There are several choices for the return trip. After you reach 765 you can turn left to Pitkin and Waunita Pass (Trail # 30). A right turn takes you over Cumberland Pass (Trail #34) to the town of Tincup. From Tincup you have the option of returning to St. Elmo via Tincup Pass (Trail # 27) or Cottonwood Pass via 765, 209, and 306.

Services: Gas in Nathrop and Pitkin. Full services in Buena Vista.

Other Activities: There are many places to fish, hike, and camp between Nathrop and St. Elmo, including three Forest Service campgrounds. The Mt. Princeton Hot Springs are also located along this stretch of road. Hiking and mountain biking are popular at several places along the trail and on the trail itself. You can also hike up to Hancock Lake to fish.

Historic Highlights: Your drive follows much of the original railroad bed that passed through the Alpine Tunnel in the 1880s. Notice the black soot that still clings to the side of the road at various points along the way. At one time you could drive to the north side of the tunnel but the road is now closed and you must hike or bike. With the closure of Williams Pass, Hancock Pass is now the only place left in this area to cross the Continental Divide.

Maps: Gunnison National Forest, Trails Illustrated Map Salida, St. Elmo #130, Colorado Atlas & Gazetteer.

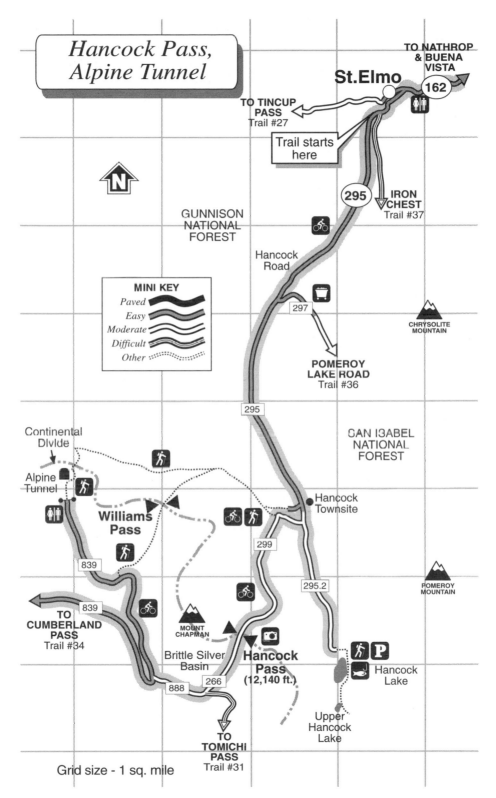

Hancock Pass, Alpine Tunnel

St.Elmo

TO NATHROP & BUENA VISTA

162

TO TINCUP PASS
Trail #27

Trail starts here

295

IRON CHEST
Trail #37

GUNNISON NATIONAL FOREST

Hancock Road

297

CHRYSOLITE MOUNTAIN

MINI KEY
Paved
Easy
Moderate
Difficult
Other

POMEROY LAKE ROAD
Trail #36

295

SAN ISABEL NATIONAL FOREST

Continental Divide

Alpine Tunnel

Williams Pass

Hancock Townsite

299

839

295.2

POMEROY MOUNTAIN

839

TO CUMBERLAND PASS
Trail #34

MOUNT CHAPMAN

Brittle Silver Basin

266

Hancock Pass (12,140 ft.)

Hancock Lake

888

Upper Hancock Lake

TO TOMICHI PASS
Trail #31

Grid size - 1 sq. mile

A single picture cannot begin to show all the switchbacks. Here are just a few.

Turn left and cross the creek for Mt. Antero.

Some prefer to walk the last half mile.

Typical example of lower part of trail.

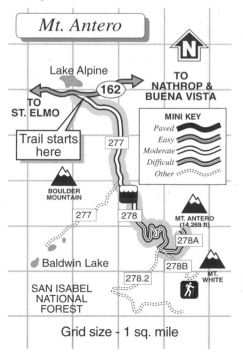

Mt. Antero

Lake Alpine

162

TO
NATHROP &
BUENA VISTA

TO
ST. ELMO

Trail starts here

277

MINI KEY
Paved
Easy
Moderate
Difficult
Other

BOULDER
MOUNTAIN

277

278

MT. ANTERO
(14,269 ft)

278A

Baldwin Lake

278B

278.2

MT.
WHITE

SAN ISABEL
NATIONAL
FOREST

Grid size - 1 sq. mile

140

Location: Southwest of Buena Vista. West of Nathrop.

Difficulty: Difficult. Except for the last half mile, the road surface is not difficult but the trail is extremely narrow above timberline. Several of the switchbacks are very tight and require backing up to make the turns. The end of the trail nears 14,000 feet, so adequate power and low range are absolutely necessary. The last half mile is for experts only. Here the road surface is soft and unstable with several large rocks at the switchback turns.

Features: No other trail in this book gives the sensation of being so high. You need not drive all the way to the top to enjoy yourself.

Time & Distance: It is 7.3 miles to the top. Allow at least 3 to 4 hours for the round trip. You can easily spend a day if you add side roads.

To Get There: From 285 south of Buena Vista, drive west 12.2 miles from Nathrop on 162. The trail is well marked to the left.

Trail Description: Set your odometer to zero at the start. The beginning is probably the rockiest part as the trail climbs through dense forest with limited views. There are several side roads to Boulder Mountain at about 1.3 miles. You continue straight. At 2.9 miles the trees thin out as you reach the fork for Baldwin Lake. Turn left and cross the creek for Mt. Antero. You climb rapidly through a pretty section until 4.3 miles when you encounter the first switchback. Watch for anyone coming down before you start up. Make sure you are in low range and begin the climb. You have the right of way going up but watch for turn-outs in case you have to back up. The terrain changes and becomes less rocky at 5.7 miles. At 6.2 follow signs for 278A. Go straight at 6.3 miles as 278B goes to the right. The road forks again at 6.7 miles. The trail to the top goes to the left. Consider walking to the top from here because the last half mile is very tough and dangerous.

Return Trip: Return the way you came. Remember to stay in low gear and use your brakes as little as possible.

Services: Gas at Nathrop. Full services in Buena Vista.

Maps: San Isabel National Forest, Trails Illustrated Salida, St. Elmo #130, Colorado Atlas and Gazetteer.

With friends at the summit on a great summer afternoon.

Looking north from the top of the pass.

These mileages are approximate.

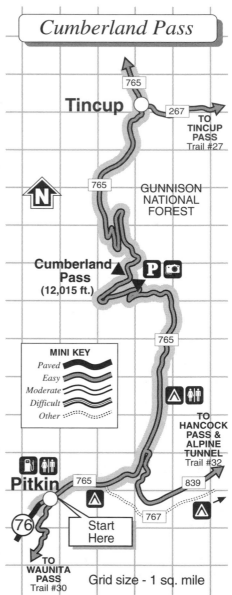

142

Cumberland Pass ㉞

Location: Between Tincup and Pitkin.

Difficulty: Easy. Suitable for passenger cars in good weather.

Features: Serves as a beautiful connecting link between Waunita Pass (Trail # 30) and Tincup Pass (Trail #27). Also serves as a link between Hancock Pass (Trail #32) and Tincup Pass. There are many great side roads in the area, including Middle Quartz Creek Road 767 just north of Pitkin.

Time & Distance: By my calculations it is about 19 miles from Pitkin to Tincup and about 16 miles from 839 to Tincup. The drive can be made in a half hour in good weather. You'll want to stop along the way so allow plenty of time.

To Get There: You reach Pitkin by completing Waunita Pass in a northerly direction or by Rt. 76 from Parlin. At the completion of Hancock Pass, as described in this book, 839 runs into Cumberland Pass Road 765. To reach Cumberland Pass from the north, take Cottonwood Pass Road 306 from Buena Vista to Taylor Reservoir and 765 south. You can also reach Tincup by driving over Tincup Pass from east to west.

Trail Description: Set your odometer at Pitkin. Just north of town is the Pitkin Forest Service Campground, followed by side road 767 to the right, which climbs a beautiful valley to the F.S. Middle Quartz Campground. Staying on 765 you reach the intersection of 839 at 2.9 miles and a mile later pass the F.S. Quartz Campground on the right. Several miles later you begin an earnest climb to Cumberland Pass, which is reached at about 11 miles. The north side descent is a little steeper and narrower so take your time going down. From the top of the pass down to Tincup is another 8 miles.

Return Trip: From Tincup return to St. Elmo via Tincup Pass (Trail #27) or continue on 765 north to Taylor Reservoir.

Services: There is gas and a general store in Pitkin. Full services in Buena Vista and Gunnison.

Maps: Gunnison National Forest, Colorado Atlas and Gazetteer, Trails Illustrated Map #130 shows most but not all of this trail.

The beginning of Old Monarch Pass just above the Monarch Ski area.

Looking northwest from the summit as the fog clears early in the morning.

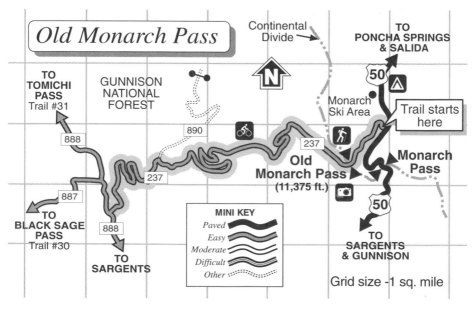

Old Monarch Pass

Continental Divide →

TO
PONCHA SPRINGS
& SALIDA

N

50

TO
TOMICHI
PASS
Trail #31

GUNNISON
NATIONAL
FOREST

Monarch
Ski Area

Trail starts
here

888

890

237

Old
Monarch Pass
(11,375 ft.)

Monarch
Pass

237

887

888

TO
BLACK SAGE
PASS
Trail #30

50

TO
SARGENTS

MINI KEY

Paved
Easy
Moderate
Difficult
Other

TO
SARGENTS
& GUNNISON

Grid size -1 sq. mile

Old Monarch Pass (35)

Location: West of Poncha Springs just north of the Monarch Ski Area.

Difficulty: Easy. Suitable for passenger cars in good weather.

Features: Links U.S. 50 to Black Sage/Waunita Pass (Trail #30). A relaxing alternative to paved road 50. Connects to Doyleville via Black Sage Pass and 877 or to Pitkin via Black Sage/Waunita Pass. This is a nice downhill mountain biking route with very little traffic.

Time & Distance: About 10.6 miles from U.S. 50 to White Pine Road 888. Takes less than half an hour under dry conditions.

To Get There: Take U.S. 50 west from Poncha Springs. Continue past the Monarch Ski Area about half a mile. Signs plainly mark the turn for Old Monarch Pass to the right. If you are coming from the south side of (new) Monarch Pass continue north downhill 1.1 miles after crossing the summit.

Trail Description: Set your odometer to zero as you turn off U.S. 50. The road is marked as F.S. 237 just shortly up the trail. Old Monarch Pass is just 1.3 miles from the start. There is a hiking trail just before you reach the pass that follows the Continental Divide above the Monarch Ski Area south to Hunt Lake and Boss Lake. As you approach Old Monarch Pass, you exit the trees, and a beautiful view of the San Juan Mountains can be seen far off to the west. There is plenty of room to park at the summit where you might want to relax and enjoy the views. The road gently descends from the pass and winds its way down the mountainside. At 7.8 miles No Name Road 890 turns to the right. It is a very inviting little side road but is unfortunately blocked several miles in. Continuing on 237 you reach White Pine Road 888 at 10.6 miles.

Return Trip: Turn left on 888 to return to U.S 50. Turn right for Black Sage/Waunita Pass (Trail # 30) and Tomichi Pass (Trail # 31.)

Services: Gas in Monarch and Sargents. There is a gift shop and restaurant at the top of (new) Monarch Pass on U.S. 50.

Maps: Gunnison National Forest Map shows this trail in its entirety. Trails Illustrated Map #130 shows only the start of the trail. The Colorado Atlas & Gazetteer cuts the trail into two parts.

The Mary Murphy Mine is a short way up the trail. The mine was active in 1875.

The trail gets tougher as you go higher.

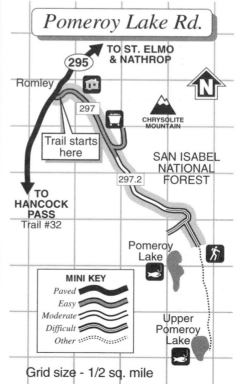

Pomeroy Lake Rd.

TO ST. ELMO & NATHROP

295

Romley

297

CHRYSOLITE MOUNTAIN

Trail starts here

SAN ISABEL NATIONAL FOREST

297.2

TO HANCOCK PASS
Trail #32

N

Pomeroy Lake

MINI KEY
Paved
Easy
Moderate
Difficult
Other

Upper Pomeroy Lake

Grid size - 1/2 sq. mile

Pomeroy Lake Road

Location: West of Nathrop. South of St. Elmo.

Difficulty: Moderate. Easy up to the Mary Murphy Mine. Moderate above the mine. A short stretch at the end is difficult.

Features: A great little trip for the family. You can see a well preserved cabin and mine within a mile of the start. There are still remnants of an aerial tramway that once carried ore down to the railroad. The hardy hiker can find fishing at the two Pomeroy Lakes.

Time & Distance: The entire trail is only 2 miles long. Driving time to the mine is minimal. The drive to the end of the trail could take an hour.

To Get There: From 285, turn west on Rt. 162 near Nathrop. Drive west 15 miles to County Road 295 and turn left up the hill. At 2.7 miles there is a detour around a decayed railroad trestle. Just after that there is a sign for Mary Murphy Mine and Pomeroy Lake to the left.

Trail Description: Set your odometer to zero as you turn off 295. The road is rocky but quite easy. Just around the corner is a small cabin next to a stream. At 0.8 miles Mary Murphy Mine is on the left. You can walk closer to the mine but don't go inside. Just past the mine a smaller road 297.2 goes to the right. The road to the left goes up the hill for a short distance and looks down on the mine. If you continue on 297.2, it gets progressively more difficult the farther you go. After 1.4 miles the trail should not be traveled by stock vehicles. The trail splits again at 2 miles. You can go a short distance more to the left before hiking is recommended. You must hike to see Pomeroy Lake or Upper Pomeroy Lake. The upper lake is a very strenuous hike.

Return Trip: Return the way you came.

Services: Gas at Nathrop. Full services in Buena Vista.

Maps: San Isabel National Forest, Trails Illustrated Salida, St. Elmo #130, The Colorado Atlas & Gazetteer.

The first half mile is the hard-core portion of the trail.

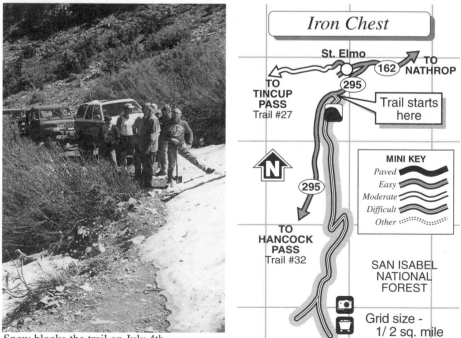

Snow blocks the trail on July 4th.

148

Iron Chest  37

Location: Southwest of Buena Vista. West of Nathrop.

Difficulty: Difficult. Most of the challenge comes within the first half mile as you pass through a large, tight boulder field. The balance of the trail is much easier but don't be surprised if snow blocks the trail early in the season. This trail is not for stock vehicles. Lifts, winches, and lockers are recommended. Don't attempt this trail by yourself.

Features: This is one of the best known and oldest hard-core trails in the state. The technical challenge is at the beginning while the upper portion is quite scenic. There are several large structures still standing at the Iron Chest Mine at the end of the trail. Watch for dangerous open mine shafts.

Time & Distance: The entire trail is only about 2.5 miles. It is very difficult to estimate the time required. Properly equipped vehicles can make the trip in an hour or two one way. If you are traveling with a group, add more time for each additional vehicle.

To Get There: From 285 turn west on Rt.162 near Nathrop. Go 15 miles and turn left on Hancock Road 295. Watch for a small parking area on the left at 0.4 miles. The trail departs from the left end of the small parking area.

Trail Description: Set your odometer to zero at the start. The trail heads to the left in the opposite direction to Hancock Road. You immediately come to an intersection. Bear to the right, almost reversing your direction again. The trail gets difficult immediately. Large boulders are strewn everywhere, and they tend to move around as you pass over and through them. Large vehicles will find it extremely difficult if not impossible to get through. Do not stack rocks to make the trail easier. Leave the trail the way you found it so others can experience the same challenge. You eventually come out of the trees as the road becomes easier. Take the left fork at 2.3 miles and proceed to the mine. Return the way you came.

Services: Gas at Nathrop. Full services in Buena Vista.

Maps: The Colorado Atlas and Gazetteer. Trails Illustrated Map #130 faintly shows part of the trail. This trail is not shown on the 1993 San Isabel National Forest Map.

AREA 4

Vail, Leadville,
Fairplay

38. West Lake Creek Rd.
39. Shrine Pass
40. Holy Cross
41. McCallister Gulch
42. Ptarmigan Pass
43. Wheeler Lake
44. Hagerman Pass
45. Mt. Lincoln

46. Mosquito Pass
47. Mt. Bross
48. Weston Pass

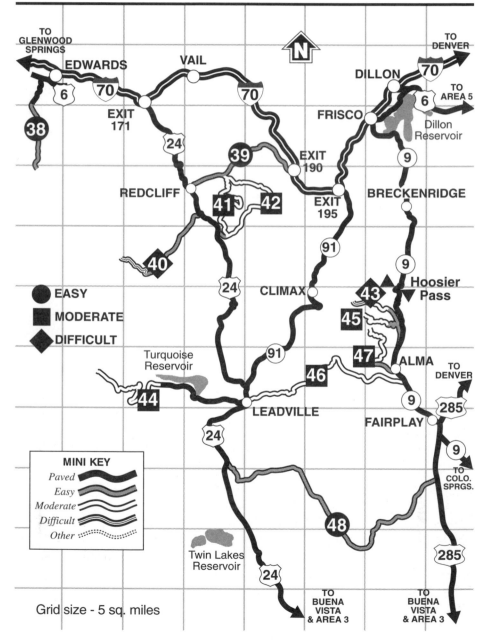

Grid size - 5 sq. miles

Vail, Leadville, Fairplay

A variety of wonderful trails are found between Buena Vista and the major ski areas along Interstate 70 between Vail and Dillon. Traveling to these trails is no farther than the typical trip to a major ski area. Like so many trails in Colorado, these were built to support mining during the boom years of the 1880s. Many trails, like Mosquito Pass (Trail #46), were abandoned within a short time of their construction by the surprisingly quick development of the railroads. The first part of Hagerman Pass Road (Trail #44) follows the same route as the first standard gauge railroad built across the Continental Divide. I discovered one of these trails, West Lake Creek Road (Trail #38), when I took a commercial Jeep ride while on a summer business trip in Vail. One of my favorite easy trails is Weston Pass (Trail # 48). It is hard to imagine that in the late 1870s, this road was clogged with stage coaches and wagons hauling people and supplies into Leadville, one of the largest and most active mining towns of its time. Some of these roads have been kept open for modern-day functional reasons, but others have been preserved for their historical and recreational value by the valiant efforts of the U.S. Forest Service and the Bureau of Land Management.

Trail #44 Hagerman Pass. Looking down on Ivanhoe Lake on the west side of the pass.

The start of the trail follows the creek.

Aspens too tall to support their own weight.

The upper section has a few rocky places.

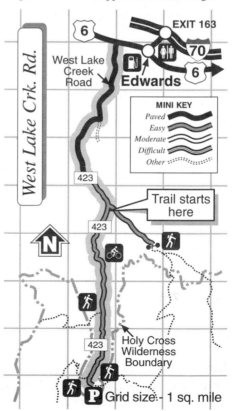

West Lake Crk. Rd.

EXIT 163

6

70

6

West Lake Creek Road

Edwards

MINI KEY

Paved
Easy
Moderate
Difficult
Other

423

Trail starts here

423

N

Holy Cross Wilderness Boundary

423

P Grid size - 1 sq. mile

West Lake Creek Road 38

Location: Southwest of Edwards and Vail.

Difficulty: Easy. Wet weather creates a few small mud holes along the way. Watch for downed trees during wet season. The last 200 feet of the trail are a little steep. Use caution if wet. Four-wheel drive required.

Features: A great way to escape the crowds of Vail. The final portion of the trail is surrounded by the Holy Cross Wilderness Area. Super hiking.

Time & Distance: A five-mile drive from route 6 to the trail start. The trail is about 4 miles one way. Allow a couple of hours for the round trip.

To Get There: Get off Interstate 70 at Edwards exit 163 and turn south. At 0.3 miles turn right on U.S. 6 at a traffic light and drive 0.7 miles to West Lake Creek Road on the left. There is a sign indicating forest service access. Head south 1.8 miles and turn right, staying on the paved road. Continue straight after the pavement ends for a total of about 5 miles from Rt. 6. When you come to a tight curve with a sign for Baryeta Cabins, follow the single lane road to right of the sign.

Trail Description: Set your odometer to zero at the start. The trail is marked as F.S. 423 after a short distance. West Lake Creek is on the left as the road begins to climb. The drainage cuts and mud holes make the ride fun. At 1.0 miles the road turns sharply to the right and begins climbing as you enter an area with aspens that are very tight to the road. In one area the aspens are so dense they have grown too tall to support their own weight and have bent to the ground. After 2 miles the terrain changes again as you enter a dark area of pine. Bear to the right at 2.8 miles. At 3 miles you cross through a rocky section. A hiking trail to New York Mountain goes to the right at 3.7 miles. You reach the end of the trail at about 4 miles as the road swings to the left and drops down into an open meadow where there is a small parking area and trailhead.

Return Trip: Return the way you came.

Services: Full services in Edwards.

Maps: White River National Forest, Trails Illustrated Eagle, Avon #121, Colorado Atlas and Gazetteer. The best of the three is Trails Illustrated.

Climbing towards the summit from the east side. A relaxing easy drive after the snow melts.

Public observation deck and outside chapel for Mt. Holy Cross.

Mt. Holy Cross.

154

Shrine Pass

Location: Between Vail Pass on Interstate 70 and Redcliff.

Difficulty: Easy. An easy drive when clear of snow, usually after July 4th.

Features: Views of Mt. Holy Cross from the west side. There is an observation deck and outdoor chapel about 1.5 miles west of Shrine Pass. This area is popular for cross-country skiing and snowmobiling in the winter.

Time & Distance: Just under 13 miles from Vail Pass on Interstate 70 to Redcliff. The drive takes about an hour one-way.

To Get There: Exit Interstate 70 at exit 190 between Copper Mountain and Vail. There is a large rest area here. Turn west then bear to the right and follow signs to Shrine Pass. The road is gated closed in the winter.

Trail Description: Set your odometer to zero at the start. A dirt road has some washboard sections but is wide and easy to drive. You reach Shrine Pass at 2.2 miles. It is easy to miss because it is wide and flat. At this point you pass from the Arapaho National Forest to the White River National Forest. As you start down the other side, the road narrows a little. At 3.7 miles a sign indicates a view of Mt. Holy Cross. There is a modern pit toilet and a small parking area to the left. You have to hike 1/4 mile to the observation deck. It is an easy trail and is wheelchair accessible although I didn't see a ramp to the deck itself. As you continue down the west side, there are several other places where Mt. Holy Cross can be seen. It has to be a clear day to see the mountain because it is far off to the west. The cross can be seen on the mountainside best when the peak is partially snow covered. At 10 miles there is a small bridge on the left that leads to McCallister Gulch (Trail #41) and Ptarmigan Pass (Trail #42). Redcliff is another 2.7 miles.

Return Trip: Return the way you came or from Redcliff take 24 north to Interstate 70 or south to Leadville.

Services: Gas at Redcliff and full services at Vail and Copper Mountain.

Maps: White River National Forest, Trails Illustrated Vail, Frisco, Dillon #108, Colorado Atlas and Gazetteer.

Looking down on Hunky Dory Lake from just beyond the end of the trail.

Obstacle #1. This tree eats hardtops.

A few cabins remain at Holy Cross City.

Obstacle #2 is a series of challenges.

Obstacle #3 at French Creek.

Location: North of Camp Hale between Leadville and Redcliff on U.S. 24.

Difficulty: Difficult. One of the most difficult hard-core trails in the state, offering the ultimate in non-stop challenge to serious four-wheelers. The final quarter mile on the right fork above Holy Cross City features Cleveland Rock, an obstacle conquered by few. Body damage is likely even for modified vehicles. Winches and lockers recommended. Do not drive this trail alone.

Features: The main feature of this trail is the consistent challenge it offers from one end to the other. The fun begins immediately and gets better with each successive mile. The trail passes through Holy Cross City and ends at the Holy Cross Wilderness area.

Time & Distance: The trail itself is just four miles long one way. I have driven the trail three times, always with at least four or five vehicles. Each time it has taken a full day because of unexpected problems.

To Get There: From exit 171 on Interstate 70 drive south on U.S. 24 past Redcliff. About a mile after the Hornsilver Campground, turn right on 703, following signs to Blodgett Campground and Homestake Reservoir. From Leadville drive north on 24 past Camp Hale. Several miles past Camp Hale you descend a tight switchback. The turn for 703 is on the left at the bottom of the hill. Follow 703 about 9 miles to the turn-off for Holy Cross trail marked as F.S. 759. The trail is just past the Gold Park Forest Service Campground.

Trail Description: Set your odometer to zero at the start of the trail. Your mileage may vary considerably due to differences in tire spinning; however, route finding is not difficult as the trail is obvious the entire way. The trail starts on loose rock and immediately enters the trees. It becomes difficult immediately as you encounter several small rock challenges around the first bend. If you don't feel comfortable with this first section, turn around immediately because this is as easy as it gets. After a mile or so of pounding rock there is a road that drops off the trail to the left. This is an easy but long road back down the mountain that can be used as a bail-out point. It connects to 704.

Continuing on the trail, you encounter many tough sections, but the first obstacle shown on the map comes at about 2.3 miles. A tree juts into the trail over a rocky section that tilts you against the tree. (See photo on page 156.) Hardtop vehicles will have difficulty here, especially coming back down. Please stay on the trail. Do not attempt to go around. About 0.3 miles later, there is a series of difficult rocks which I show as obstacle #2. At 2.8 miles you cross French Creek with obstacle #3 on the opposite bank. It is especially difficult because your tires will be wet after crossing the stream. Stop here and register at a Forest Service sign-in station.

Around the corner and several tough sections later, you'll see a large sign indicating that the trail was restored at this point by the Big Horn Jeep Club of Denver. This spot was once a giant impassable mud bog. You must stay on the trail through this section. After this point, Holy Cross City is about 0.7 miles. Before reaching the city you pass through what is left of the once very large Holy Cross mill. Only rusting boilers and small stretches of corduroy roads remain. At this point bear to the right and head up the hill. After a short muddy stretch, a small trail goes to the right back to a few cabins remaining of Holy Cross City. Please hike to the cabins, don't drive. There is a small place to park on the left.

Just after that, the main trail splits. The left fork, not noteworthy, goes up the hill about 0.3 miles to a hiking trail. Those looking for the ultimate challenge take the right fork to obstacles #4 and #5. You might want to walk up and take a look before you try it. It's very tough. This fork ends 0.3 miles later at the boundary to the wilderness. From there you can take a short hike to see Cleveland Lake. Hunky Dory Lake can also be seen below. (See photo on page 156.)

Return Trip: Return the way you came.

Services: The closest gas is in Redcliff. Full services in Leadville.

Other Activities: This is a very popular hiking area. Please be courteous and give way to all hikers. Let's enjoy this area together.

Historical Highlights: Holy Cross City once had a population of about 300, a school, and a hotel. Look around and you should be able to count about 17 foundations along with the few remaining cabins. It survived only a few short years during the 1880s and early 1890s when it became evident that the quality of its ore would not sustain a profit.

Maps: White River National Forest, Trails Illustrated Holy Cross, Ruedi Reservoir #126, Colorado Atlas and Gazetteer.

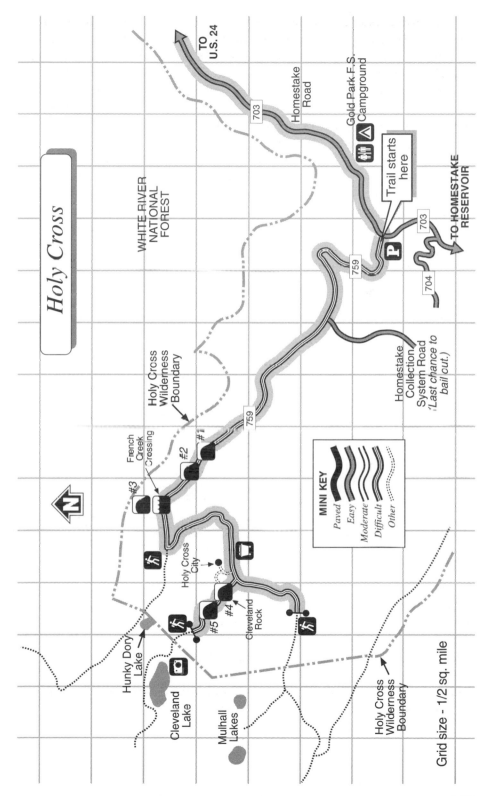

Holy Cross

N

WHITE RIVER NATIONAL FOREST

Holy Cross Wilderness Boundary

French Creek Crossing

TO U.S. 24

Homestake Road

703

Gold Park F.S. Campground

Trail starts here

703

TO HOMESTAKE RESERVOIR

P

759

704

Homestake Collection System Road
(Last chance to bail out.)

759

#1

#2

#3

MINI KEY
Paved
Easy
Moderate
Difficult
Other

Holy Cross City

#4

Cleveland Rock

#5

Hunky Dory Lake

Cleveland Lake

Mulhall Lakes

Holy Cross Wilderness Boundary

Grid size - 1/2 sq. mile

159

A fantastic 360 degree view from the top of Resolution Mountain. (11,905 ft.)

Although fairly steep in places, the wooded portion of the drive is very enjoyable.

McCallister Gulch

Location: North of Leadville and Camp Hale. South of Shrine Pass Road (Trail #39).

Difficulty: Moderate. The lower wooded portion on the south side is steep in places, with moguls that require careful tire placement to maintain traction. This trail, although challenging, is suitable for stock sport utilities. This trail is often snow covered in June because the snow melts slowly in shade of the trees. It is best to drive this trail later in the summer when it is dry.

Features: This is one of my favorite trails because it offers a wide variety of moderately challenging driving situations for modern sport utility vehicles, while simultaneously featuring some of the finest scenery in Colorado. I was first introduced to this trail several years ago when I attended *Camp Jeep*® sponsored by Chrysler Corporation. I was taken on this trail along with many novice drivers. Everyone managed to get to the top of Resolution Mountain without incident and we all had a great time. People coming from other parts of the U.S. were awestruck by the beauty of the area. They were also quite surprised to discover how capable a stock SUV can be.

Time & Distance: The trip is a little more than 10 miles. Add half a mile for the side trip to the top of Resolution Mountain. Allow 2 to 4 hours for the complete trip.

To Get There: Head south from Interstate 70 (exit 171) on U.S. 24 to Pando, which is at the north entrance to Camp Hale. From Leadville, drive north on 24 past Camp Hale to the north entrance. Turn into the entrance and head east about 0.1 miles and bear to the right, following a well worn paved road. Go about 0.5 miles and turn left across a bridge. Make two quick left turns in another 0.4 miles. McCallister is marked as F.S. 708 and heads north. The other road going up the hill to the right is Resolution Road to Ptarmigan Pass (Trail #42). Note: if you drive McCallister Gulch in the opposite direction described here, the entrance is off Shrine Pass Road (Trail #39) north of Redcliff. Follow directions to Ptarmigan Pass (Trail #42), which is described starting from the north end. Trail #42 can be driven as a loop combined with McCallister.

Trail Description: Set your odometer to zero at the start of the trail. Head north on a bumpy road about 0.8 miles and turn right. At 1.3 miles turn right again up a smaller road with signs indicating McCallister Gulch. This road is just one lane wide and crosses an easy ledge until it enters the trees at 1.7 miles. You pass by some private property on the left. The road becomes steeper as you begin climbing through the trees. Views are limited by the dense trees. This stretch lasts for about three miles and gets steeper the higher you go. You may have to make several attempts on some of the sections until you discover the best line that keeps your tires on the ground. It can be done with a stock vehicle even if a little wet. Don't attempt, however, if extremely muddy or if any snow is present.

At 4.6 miles you begin to come out of the trees. On a clear day you can see Mt. Holy Cross quite prominently to the west. At 4.9 miles there is a road that goes up the hill to the right. This is a short side trip to the top of Resolution Mountain with a spectacular 360 degree view. The trail is a little tougher but still manageable by stock vehicles. You may also choose to hike to the top. My mileage from this point does not count the 0.5 miles for this side trip.

Continuing on from this intersection, you begin to descend across a wide beautiful sloping area on your way down to Hornsilver Mountain. At 7.4 a road goes to the left. Continue straight. At 8.5 miles a road joins the main trail from the left. Continue straight down the hill. At 9.5 turn left after crossing a creek. The road weaves its way back and forth across the creek a few times before crossing a bridge to Shrine Pass Road (Trail #39).

Return Trip: Turn left at Shrine Pass Road to get back to Redcliff and U.S. 24. Turn right at Shrine Pass Road to get back to Vail Pass at Interstate 70. If you want to do a loop trail back to the starting point of McCallister, turn around and head back up the trail. When you get to the point where you crossed the creek at 9.5 miles, go straight.

Services: Gas in Redcliff. Full services in Leadville and Vail.

Other Activities: This is a popular winter recreation area. The road itself can be hiked and biked.

Maps: White River National Forest, Trails Illustrated Maps #108 and #109, Colorado Atlas & Gazetteer.

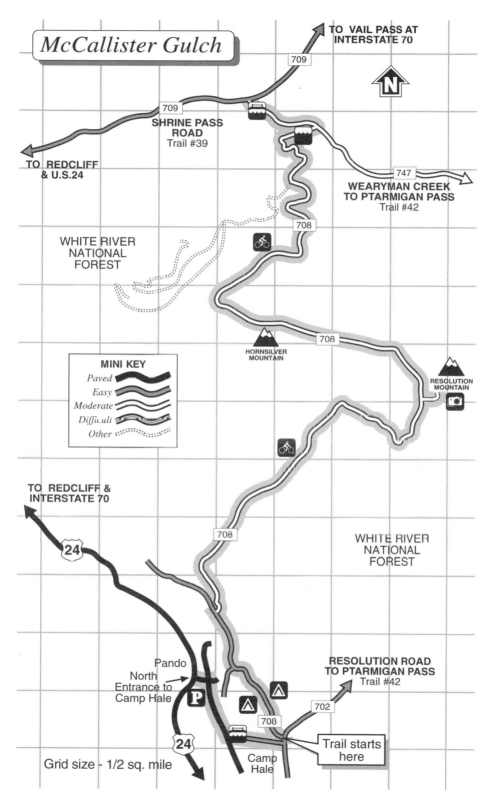

McCallister Gulch

TO VAIL PASS AT INTERSTATE 70

709

N

709

SHRINE PASS ROAD
Trail #39

TO REDCLIFF & U.S. 24

747

WEARYMAN CREEK TO PTARMIGAN PASS
Trail #42

708

WHITE RIVER NATIONAL FOREST

708

HORNSILVER MOUNTAIN

RESOLUTION MOUNTAIN

MINI KEY
Paved
Easy
Moderate
Difficult
Other

TO REDCLIFF & INTERSTATE 70

24

708

WHITE RIVER NATIONAL FOREST

Pando
North
Entrance to
Camp Hale

P

24

RESOLUTION ROAD TO PTARMIGAN PASS
Trail #42

702

708

Trail starts here

Camp Hale

Grid size - 1/2 sq. mile

Resolution Road 702 (Foreground) is easy. The road going up the hill in the distance is 751.

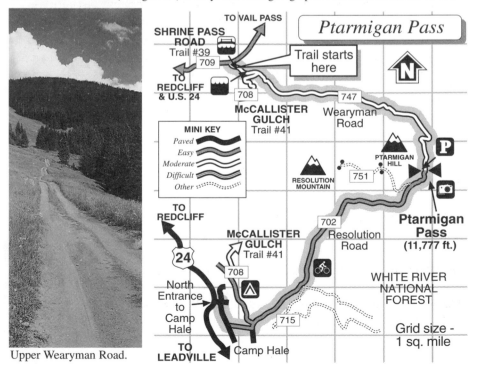

Upper Wearyman Road.

TO VAIL PASS

Ptarmigan Pass

SHRINE PASS
ROAD
Trail #39
709

Trail starts
here

N

TO
REDCLIFF
& U.S. 24

708

747

McCALLISTER
GULCH
Trail #41

Wearyman
Road

MINI KEY
Paved
Easy
Moderate
Difficult
Other

RESOLUTION
MOUNTAIN

751

PTARMIGAN
HILL

P

TO
REDCLIFF

24

McCALLISTER
GULCH
Trail #41

708

702

Resolution
Road

**Ptarmigan
Pass**
(11,777 ft.)

North
Entrance
to
Camp
Hale

WHITE RIVER
NATIONAL
FOREST

715

Grid size -
1 sq. mile

TO
LEADVILLE

Camp Hale

164

Ptarmigan Pass 42

Location: Between Camp Hale and Shrine Pass Road (Trail #39).

Difficulty: Moderate. Rating applies to the Wearyman Creek side only. Resolution Road on the south side is easy. Overall this trail is much easier than McCallister Gulch (Trail #41). Brush is tight in places. Stay off this trail if snow covered.

Features: Provides a nice return loop for McCallister Gulch.

Time & Distance: About 12 miles from Shrine Pass Road to Camp Hale. Allow about an hour and a half in good weather.

To Get There: Turn off Shrine Pass Road 709 about 3 miles northeast of Redcliff or about 10 miles southwest of Vail Pass exit 190. Watch for a small bridge on the south side of the road.

Trail Description: Set your odometer to zero at the start. Cross the small bridge heading south. The hardest part of the trail is at the beginning. The first half mile winds in and out of Wearyman Creek. Do not attempt this trail during spring run off because the creek can be deep and fast moving. The road is quite narrow as it cuts into the steep valley wall. Passing can be inconvenient but is seldom necessary because there is usually little traffic. At 0.7 miles McCallister Gulch (Trail #41) goes to the right. The climb is constant as the road twists in roller coaster fashion up the valley and eventually climbs above the trees. Ptarmigan Pass is reached at 5.6 miles. It is a wide flat open area. Resolution Road on the south side of the pass is a two-lane graded road most of the way. Bear left at 6.2 miles as 751 goes to the right. At 9.8 miles road 715 goes to the left. You drive past the start of McCallister Gulch at 11.2 miles. After that, two right turns and one left turn will take you to U.S. 24.

Return Trip: At 24 turn left for Leadville and right for Redcliff and Interstate 70.

Services: Gas at Redcliff. Full services in Vail and Leadville.

Maps: White River National Forest, Trails Illustrated #108 and #109, Colorado Atlas & Gazetteer.

The last obstacle just before the lake is the toughest. You will need help without lockers.

Wheeler Lake. The sport utilities pictured here are not stock. Hike to a smaller lake above.

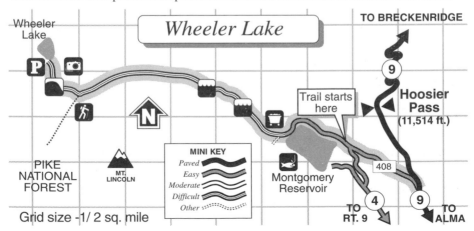

Wheeler Lake

TO BRECKENRIDGE

9

Hoosier Pass
(11,514 ft.)

Trail starts here

PIKE
NATIONAL
FOREST

MT.
LINCOLN

N

MINI KEY
Paved
Easy
Moderate
Difficult
Other

Montgomery
Reservoir

408

Grid size -1/ 2 sq. mile

TO
RT. 9

4

9

TO
ALMA

Wheeler Lake

Location: West of Route 9 between Alma and Hoosier Pass.

Difficulty: Difficult. There are several obstacles along the way that can be managed by stock vehicles. However, the last obstacle before the lake requires lockers, a winch, or a friend with a tow strap. Brush is very tight in places along the trail.

Features: For hard-core four-wheelers, the main feature of this trip is the last obstacle. Other interesting features include Montgomery Reservoir, the Magnolia Mill, and Wheeler Lake.

Time & Distance: The total length of the trail is 4.3 miles. Allow at least a half day for the round trip.

To Get There: From the north, take Route 9 south from Breckenridge and turn right on F.S. Road 408 about a mile south of Hoosier Pass. Go another mile or more to Montgomery Reservoir. The trail is on the north side of the reservoir. If you are approaching from the south, you can take County Rd. 4 prior to 408.

Trail Description: Set your odometer to zero at the gate above Montgomery Reservoir. Follow the road around the back of the lake. When the road starts to climb, bear to the right up a couple of switchbacks. At 1.1 miles you literally pass under part of the Magnolia Mill. There is a challenging spot after the mill. Stock vehicles should stay to the left side. The trail stays fairly rocky and at 1.6 miles you pass through some water as you skirt the edge of the Middle Fork of the South Platte. This happens again at 2.2 miles. In the spring, these places can get pretty deep. Stock vehicles should go no farther than 3.8 miles. Bear to the right as you climb up a narrow ledge of loose rock. At 4.0 miles the trail bends to the right and you see the final obstacle. The lake is another 0.3 miles past this point. There is plenty of room to park at the lake.

Return Trip: Return the way you came.

Services: Gas at Alma. Full services in Breckenridge and Fairplay.

Maps: Pike National Forest, Trails Illustrated Breckenridge, Tennessee Pass #109, Colorado Atlas and Gazetteer.

Looking east at Turquoise Reservoir with Hagerman Pass Road below.

Looking west from just below Hagerman Pass. Ivanhoe Lake is on the left.

East side approach to Hagerman Pass. The road gets a little tougher than this in places.

Hagerman Pass

Location: West of Leadville and southeast of Turquoise Reservoir.

Difficulty: Moderate. This trail is fairly easy except for a few spots that raise the rating to moderate.

Features: With three outstanding wilderness areas as a backdrop, Turquoise Reservoir serves as a focal point for a vast number of recreational activities. Many great hiking trails, including the Colorado Trail, crisscross the area. In addition, there are two historically significant railroad tunnels (See Historical Highlights section). If you visit this area around Memorial Day, you may have an opportunity to drive through deep snow tunnels at the summit.

Time & Distance: The trail is described here from Turquoise Reservoir to F.S. Road 527. This 12-mile stretch can be driven in about an hour one way. You could easily spend an entire day hiking or exploring a vast number of side roads on the west side of the pass.

To Get There: Take 6th Street west from Leadville and bear right at the end where a major paved road heads west to the lake. Follow this road 4 miles until you enter the San Isabel National Forest and see signs for Turquoise Reservoir. Just south of the lake, the road splits. Go left over the dam and around the south side of the lake. At 3.4 miles turn left up F.S. 105, a smooth gravel road to Hagerman Pass.

Trail Description: Set your odometer to zero as you start up the road. The first few miles remain smooth and then it gets a little bumpier with more frequent narrow sections. The main trail is obvious so route-finding is not a problem. Short of 4 miles the road turns sharply to the right. At this point you pass the sealed entrance to the Carlton Tunnel. As you climb higher, there are several places to pull over, offering fantastic views of Turquoise Reservoir. You pass a large sign on the left explaining some of the history of the Colorado Midland Railway. There is a trailhead here that leads to the Hagerman Tunnel.

After 5 miles, the road swings left back into the mountain. It is rocky and narrow in places but represents no threat when dry. At about 8 miles you reach the summit at 11,925 feet. As you start down the west side a wide vista opens up, exposing the upper Fryingpan Valley and Ivanhoe Lake. As you continue down into the valley, road conditions improve quickly. At 11.1

miles there is a small stream that can be deep in the spring. At 11.8 miles you reach the intersection of 527. Going left takes you on an easy road to Ivanhoe Lake. This road follows the original railroad bed to the west entrance of the Carlton Tunnel. The road continues past the tunnel to Lily Pond Lake and another hiking trail into the Fryingpan Wilderness.

Return Trip: Most people return the way they came. However, if you turn right where 105 intersects with 527, 105 continues and connects with paved road 4 which takes you by Ruedi Reservoir and into Basalt.

Services: Full services in Leadville.

Other Activities: Turquoise Reservoir is large with many nice Forest Service Campgrounds. Good sized boats are allowed on the lake for fishing and other water activities. Fishing is also allowed on Ivanhoe Lake. Hiking and biking trails are everywhere.

Historical Highlights: The Hagerman Tunnel was completed in 1886 and connected Colorado Springs to Aspen. It was the first standard gauge railroad to cross the Continental Divide. Due to high maintenance costs, the Busk-Ivanhoe Tunnel was built at a lower altitude seven years later. It too proved to be impractical for railroad use and was later bought by mining magnate Albert Carlton. He renamed the tunnel after himself and converted it to automobile use. It served as such between 1924 and 1937. A third tunnel at yet a lower altitude was built in the 1960s by the Corps of Engineers to divert water from the Fryingpan Wilderness to the Turquoise Reservoir. Known as the Charles H. Boustead Tunnel, it is four miles long and runs perpendicular to the other tunnels.

Maps: San Isabel National Forest, White River National Forest, Trails Illustrated Holy Cross, Ruedi Reservoir #126, Colorado Atlas & Gazetteer.

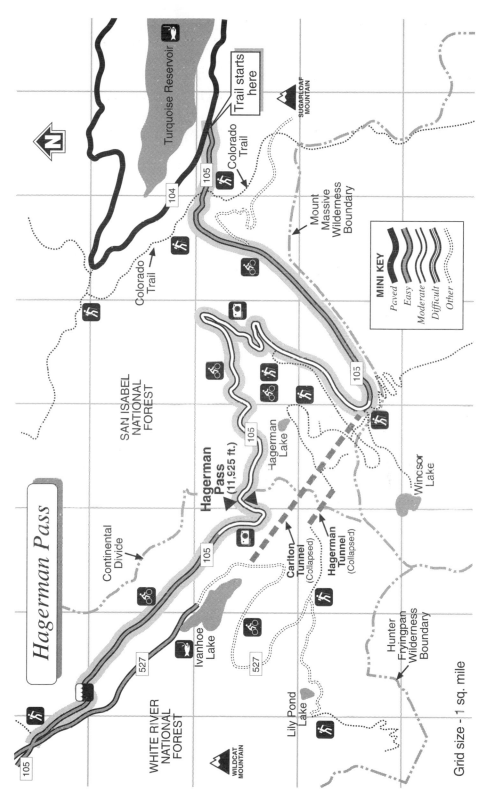

Hagerman Pass

MINI KEY
Paved
Easy
Moderate
Difficult
Other

Turquoise Reservoir

Trail starts here

Colorado Trail

104

105

SUGARLOAF MOUNTAIN

Mount Massive Wilderness Boundary

Colorado Trail

SAN ISABEL NATIONAL FOREST

105

105

Hagerman Lake

105

Windsor Lake

Hagerman Pass (11,925 ft.)

Continental Divide

Carlton Tunnel (Collapsed)

Hagerman Tunnel (Collapsed)

527

105

Ivanhoe Lake

527

WHITE RIVER NATIONAL FOREST

WILDCAT MOUNTAIN

Lily Pond Lake

Hunter Fryingpan Wilderness Boundary

105

Grid size - 1 sq. mile

171

Mt. Lincoln Road as seen from Mt. Bross. The road is clearly defined until you reach the top.

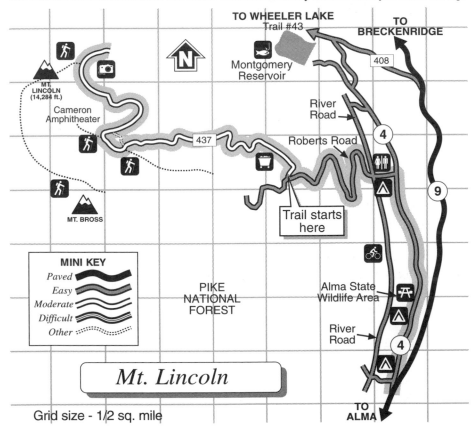

TO WHEELER LAKE
Trail #43

TO
BRECKENRIDGE

408

Montgomery
Reservoir

River
Road

Roberts Road

4

MT.
LINCOLN
(14,284 ft.)

Cameron
Amphitheater

437

9

Trail starts
here

MT. BROSS

MINI KEY

Paved
Easy
Moderate
Difficult
Other

PIKE
NATIONAL
FOREST

Alma State
Wildlife Area

River
Road

4

Mt. Lincoln

Grid size - 1/2 sq. mile

TO
ALMA

172

Location: Northwest of Alma. Southwest of Hoosier Pass.

Difficulty: Moderate. This rating is based on the road surface which is equivalent to other moderate trails in this book. Some drivers might find the trail more difficult because of the extreme high elevation and narrowness of the trail at the top. If this is the case for you, consider going only part way up. Descend immediately at the first sign of stormy weather.

Features: An extremely short drive to the top of a fourteener.

Time & Distance: About 3 miles from the start to the top. Allow about an hour one-way in clear weather.

To Get There: Follow directions carefully because the start of this trail is difficult to find. Look for County Road 4. It exits Route 9 about 2 miles north of Alma and about 3.5 miles south of Hoosier Pass. Once on Rt. 4, go about 2 miles north and turn left across the river. Look for the intersection of River Road and Roberts Road. Set your odometer to zero and head up the hill on Roberts Road. At 1.7 miles turn right on a single-lane dirt road that crosses a field before it enters the forest. Stay on the Forest Service road for the first half mile as it cuts through private property. Please respect the rights of the property owners.

Trail Description: Set your odometer to zero at the start. The road winds through the forest at a fairly steep grade as you climb quickly above timberline. Bear left at about 0.6 miles. The main road is well defined until you pass through a gate above the Cameron Amphitheater. Do not feel compelled to continue if you feel uncomfortable with the elevation. Find a wide spot and turn around if necessary. The road splits in many directions the higher you go. Without exact mileages, directions may do more harm than good. Just find your way to the top as best you can. You can't get too far off course. Once at the top, you can see Wheeler Lake to the north.

Return Trip: Return the way you came.

Services: Gas at Alma. Full services in Fairplay and Breckenridge.

Maps: Pike National Forest, Trails Illustrated Breckenridge, Tennesee Pass #109, Colorado Atlas & Gazetteer.

The lower east side approach is a beautiful easy drive.

Approaching the summit on the west side.

The east side climb begins.

The east side approach is still easy at this point. It's a little tougher higher up.

Location: Northwest of Fairplay between Alma and Leadville.

Difficulty: Moderate. The upper portion of the trail is narrow and rocky on both sides but suitable for stock sport utility vehicles when dry. Do not attempt if snow covered. Snow can be present on this extremely high pass well into late summer. Check with the Bureau of Land Management or the Pike National Forest Ranger District for road conditions.

Features: The highest pass road in Colorado open to travel. There are many interesting, well preserved mines along the way. Views from the 13,186 ft. summit are impressive on a clear day.

Time & Distance: From Route 9 to Leadville is about 17 miles one way. Allow 1 to 2 hours under dry conditions.

To Get There: This trail is described from east to west. Find County Road 12 one mile south of Alma on Route 9. Alma is between Hoosier Pass and Fairplay. If you are starting from the west side, head east from Leadville on 7th Street. At about 4 miles, dirt roads go in several directions. Bear left at all intersections until you reach the Diamond Mine. The road to the pass goes left of a gate at this point.

Trail Description: Reset your odometer as you turn off Route 9. After 2 miles you pass through a small residential area called Park City. At 4.6 a road to the South London Mine goes to the left. Bear right, following signs to Mosquito Pass. At 7 miles, a lesser road marked as 856 goes right to the Champaign Mine. Bear left on the main road and cross a small stream. After the stream there is a large sign on the right for the Mosquito Pass road. At 8.1 miles a lesser road goes to the right up to Cooney Lake. Stay on the main road and you soon pass a mine on the left. The road starts getting rockier and a little narrower in places. At about 8.6 a road coming from the South London Mine joins the trail on the left. If there is any leftover snow on the trail, this is where it usually accumulates. Don't be concerned if the snow is off to the side of the trail, provided the trail is clear. There is a tough section at 8.9 miles. After that it levels off before reaching the summit at 9.7 miles. At the summit there is a side road that heads north to Mosquito Peak. Stay off this road.

The descent down the west side can be a little unnerving at first due to the narrowness of the trail. Check to make sure the trail is clear of vehicles before starting down. Anyone coming up has the right of way and passing can be tricky in places. There are several small side roads on the way down. Just follow the main part of the trail. From above, you can see a long side road that heads north. This is called Birdseye Gulch and connects to Route 91 to Climax. This trail is for hard-core wheelers only. The turnoff for Birdseye Gulch is just after 11 miles. Bear left and continue to head down the hill. It is pretty rocky down through this lower section but should be no problem if you take your time. At 12.8 miles you pass the active Diamond Mine on the left. Bear right for the next few side roads and you eventually find yourself on a major dirt road that takes you into Leadville on 7th Street. You reach Harrison Avenue which is Route 24 at about 17 miles.

Return Trip: The quickest way to get back to the starting point is to return the way you came. A longer alternative would be to take Weston Pass Road (Trail #48) which is south of Leadville on 24. To get to Denver take 91 to Interstate 70.

Services: Full services at Fairplay, Alma, and Leadville.

Other Activities: Mountain biking is popular on the lower elevation portions of the the trail. Check with the Leadville Visitors Center on Harrison Avenue north of 7th Street. There are many summer activities in the area including the Leadville 100 endurance run and the World Championship Mosquito Pass Burro Race from Leadville to Fairplay. Call the Leadville Chamber of Commerce for details. (See Appendix.)

Historical Highlights: This short-lived trail was actively used in the 1870s as the quickest way to reach western mining activities. Like so many of these high pass roads, travelers eventually found it easier to take longer but lower routes like Weston Pass.

Maps: San Isabel National Forest, Pike National Forest, Trails Illustrated Breckenridge, Tennessee Pass #109, Colorado Atlas & Gazetteer.

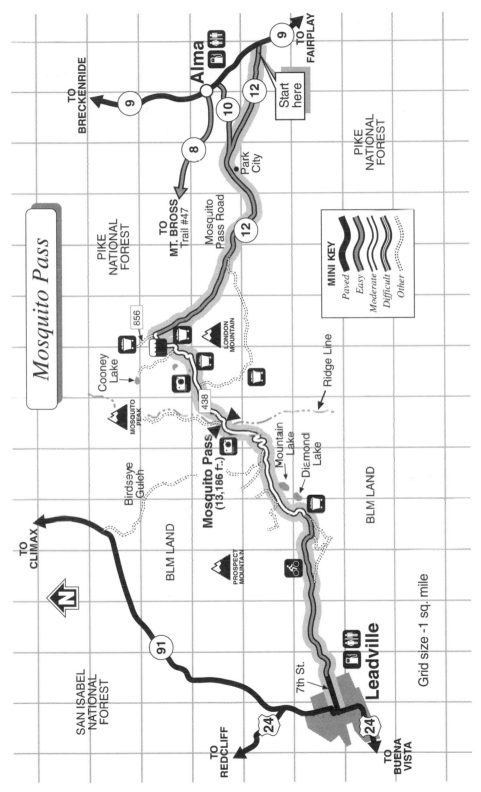

Mosquito Pass

MINI KEY
Paved
Easy
Moderate
Difficult
Other

Grid size - 1 sq. mile

Near the summit of Mt. Bross. Alma can be seen in the distance upper left.

Road washed out near the top.

1,000 year old Bristlecone Pine.

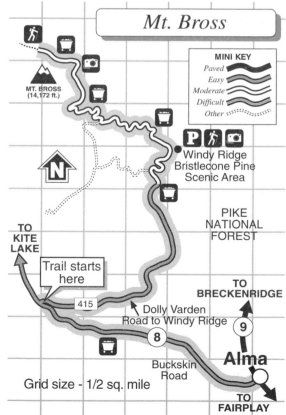

Mt. Bross

MT. BROSS
(14,172 ft.)

MINI KEY
Paved
Easy
Moderate
Difficult
Other

N

Windy Ridge
Bristlecone Pine
Scenic Area

PIKE
NATIONAL
FOREST

TO
KITE
LAKE

Trail starts
here

415

Dolly Varden
Road to Windy Ridge

TO
BRECKENRIDGE

9

8

Buckskin
Road

Alma

Grid size - 1/2 sq. mile

TO
FAIRPLAY

178

Location: West of Alma. Northwest of Fairplay.

Difficulty: Moderate. This rating is based on the road surface, which is equivalent to other moderate trails in this book. Some drivers might find the trail more difficult because of the extreme elevation. If this is the case for you, consider going up only part way. Descend immediately at the first sign of stormy weather.

Features: Numerous mines and spectacular views. Stop at the Bristlecone Pine Scenic Area and see 1,000-year-old trees.

Time & Distance: About 7 miles to the summit from Buckskin Road. Allow about two hours for the round trip.

To Get There: From Alma, head west on Buckskin Road 8 from the center of town across from the gas station. Just under 3 miles, turn right following signs to Windy Ridge. I found the road marked as F.S. 415 but newer maps show the road as County Road 787.

Trail Description: Reset your odometer at the start. The first 2.8 miles can be driven by passenger car. After that you pass a mine and the road gets tougher. Bear right at 2.9 miles. A difficult road goes to the left. There is a small parking area at 3.5 for the Bristlecone Pine Scenic Area. Stop here and read about these very old trees and do some hiking if you have time. From this point you climb above timberline. Bear left at 3.8 and right again at 4.8. Go straight at 5.6 miles. At 5.7 you should see a cave to a mine on the left. The road gets narrower and steeper in places. Bear right at 5.8 miles. Continue straight at 6.2 and left at 6.4. I had to stop near the top because a section of the road had collapsed at 6.7 miles. To your right you should see the road going up to the top of Mt. Lincoln. You can hike over to Mt. Lincoln from Mt. Bross.

Return Trip: Return the way you came.

Services: Gas at Alma. Full services in Fairplay and Breckenridge.

Maps: Pike National Forest, Trails Illustrated Breckenridge, Tennesee Pass #109, Colorado Atlas & Gazetteer.

There are excellent views of the Sawatch Mountain Range coming down the west side.

There are two forest service campgrounds plus many other places to camp along the way.

TO
LEADVILLE

Weston Pass

TO
FAIRPLAY
& DENVER

285

MINI KEY
Paved
Easy
Moderate
Difficult
Other

7

N

PIKE
NATIONAL
FOREST

7

Mt
Massive
Lakes

Weston Pass
(11,921 ft.)

5

Start
here

24

SAN ISABEL
NATIONAL
FOREST

Buffalo
Peaks
Wilderness
Boundary

22

285

22

22

TO
BUENA
VISTA

Grid size - 2 sq. mile

TO
BUENA
VISTA

Location: South of Fairplay and Leadville between Routes 285 and 24.

Difficulty: Easy. Suitable for passenger cars in good weather on the east side. High clearance is needed on the west side.

Features: A beautiful drive along the south fork of the South Platte River. There are two forest service campgrounds on the east side of the pass plus numerous other camping places on both sides of the pass. Several hiking trails lead to the nearby Buffalo Peaks Wilderness. In 1879 this was a busy stage coach route with hundreds of passengers making the trip to Leadville everyday.

Time & Distance: Almost 27 miles from 285 to 24. Allow about 1 1/2 hours one way.

To Get There: Take 285 south from Fairplay. Watch for well marked County Road 5 on the right. If coming from the south, you can enter via County Road 22. From Leadville, head south on 24 to Rd. 7.

Trail Description: Set your odometer to zero as you turn off U.S. 285 Route finding is very easy on this road. Just follow the obvious main road. Head west on well-graded Rd. 5 across a wide flat valley. You pass several hiking trails before reaching the Weston Pass Campground at 11 miles. There are many camping spots along the side of the road from this point. The South Fork Campground is at 15 miles. At 16 miles you begin the descent on the other side of the pass. The road is not maintained west of the pass and requires higher ground clearance. Views of the Sawatch Mountains in the distance are impressive. The road becomes paved at 24.3 as you enter the Mt. Massive Lakes residential area. Bear right as you pass through the lakes area and follow Rd. 7 out to 24 at 26.6 miles.

Return Trip: Return the way you came or take 24 north to I-70 or south to Buena Vista. If open, consider the more difficult Mosquito Pass (Trail #46) as a possible return route.

Services: Full services in Fairplay and Leadville.

Maps: Pike National Forest, San Isabel National Forest, Trails Illustrated Leadville, Fairplay #110, Colorado Atlas and Gazetteer.

AREA 5

Breckenridge,
Dillon, Como,
Idaho Springs

49. Boreas Pass
50. Georgia Pass
51. Webster Pass
52. Red Cone
53. Lamartine, Saxton Road
54. Spring Creek
55. Guanella Pass

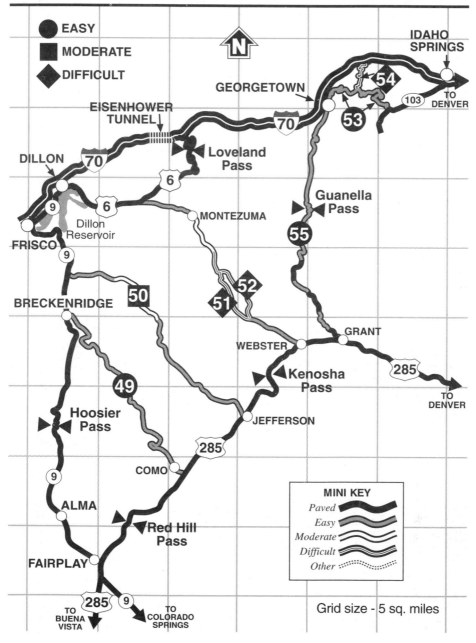

182

Breckenridge, Dillon, Como, Idaho Springs

The great thing about Colorado is that you don't have to go far to find exciting backcountry drives. Scenes like the one below are within a short drive of Denver and Colorado Springs. Five of the trails in this area cross the Continental Divide between U.S. 285 and Interstate 70 and connect to the major resort towns of Breckenridge, Keystone, and Georgetown. The other three trails are less than an hour west of Denver and literally look down on the interstate. All of these trails have been in existence for a very long time and are rich in mining and railroad history. For example, Boreas Pass road (Trail #49) literally follows what was the original railroad route between Como and Breckenridge. All levels of difficulty are possible because each of the trails crosses the Continental Divide at a different altitude. Guanella Pass (Trail #55) is the easiest route in this book and can be traversed by passenger car in good weather. Red Cone (Trail #52) is perhaps the most terrifying drive in the state. Remember that the higher mountain passes may be closed well into summer during years of heavy winter snows.

Looking down on Webster Pass (Trail #51). Radical Hill in the distance. Red Cone to right.

183

Boreas Pass Road climbs high above Breckenridge. The sun sets on the ski area.

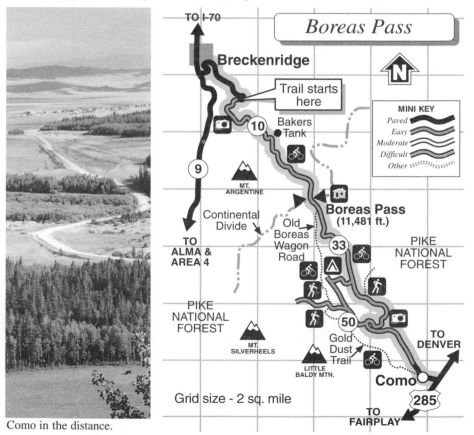

Como in the distance.

Boreas Pass

TO I-70

Breckenridge

Trail starts here

N

9

10

Bakers Tank

MINI KEY
Paved
Easy
Moderate
Difficult
Other

MT. ARGENTINE

Continental Divide

Old Boreas Wagon Road

Boreas Pass
(11,481 ft.)

33

PIKE NATIONAL FOREST

TO ALMA & AREA 4

PIKE NATIONAL FOREST

MT. SILVERHEELS

50

LITTLE BALDY MTN.

Gold Dust Trail

TO DENVER

Como

Grid size - 2 sq. mile

285

TO FAIRPLAY

184

Boreas Pass ㊾

Location: Between Breckenridge and Como.

Difficulty: Easy. Bumpy in places but suitable for passenger cars when dry.

Features: Beautiful views the entire trip, especially at the start and finish. Historically significant. Once a railroad, converted to auto traffic in 1952.

Time & Distance: About 21 miles from Rd. 9 in Breckenridge to 285 at Como. Driving this road fast will loosen a few bolts in your vehicle. Allow more than an hour plus stopping time.

To Get There: From I-70 take Rt. 9 to Breckenridge. Just south of downtown, Boreas Road goes to the left and is marked by a normal street sign.

Trail Description: Reset your odometer as you turn off Rt. 9. Follow this paved road as it climbs above the city. It becomes a dirt road at 3.6 miles. A gate here will tell you if the road is open. There is an overlook at 4.6 miles, followed by Bakers Tank at 6.6. The summit is reached at 10 miles. This was once the town of Boreas, now partially restored. Stop here and read about the history of this road. At 13.8 there is a turn-off for North Tarryall Creek and the Selkirk F.S. Campground. At 15.6 you can pull over at the Davis Overlook. You join Rd. 50 at 17.1 miles. Turn left and at 20 miles you hit pavement before entering the little town of Como. Rt. 285 is just south of Como at 20.9 miles.

Return Trip: Return the way you came or turn left at 285 to head back to Denver. Right on 285 takes you to Fairplay.

Services: Full services at Breckenridge. Gas is available at Jefferson on 285 northeast of Como about 6 or 7 miles.

Other Activities: This is a very popular road for mountain biking. About a half mile south of the pass there is a one-way biking and hiking trail that follows the Old Boreas Wagon road. It connects to the Gold Dust Trail and goes all the way to Como. There are several side roads to explore in the Tarryall Creek area.

Maps: Pike National Forest, Trails Illustrated Breckenridge, Tennesee Pass #109, Colorado Atlas and Gazetteer.

This side trip is above and east of Georgia Pass. The pass is in the upper right of this picture.

The correct way down the north side is the least impressive route from the top of the pass.

The north side is steep in places with some moderately rough terrain.

Georgia Pass 50

Location: Between Breckenridge and Jefferson. Jefferson is on Route 285 southwest of Denver.

Difficulty: Moderate. This rating is based on a 3-mile stretch on the north side of the pass. The south side approach is easy. The entire route is very suitable for stock sport utility vehicles unless snow covered, in which case the pass will be gated closed. The trail may be closed later in the spring because of one wet area on the upper north side.

Features: This trail is an interesting backcountry shortcut to Breckenridge from Denver if you are looking for a little adventure and a change in routine. You can access some fairly remote highlands from the south side via an easy road. There are several nice forest service campgrounds on the south side of the pass on a side road to Jefferson Lake.

Time & Distance: About 23 miles from Route 285 to Route 9 above Breckenridge. Allow at least 2 hours one way.

To Get There: Take 285 southwest from Denver to Jefferson. Jefferson is about an hour from Denver depending on where you start. Turn right at Jefferson on Michigan Creek Road across from the gas station. If you are starting from the Breckenridge end, Tiger Road is several miles north of Breckenridge off Route 9. Follow signs to the golf course on County Rd. 6.

Trail Description: Reset your odometer as you turn off 285. Michigan Creek Road is paved at the start but quickly becomes a smooth dirt road. At 2.2 miles continue straight past Rd. 37 which goes right to Jefferson Lake. At 3.1 miles bear to the right on County Road 54, a slightly rougher road. There should be a sign here for Georgia Pass 9 miles. At 5.3 miles you enter the Pike National Forest and about a mile farther you go by the Michigan Creek F.S. Campground on the left. At 11 miles the road narrows as you complete the last mile to the pass. At about 12 miles you reach a wide flat area with roads going in several directions. There is a large sign to your left indicating that you have reached Georgia Pass and the Continental Divide. There is a short side road behind you that heads west in the direction of Mt. Guyot, a distinctive cone-shaped peak. Directly ahead is another road that heads east and splits. The road you are looking for is to your left and is almost indistinguishable as it heads down the north side across a wide barren area.

Reset your odometer to zero at the pass. (Note: read the last part of this section for a description of an interesting side trip from the top of the pass.) As you head down the north side, the road is not obvious as it splits in several directions. Just pick the one with which you feel most comfortable because they all funnel back together. The next few miles are the roughest part of the trip as you drop down quickly over some fairly bumpy terrain. At 0.7 miles you come to a meadow that can be muddy in the spring and is usually closed if too wet. Use caution through this area. There is also some brush here that may lightly touch your vehicle. Bear to the right at 0.9 miles. At 1.1 there is a gate that should be open; otherwise the pass would have been closed on the other side. At 1.3 miles the road splits and then comes back together again. Keep to the right. You pass a small stream and a road that goes to the right at 1.5 miles. Follow the main road at 1.7 miles. At about 3.5 miles you cross a bridge followed by an intersection. Bear right. At 4.5 turn right and cross the Swan River through an area of tailings piled high everywhere. When you reach the other side of the river, turn left and follow Tiger Road about 6 more miles to Route 9 north of Breckenridge.

An interesting side trip from the top of the pass is to go west, taking the fork to the right. It takes you to a three-way intersection at 0.8 miles. Don't go left. This goes into some difficult terrain across Glacier Ridge. The fork to the right goes around in circles but is fun to explore. The center fork, pictured on the top of page 186, goes to the top of the hill with some beautiful views. It's rocky but suitable for sport utilities. See photo on back cover.

Return Trip: At Route 9 head north to I-70 or south to Breckenridge.

Services: Full services in Breckenridge. Gas in Jefferson.

Other Activities: There is a vast network of trails to explore on the Breckenridge side; however, be careful as some of the trails can be quite difficult. This side is also a popular mountain biking area. You can also hike the pass over the Colorado Trail shown on the map.

Historical Highlights: Georgia Pass was the most popular way to reach Breckenridge from the south in the early 1860s as thousands of crazed miners brought their wagons over the pass and down through the Swan River Valley. Eventually Hoosier Pass and Boreas Pass became the more popular routes, and Georgia Pass was abandoned.

Maps: Pike National Forest, Colorado Atlas & Gazetteer. Unfortunately, this trail is spread across four different Trails Illustrated maps, # 104, #105, #108, and #109.

188

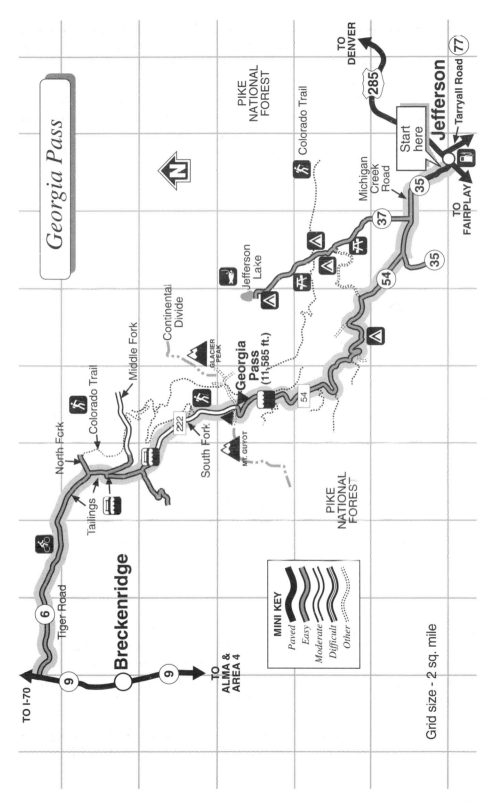

Georgia Pass

TO DENVER

TO
DENVER

285

Jefferson

77

Tarryall Road

PIKE NATIONAL FOREST

Start here

N

Colorado Trail

35

Michigan Creek Road

37

TO FAIRPLAY

54

35

Jefferson Lake

Continental Divide

Middle Fork

GLACIER PEAK

Georgia Pass (11,585 ft.)

Colorado Trail

North Fork

222

South Fork

54

MT. GUYOT

PIKE NATIONAL FOREST

Tailings

6

Tiger Road

Breckenridge

9

9

TO I-70

TO ALMA & AREA 4

MINI KEY
Paved
Easy
Moderate
Difficult
Other

Grid size - 2 sq. mile

These switchbacks are the most difficult part of Webster Pass. Shot taken from Red Cone.

This part of the trail is extremely narrow.

Stream crossing above Montezuma.

Location: Between the Keystone Ski Area and Webster on U.S. 285.

Difficulty: Difficult. The switchbacks coming down from the south side of the pass are extremely narrow. I would not recommend this trail for full-sized vehicles. This section can be blocked with snow most of the year. If any snow is present, the trail is impassable. Your best chance to get through is in late August and early September. The lower end of the trail has some challenging sections and several muddy areas.

Special note: Road signs in the area do not match published Forest Service and Trails Illustrated maps. The following map shows the actual route numbers that were posted on the trail.

Features: The views from both sides of the pass are impressive. There are many side roads in the area to explore, but be careful because some are extremely difficult.

Time & Distance: About 21 miles from Keystone to Webster. Allow about 3 hours one way. From Montezuma to where the trail meets County Road 60 is about 10 miles.

To Get There: Follow signs to Montezuma Road off Route 6 east of the Keystone Ski Area. After you get off 6, go straight at the stop sign. You pass one private road on the left before Montezuma Road swings to the left. The road stays paved all the way to Montezuma. Continue through Montezuma. Webster Pass Road, marked as F.S. 285, turns left less than a mile east of Montezuma. If you are driving the trail in the opposite direction, see Red Cone (Trail #52).

Trail Description: Set your odometer to zero at the start of the trail. Stay on the main road F.S. 285 as lesser roads go to the left. A gate may close the road at 0.6 miles. At 1.4 bear to the right and cross a stream. (See photo opposite page.) To this point the road is of intermediate difficulty. Nice camping spots in this area can be reached by stock vehicles. Bear left at 2.6 miles. A very difficult road marked as 286 goes to the right up Radical Hill. At 3.1 miles F.S. 285 widens as it begins to climb several easy switchbacks. You reach the summit of Webster Pass at 4.1 miles. The road coming down from the left is Red Cone. It is one-way because it is too steep to go up. Before you start down the south side of Webster make sure no one is coming up. They would have the right of way and there is no place to pass. Backing up is difficult and dangerous. Also make sure that the trail is clear of snow. If dry, the trail is relatively smooth with no major obstacles. A couple of spots are a little off-camber. You complete the switchbacks at 5.3 miles. At 5.6 there is a small stream crossing followed by an area of moguls where higher ground clearance is necessary. You pass through an area of scree followed by another stream. The color of the soil changes dramatically at different points along the way.

Bear to the right of a big mud hole at 6.2 miles. At 6.4 you must pass through a mud bog. Fences have been built on each side of the trail to keep vehicles on the trail. You pass by some abandoned vehicles before a fenced meadow at 7.5 miles. Follow the wider part of the road until 8.4 miles, where F.S. Rd. 565.2 shortcuts over to Red Cone. Turn left here if you plan to drive Red Cone. Straight downhill is the shortest way back to 285. This part of the trail bounces you around quite a bit. At 8.8 there is an unmarked fork to the left that goes over to Red Cone. Bear right. At 8.9 you reach the point where Webster meets Red Cone.

Return Trip: You can return via Red Cone (Trail # 52). *Special caution advised.* Or you can follow the road you are on, which is marked as F.S. 121. It becomes County Rd. 60 before it gets to U.S. 285 in another 5 miles.

Services: Full services in Keystone, Dillon, and Silverthorne.

Other Activities: Mountain biking is popular on the north side. Due to the roughness of the terrain, many of the side roads are also used for hiking.

Historical Highlights: The mining camp of Montezuma was founded in 1865 and reached its peak in the 1890s with a population of more than 700. Over the years the town has been destroyed by fire many times, but some part has always survived to rekindle new growth.

Maps: The Arapaho National Forest map is the only map I could find that shows this trail in its entirety. Trails Illustrated Map #104 shows only the northern portion of the trail. The Colorado Atlas and Gazetteer shows the trail across two pages.

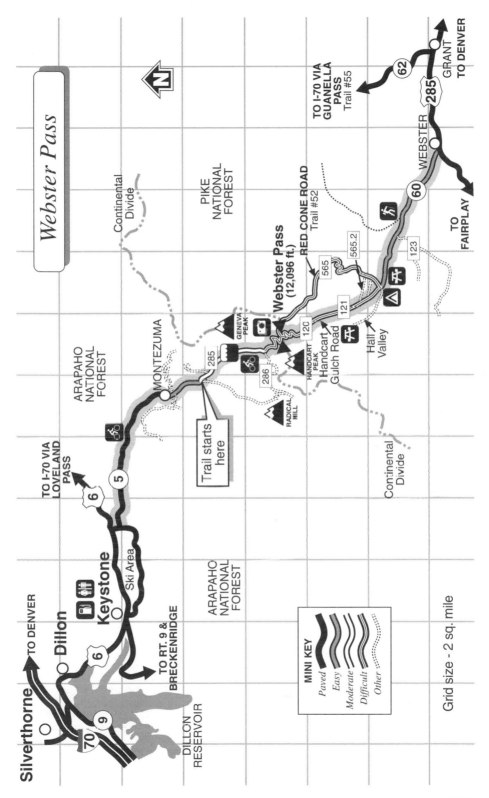

Webster Pass

N

Silverthorne

TO DENVER

Dillon

Keystone

70

9

6

6

5

Ski Area

TO RT. 9 &
BRECKENRIDGE

DILLON
RESERVOIR

TO I-70 VIA
LOVELAND
PASS

ARAPAHO
NATIONAL
FOREST

ARAPAHO
NATIONAL
FOREST

Continental
Divide

PIKE
NATIONAL
FOREST

MONTEZUMA

Trail starts
here

285

286

RADICAL
HILL

GENEVA
PEAK

HANDCART
PEAK

Webster Pass
(12,096 ft.)

120

121

565

565.2

RED CONE ROAD
Trail #52

Handcart
Gulch Road

Hall
Valley

Continental
Divide

123

60

62

WEBSTER

GRANT

285

TO I-70 VIA
GUANELLA
PASS
Trail #55

TO
FAIRPLAY

TO DENVER

MINI KEY

Paved
Easy
Moderate
Difficult
Other

Grid size - 2 sq. mile

The last part of Red Cone (on left) is one-way down. It is too steep to drive up.

No photo can capture the steepness of this most talked-about section of Red Cone.

The lower part is a little tight in spots.   Loose rock is a challenge during the climb.

Location: Between Webster on U.S. Route 285 and the Keystone Ski Area.

Difficulty: Difficult. To drive this trail, you must have surpreme confidence in your vehicle and your driving skills. This trail's notoriety is based on an extremely steep 3/4-mile long, one-way descent from the top of Red Cone down to Webster Pass (Trail #51). This stretch is so steep it is difficult to walk down in places. It is extremely dangerous because your vehicle will likely roll if it gets sideways on the hill. Before descending, make sure there is no snow blocking your continued descent from Webster Pass, because you cannot turn around and drive back up Red Cone. Your best chance of a snow-free trip is in late August or early September.

Special note: Road signs in the area do not match published Forest Service and Trails Illustrated maps. The following map shows the actual route numbers that were posted.

Features: The trip up is challenging and fun. You reach an elevation of over 12,800 feet with a spectacular 360-degree view.

Time & Distance: About 22 miles from Webster to Keystone. Allow about 3 1/2 hours one way. From the start of the trail to Montezuma is about 11 miles.

To Get There: Take U.S. 285 west to Webster. Head north on County Road 60. Bear right at 3.2 miles. You enter the Pike National Forest at 3.7 miles. There is a Forest Service Campground at 4.8 miles. At 5.1 signs direct you to various trails and campgrounds. The mileage to Webster Pass was indicated as 3.4 miles. My actual mileage was 4.8 miles. At 5.2 the road forks. This is the start of Red Cone. Signs indicate Webster and Red Cone both to the right. This is because there are two places to cross over to Webster from Red Cone trail 565.

Trail Description: Set your odometer to zero at the start of the trail. Bear to the right for Red Cone, following signs for F.S. 565. You pass a sign indicating this trail is for experienced drivers only. In no time at all you find yourself on tough terrain. If you want to get to Webster, take the second crossover to the left marked as 565.2. You cross a small stream at 0.9 miles followed by some difficult spots. At 2.1 you get into an area where long wheel-based vehicles will find it a little tight through the trees. I had to back up to make some of the turns. You eventually climb above timberline. The trail is very rocky and jarring most of the way. There is a sign at 3.7 miles that reminds you to stay on the original road. Be responsible. Do not drive off the trail. You begin to see the trail stretching out in front of you across the ridge line to Red Cone. At 4.6 miles you descend before the final steep climb to the top of Red Cone. The summit is reached at 5.5 miles.

The next part is the tough part. Get out of your vehicle and look at the descent. If you are not confident, you can still turn around. Once you start down, there is no turning back. The slope is almost too steep to walk down. If you go down, you must go straight down without hesitation like a skier on a mogul run. Put your vehicle in first gear low range. Keep your foot off the brake as much as possible. If you must use your brake, do it very lightly. Your wheels must not lock up or you will lose your abililty to steer. If you feel the back of your vehicle start to slide sideways, you may actually have to accelerate a little to stop the slide. There are several more steep sections like this before you get down to Webster Pass at 6.2 miles.

Return Trip: Reset your odometer at Webster Pass. You can return via Webster Pass Road to the left (Trail # 51), or you can go north to Keystone and I-70. To get to Keystone, turn right at the top of the pass and follow F.S. 285. Go straight at 1.5 miles. Bear right and cross a stream at 2.7 miles. Bear left after the stream. Continue to follow the main road, and at 4.1 miles you reach a larger gravel road. Turn right for Montezuma. After Montezuma the road is paved and runs into Route 6 at the east end of the Keystone Ski Area.

Services: Full services in Keystone, Dillon, and Silverthorne.

Other Activities: Mountain biking is popular on the north side. Due to the roughness of the terrain, many of the side roads are also used for hiking. Always give way to hikers.

Maps: The Arapaho National Forest map is the only map I could find that shows this trail in its entirety. Trails Illustrated Map #104 shows only the northern portion of the trail. The Colorado Atlas and Gazetteer shows the trail across two pages.

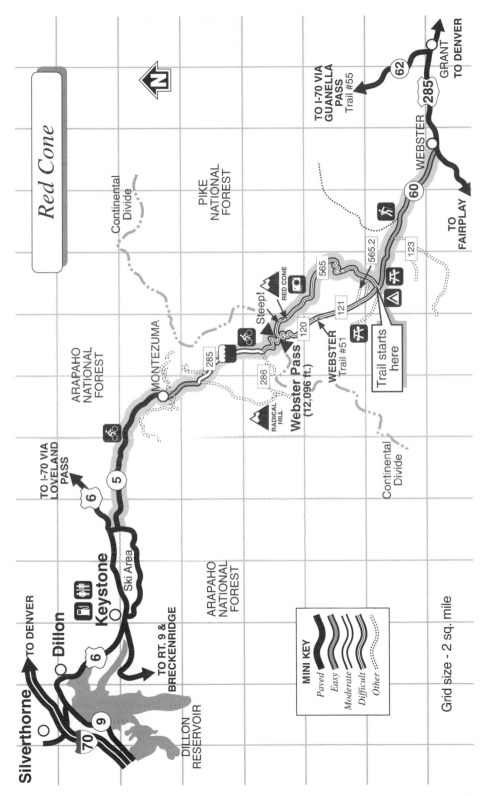

Red Cone

N

Silverthorne
TO DENVER
Dillon
Keystone
Ski Area

70
9
6
6
5

TO I-70 VIA
LOVELAND
PASS

TO RT. 9 &
BRECKENRIDGE

DILLON
RESERVOIR

ARAPAHO
NATIONAL
FOREST

ARAPAHO
NATIONAL
FOREST

MONTEZUMA

285
286

RADICAL
HILL

Continental
Divide

Continental
Divide

PIKE
NATIONAL
FOREST

Steep!
RED CONE

Webster Pass
(12,096 ft.)

120
121
565
565.2
123

WEBSTER
Trail #51

Trail starts
here

60
WEBSTER
285
GRANT

62

TO I-70 VIA
GUANELLA
PASS
Trail #55

TO DENVER

TO
FAIRPLAY

MINI KEY
Paved
Easy
Moderate
Difficult
Other

Grid size - 2 sq. mile

197

Saxton Road. This is what five miles of road looks like squeezed into a two-mile distance.

Not much remains of the Lamartine Mine except tailings. Even less remains of the town.

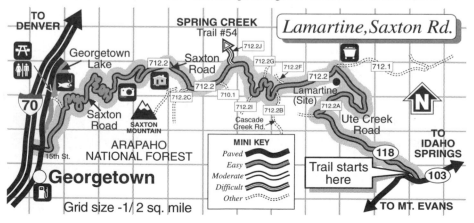

Lamartine, Saxton Rd.

SPRING CREEK Trail #54

TO DENVER

Georgetown Lake

Saxton Road

712.2

712.2J

712.2G

712.2F

712.1

712.2

712.2

710.1

712.2C

Saxton Road

SAXTON MOUNTAIN

712.2I

712.2B

Cascade Creek Rd.

Lamartine (Site)

712.2A

Ute Creek Road

N

ARAPAHO NATIONAL FOREST

15th St.

Georgetown

MINI KEY
Paved
Easy
Moderate
Difficult
Other

Trail starts here

118

TO IDAHO SPRINGS

103

TO MT. EVANS

Grid size -1/2 sq. mile

198

Lamartine, Saxton Road 53

Location: West of Denver between Idaho Springs and Georgetown.

Difficulty: Easy. The toughest easy trail in the book. Several rocky sections require careful driving. I did it in my stock Grand Cherokee with no problems. Go slow and place tires on high points. Easy to get lost. Best done later in the summer when it is drier.

Features: A short drive from Denver. Interesting mining history.

Time & Distance: About 14 miles from the beginning of Ute Creek Road to Interstate 70 at Georgetown. Allow about 2 hours driving time.

To Get There: Get off I-70 at Idaho Springs Exit 240 and follow signs to Mt. Evans on Route 103. Ute Creek Road 118, on the right, is about 5 miles from the Interstate.

Trail Description: Follow Ute Creek Road 118 up through a developed area. Go straight at 1.1 miles. Turn right at 2.3 miles at sign marked Lamartine/Cascade. The road narrows as you eventually pass under a power line. When you reach the top of the hill at 4.0 miles, **reset your odometer** and turn left on 712.2. At 0.8 miles bear left as 712.2F goes right. At 1.0 miles bear right as Cascade Creek Road enters from the left. The road switchbacks up the hill. Bear left at 1.5 miles and right at 1.7 miles. This is the toughest part of the trail. You pass through a more open area as you climb and go by Spring Creek (Trail #54) on the right at 2.5 miles. Continue straight as you pass through dense trees. Bear right at 3.1 as 710.1 intersects 712.2. You reach Saxton Road at 3.3 miles. **Reset your odometer** and turn right as you head downhill towards Georgetown. When you reach Main Street (a dirt road) at 5.7 miles, turn left. At 6.1 miles turn right on 15th Street and go straight to the freeway. Just before the freeway, you may want to turn left on Alvarado to visit the wonderful downtown area of Georgetown. Also, Guanella Pass, (Trail #55) is west of Georgetown past the downtown area.

Return Trip: Take Interstate 70 in your desired direction.

Services: Full services in Georgetown and Idaho Springs.

Maps: Arapaho National Forest, Trails Illustrated Idaho Springs, Georgetown, Loveland Pass #104, The Colorado Atlas and Gazetteer.

The town of Empire and Route 40 as seen from part way up the trail.

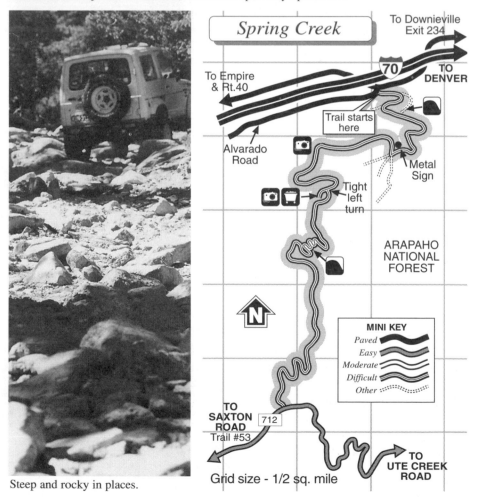

Spring Creek

To Downieville
Exit 234

To Empire
& Rt.40

70

TO
DENVER

Trail starts
here

Alvarado
Road

Metal
Sign

Tight
left
turn

ARAPAHO
NATIONAL
FOREST

N

MINI KEY
Paved
Easy
Moderate
Difficult
Other

TO
SAXTON
ROAD
Trail #53

712

TO
UTE CREEK
ROAD

Grid size - 1/2 sq. mile

Steep and rocky in places.

200

Location: Southwest of the Downieville exit on Interstate 70. Downieville is about 7 miles west of Idaho Springs.

Difficulty: Difficult. Steep climbs, narrow shelf roads, and boulder fields.

Features: A fun hard-core trail within a short drive of Denver.

Time & Distance: About 5 1/2 miles from the start to where the trail intersects with F.S. 712 at the top of the mountain. Allow 2 or 3 hours one way. Add an hour or two more to get back down off the mountain.

To Get There: Get off Interstate 70 at Donnieville exit 234 west of Idaho Springs. Go west on the access road. It starts on the north side and passes under the freeway. At 1.1 miles from the exit, turn left on Alvarado Road. Cross the bridge and immedialtely pull over to the left. Follow the trail up the hill.

Trail Description: Set your odometer to zero at the start of the trail. At 0.3 miles the main road switchbacks up the hill to the right. If you are looking for maximum challenge, turn left here on the lesser road. It rejoins the main road but not before climbing a steep obstacle. If you continue on the main trail, bear left at the next fork at 0.4 miles and begin a steep rocky climb. At 1.3 miles turn right at a metal sign indicating the Spring Creek Trail. Follow the narrow trail as it cuts across the mountain and switchbacks uphill. At about 3.9 miles you have to make a tight left turn up the hill. If you miss this turn, the trail will quickly end at an overlook. After a downhill stretch, you pass through a long and difficult boulder field at 4.5 miles. It smooths out at about 5.2 as you enter a meadow before reaching the end of the trail at 5.3 miles where it joins F.S. 712.

Return Trip: Go back the way you came or turn right to reach Georgetown via Saxton Road (Trail #53). You can also go left to the Lamartine townsite and head downhill via Ute Creek Road (Trail #53).

Services: Full services in Gerogetown and Idaho Springs.

Maps: Arapaho National Forest, Trails Illustrated maps #103 and #104, Colorado Atlas and Gazetteer.

This mountain ridge, east of the pass, is simply called "The Sawtooth."

Georgetown from Leavenworth Mountain.

Duck Lake southwest of the pass.

Guanella Pass

TO DENVER

Georgetown

I-70

LEAVENWORTH MOUNTAIN

Trail starts here

381

N

ARAPAHO NATIONAL FOREST

Continental Divide

Guanella Pass
(11,669 ft.)

MT. EVANS

Duck Lake

MINI KEY
Paved
Easy
Moderate
Difficult
Other

TO WEBSTER PASS
Trail #51

PIKE NATIONAL FOREST

62

Grant

Webster

285

TO DENVER

Grid size - 2 sq. mile

202

Guanella Pass 55

Location: Between Georgetown and Grant.

Difficulty: Easy. Suitable for passenger cars most of the year. Some of the road is paved. Plowed in the winter.

Features: Many Forest Service campgrounds, picnic areas, hiking trails, lakes, and side roads. A very popular area due to its beauty, extensive recreational activities, and its close proximity to Denver. Also serves as a well traveled link between I-70 and U.S. 285 and is usually kept open all year.

Time & Distance: About 24 miles. Takes less than an hour to drive.

To Get There: Starting from the north end, exit Interstate 70 at Georgetown and head south toward the downtown area. Follow signs to Guanella Pass. Starting from the south end, take U.S. 285 from Denver to Grant and turn north on County Road 62.

Trail Description: Described north to south. Set your odometer to zero as you start up Leavenworth Mountain on a paved road at the south end of Georgetown. The road winds up the hill between several lakes and a power plant. The pavement ends at Clear Lake Campground, but several more places are paved on the south side descent. Guanella Pass Campground is encountered at 8.6 miles before reaching the summit at 10.7. The pass has several nice hiking trails and plenty of parking area. At 16.7 a picnic area marks a road to the right that goes to the old Geneva Basin ski area, which is now closed for downhill skiing. There is another campground at 18.3, followed by a hiking trail with a nice parking area. At 20.9 there is another hiking trail to the Mt. Evans Wilderness. There are several more campgrounds and picnic areas before you reach the town of Grant on 285 at 23.8 miles.

Return Trip: From Grant, head east to Denver on 285. From Georgetown, head east on I-70.

Services: Full services in Georgetown.

Maps: Arapaho National Forest, Trails Illustrated Idaho Springs, Georgetown, Loveland Pass #104, Colorado Atlas and Gazetteer. Only the south side is shown on the Pike National Forest Map.

AREA 6

Pikes Peak Region

56. La Salle Pass
57. Mt. Herman Road
58. Longwater Gulch
59. Hackett Gulch
60. Rampart Range Road
61. Mt. Baldy
62. Phantom Canyon, Shelf Road

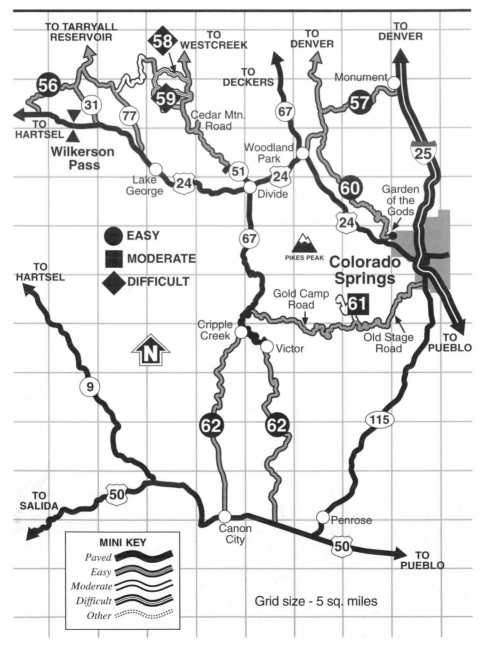

204

Pikes Peak Region

Area 6 offers an incredible array of driving adventure within a few short miles of the front range. Two of the trails, Mt. Herman Road (Trail #57) and Rampart Range Road (Trail #60) literally depart from the edge of metropolitan areas. Because many of these trails are at lower elevations, the driving season is extended longer than any other area. The trails range in difficulty from extremely easy (Phantom Canyon, Trail #62) to very difficult (Hackett Gulch, Trail #59). There is a vast amount of information available on this area because it has been a major tourist attraction for many years. I would suggest you obtain a copy of the the newer Pike National Forest map. The back side of the map is extremely informative. Trails Illustrated map #137 is an expanded version and covers many of the driving attractions in great detail. Well known attractions like the Pikes Peak Highway are not covered here since this information is available in many other places. A word of caution regarding safety: Just because you are within what seems like shouting distance from Colorado Springs, don't assume there is less danger. You must treat each trail with the respect it deserves. Plan your trip carefully and be prepared for any eventuality.

F.S. Rd. 540 along the S. Platte River between Longwater & Hackett Gulches (Trails 58, 59).

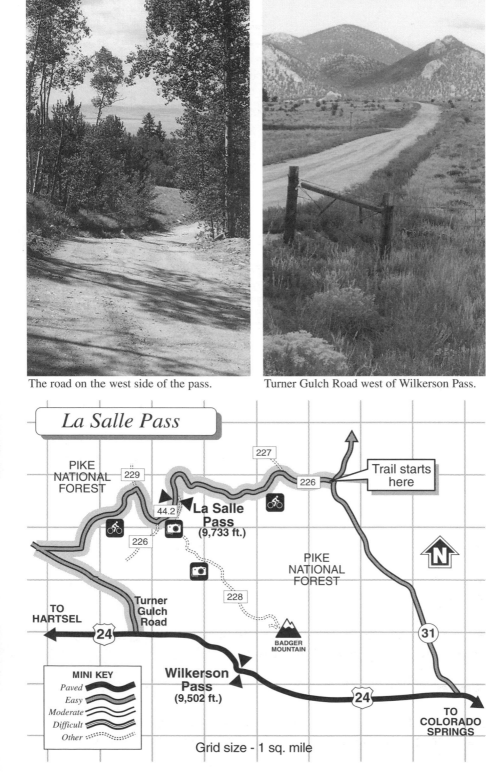

The road on the west side of the pass.

Turner Gulch Road west of Wilkerson Pass.

La Salle Pass

PIKE NATIONAL FOREST

227

229

226

Trail starts here

44.2

La Salle Pass
(9,733 ft.)

226

PIKE NATIONAL FOREST

N

228

TO HARTSEL

Turner Gulch Road

24

BADGER MOUNTAIN

31

MINI KEY
Paved
Easy
Moderate
Difficult
Other

Wilkerson Pass
(9,502 ft.)

24

TO COLORADO SPRINGS

Grid size - 1 sq. mile

La Salle Pass 56

Location: West of Colorado Springs near Wilkerson Pass off Rt. 24.

Difficulty: Easy. High ground clearance recommended. Four-wheel drive might be needed in wet weather.

Features: A fun and relaxing alternative to paved Wilkerson Pass. There are many easy side roads to explore.

Time & Distance: A little more than 9 miles from County Road 31 to Route 24. Takes about an hour. Add time for the side trip to Badger Mountain.

To Get There: Head west on 24 from Colorado Springs towards Wilkerson Pass. Turn right on County Road 31 about 1/2 mile west of the Round Top Mountain Forest Service Campground. Drive north 5 miles on 31 and watch for the turn-off for La Salle Pass on the left.

Trail Description: Set your odometer to zero as you turn off 31 onto F.S. 226. As you start up this trail, you go by a ranch on the left. This road is single lane with an occasional mud hole. Do not make the road wider by trying to go around these minor mud holes. Getting your vehicle dirty is part of the fun. Bear left at 0.8 miles. The road passes through private land until you reach the Pike National Forest at 3.1 miles. There are some nice places to camp in this area. You reach the pass at 4.1, where a road goes left to the top of Badger Mountain. This road is a little rocky but still easy. There are some nice views of South Park about half way up but no views at the top. Continuing west from La Salle Pass, the road becomes F.S. 44.2. At 4.6 miles bear right on F.S. 44. Bear left at 5.0. You pass through an open fence under a power line at 5.3. After that bear left on 44.2A, following the power line. You leave the forest at 6.7 miles. Make sure to close the gate. Turn right after the gate. At 7.2 miles turn left. This is Turner Gulch Road. Bear right at 8.6 before reaching U.S. 24 at 9.3 miles.

Return Trip: Turn left for Wilkerson Pass and Colorado Springs. Right takes you to Hartsel, Buena Vista, and Breckenridge.

Services: Full services at Woodland Park. Gas at Lake George and Hartsel.

Maps: Pike National Forest, Colorado Atlas and Gazetteer. Only the east side of the pass is shown on Trails Illustrated Pikes Peak, Canon City #137.

Looking back towards the front range from several miles up Mt. Herman Road.

North side of Pikes Peak as seen from the top of Mt. Herman Road.

One of many interesting rock formations along the way.

Mt. Herman Road ⑤⑦

Location: Between Monument and Woodland Park.

Difficulty: Easy when dry. This road is well maintained; however, drainage cuts and naturally rocky terrain make it more interesting than the typical gravel road. There are many switchbacks with blind narrow curves. Much more difficult if snow packed or icy.

Features: A beautiful and exciting drive, especially in the early fall when the trees are turning. There are views of the front range and the Air Force Academy at the beginning and Rampart Range and Pikes Peak at the top. Provides access to more difficult trails. This is a great trail for a first time four-wheeler. It has a little of everything without having to travel deep into the mountains. Its lower altitude permits travel early and late in the season.

Time & Distance: Mt.Herman Road is about 10 miles and takes about an hour one way. You can spend any amount of time exploring a vast number of side trails.

To Get There: Get off Interstate 25 at Monument exit 161 and head west on 3rd Street. Follow 3rd until it swings left and runs into 2nd. Turn right on 2nd and cross the railroad tracks to Mitchell Avenue and turn left. Go about 0.5 miles and turn right on Mt. Herman Road. Follow Mt. Herman Road until it forks at 2.5 miles and bear left. This is the start of the trail and is marked as F.S. Road 320.

Trail Description: Set your odometer to zero at the start of the trail. It begins as a gradual climb across the east face of Mt. Herman. The condition of the trail is usually very good with just enough bumps, rocks, and ruts to make it fun. There is a great view of the Air Force Academy at 1.1 miles. The trail gradually turns west and becomes a shelf road as it heads up a scenic valley. Watch for washed-out areas which can cut into the roadway. At 2.3 miles you pass the Mt. Herman hiking trail on the right. As you continue, you see many side roads to explore. You may do so only on those that have Forest Service white arrows. At about 5.4 you begin to see vistas to the north and interesting rock formations. This is a very popular area for dirt bikes so approach tight curves cautiously. It's always helpful to have your windows down and your radio off so you can hear dirt bikes and other cars approaching. At 6.4 miles there is a white arrow trail on the left marked as F.S. 318. This is Power Line Road and is a difficult hard-core trail. It is narrow and extremely steep with deep washed out areas.

At the 8-mile point, you can continue straight two more easy miles to Rampart Range Road 300. Or you can try either of two interesting side roads. The road to the left is 315. It has several moderate sections with many spurs making it easy to get lost. My favorite route is to go right on 322A. It is a **moderate** trail and begins by dropping down a narrow road with deep drainage cuts. After winding through a small valley, it joins 322 Balanced Rock Road at 1.9 miles. A left turn here takes an easy and very scenic route back to Rampart Range Road 300. Turning right takes you on a long but fun descent back down the mountain. There are several steep rutted and narrow sections, but they are manageable by stock sport utilities under dry conditions. This way dead ends at a hiking trail to Palmer Lake after about 5 miles. Turn around and head back to 322A, but continue straight at that point until you reach Rampart Range Road 300.

Return Trip: Any of the three routes described above will get you back to Rampart Range Road 300. Turning left (south) on 300 will take you back to Woodland Park or Colorado Springs. To get to Woodland Park off 300 take paved 393 to the right. It becomes Baldwin Road, which connects to Route 24. To get to Colorado Springs via Rampart Range Road, see Trail # 60.

Services: Full services in Monument and Woodland Park.

Other Activities: There are several nice hiking trails in the area. One trail takes you on a steep but short hike to the top of Mt. Herman, where there are beautiful views of the front range and the Air Force Academy. Although there are no Forest Service campgrounds on Mt. Herman Road, there are many nice camping spots along the way.

Maps: Pike National Forest, Trails Illustrated Pikes Peak, Canon City #137, the Pikes Peak Atlas Map by Robert Ormes & Robert Houdek, Colorado Atlas and Gazetteer.

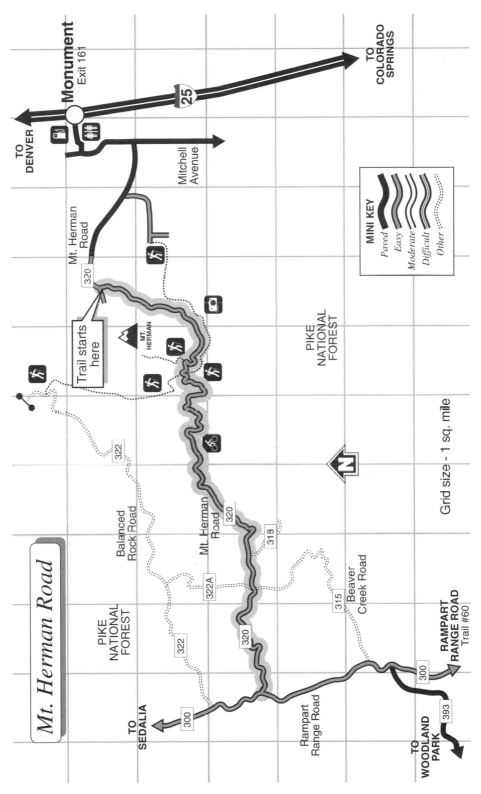

Mt. Herman Road

MINI KEY
Paved
Easy
Moderate
Difficult
Other

Grid size - 1 sq. mile

211

Crossing the Platte River at the bottom of the trail. Water is much deeper in the spring.

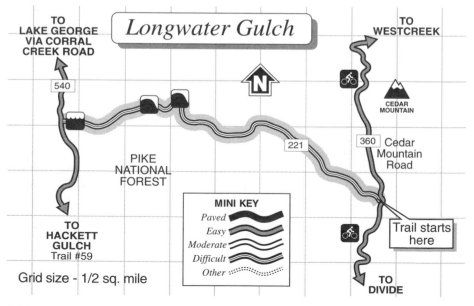

Longwater Gulch

Location: Northwest of Colorado Springs and Divide.

Difficulty: Difficult. Going downhill is easier than going up. There are several spots where the moguls are large with loose soil, requiring lockers or winching going up. There is one big rock obstacle that is smooth but steep. The river crossing at the bottom varies from bumper deep to too deep.

Features: A very popular trail with the hard-core crowd. The steep rolling and twisting trail is extremely fun to drive.

Time & Distance: The total length of the trail is 4.7 miles. Going down takes less than an hour. Coming back up can take a lot more time. Allow additional time to wait for others on the trail.

To Get There: Take Route 24 west from Colorado Springs about 20 miles to Divide. Turn right at the light on County Road 5 in the center of Divide. Bear left at 0.5 onto Rd. 51. Turn right after another 3 miles on a wide gravel road still marked as 51. Drive 6.7 miles until you come to an X intersection. Bear left but not sharp left on F.S. 360 Cedar Mountain Road. After 7 miles watch for a small sign on the left for Longwater Gulch, less than 2 miles after Hackett Gulch (Trail #59).

Trail Description: Reset your odometer at the start. The road drops quickly like a roller coaster. At 2.9 miles you reach a large slab of tilting rock that you must drive across. Select your line carefully. After this obstacle there is a steep run of moguls in loose soil. At 3.6 miles, after passing under a power line, the road splits for a short distance. Left is more difficult. You reach the river at 4.7 miles. It is often too deep to cross in the spring.

Return Trip: There are three options: 1. Return the way you came. 2. Cross the river and turn right on easier F.S. 540. When you reach Corral Creek road 211 turn left on a long stretch to County Rd. 77. A left turn at 77 takes you back to Rt. 24 near Lake George. 3. Cross the river and turn left following 540 to difficult Hackett Gulch. This way has two deep water crossings.

Services: Full services in Woodland Park. Gas in Divide and Lake George.

Maps: Pike National Forest, Trails Illustrated Pikes Peak, Canon City #137, Colorado Atlas and Gazetteer.

This obstacle is known as Hackett Rock and is more difficult than this picture shows.

One of many difficult mogul runs. This one is located on F.S. 220A.

This optional obstacle is very dangerous and nearly impossible to climb without winching.

Hackett Gulch

Location: Northwest of Colorado Springs and Divide.

Difficulty: Difficult. The condition of this trail varies considerably depending upon how recently the road has been maintained. The steep hillsides combined with loose soil conditions create moguls that can be quite severe. There are several rock obstacles that are always difficult. The Platte River crossing at the bottom of the trail can be fairly deep. In the spring it may be impassable.

Features: In addition to many outstanding hard-core obstacles, this trail is just plain fun to drive. It twists and falls down the mountainside so aggressively you'll want to come back and drive it again.

Time & Distance: The traditional route from the top to the Platte River at the bottom is about 5 miles. This portion can be driven in less than an hour downhill with a properly equipped vehicle. However, it is rare for anyone to drive it so quickly because of the many exciting attractions along the way. Most people don't realize that Hackett Road F.S. 220 actually forks to the left towards the bottom and returns to Cedar Mountain Road by connecting with Sportsman Road 897. The reason few people go this way is that there is an extremely steep and dangerous obstacle as you start back up the trail from the river. The most common route is to turn right at 220A and cross the river to 540, which links to Longwater Gulch (Trail #58) and Corral Creek Road. With all these connecting side trips, you can spend a full day or even the weekend exploring the area.

To Get There: Take 24 west from Colorado Springs about 20 miles to Divide. Turn right at the light on County Road 5 in the center of Divide. Bear left at 0.5 miles onto Rd. 51. Turn right after another 3 miles on a wide gravel road still marked as 51. Drive 6.7 miles until you come to an X intersection. Bear left but not sharp left on F.S. 360 Cedar Mountain Road. After about 5 miles watch for a small sign on the left for Hackett Gulch.

Trail Description: Set your odometer to zero at the start. The trail begins gently for the first mile and a half before you are greeted by a rocky section that is fairly rough and steep. At the end of this section is Hackett Rock, which is bordered by a wall of timber on the left. Those without lockers or a winch can take a bypass just before the rock. The best route I find is to hug the right side at the bottom of the rock and let the rocks push you sideways as you go up.

After Hackett Rock you start a steeper descent down the mountain. After a ridge the road splits at about 3.5 miles. Most people go to the left first then return to this point. There are several nice obstacles to the left and a small stream crossing before you come to a clearing by the river. You can cross the river to a nice camping spot on the other side. Hackett Road actually continues to the left of this clearing up a very steep hill. There is a large rock that you must drive over about a hundred feet up. Few vehicles can get up this section without winching. Vehicles with short wheel bases are prone to rollovers going either up or down. With my long wheel-based Cherokee and ARB lockers, I was able to successfully drive over this obstacle. After the rock it is a tricky drive until you connect to Sportsman Road 897 back to Cedar Mountain Road. Chances are you will turn around at this tough rock obstacle and return to the point where 220A splits to the right. From this point to the river, more challenges remain, including a very steep down-hill slab of rock, a long climb up a steep hill of moguls, and a final long descent down a long hill of moguls to the river.

Return Trip: From the river crossing at the bottom of 220A, you can turn around and head back up Hackett Road or cross the river and bear right. This takes you along the other side of the river where there is a tough water crossing at Tarryall Creek. It is not wide but it can be deep and swift. After the creek, you reach Longwater Road (Trail #58). To return via Longwater, turn right and cross the river. An easier but longer way out of this valley is to continue north on 540 to Corral Creek Road 211. Bear left at 211 until you reach Tarryall Road 77. Bear left on 77 to U.S. 24 near Lake George.

Services: Full services in Woodland Park. Gas and food at Lake George and Divide.

Other Activities: Mountain biking and camping are popular on Cedar Mountain Road. This is also a very popular area for ATVs and motorbikes. There is excellent fishing on the Platte River.

Maps: Pike National Forest, Trails Illustrated Pikes Peak, Canon City #137, Colorado Atlas and Gazetteer.

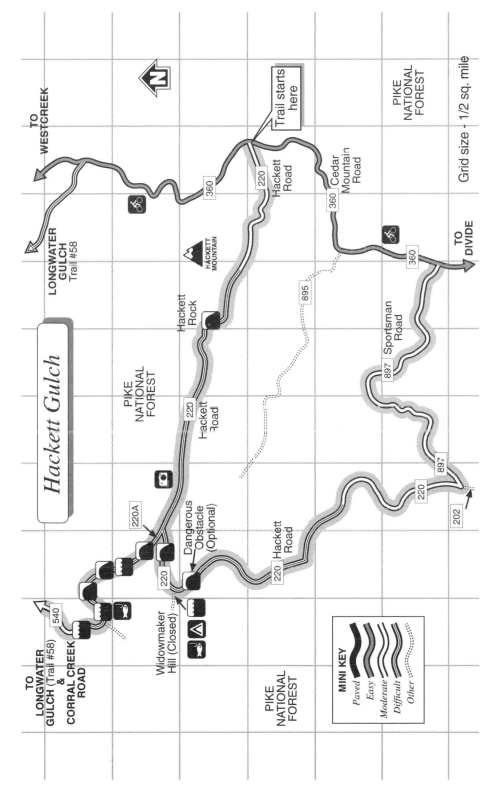

Hackett Gulch

TO WESTCREEK

TO LONGWATER GULCH (Trail #58) & CORRAL CREEK ROAD

LONGWATER GULCH Trail #58

Trail starts here

Hackett Mountain

Hackett Rock

360

220

Hackett Road

Cedar Mountain Road

360

895

PIKE NATIONAL FOREST

220 Hackett Road

Sportsman Road

897

897

TO DIVIDE

360

220

202

220A

Dangerous Obstacle (Optional)

220

220 Hackett Road

540

Widowmaker Hill (Closed)

PIKE NATIONAL FOREST

PIKE NATIONAL FOREST

Grid size - 1/2 sq. mile

MINI KEY
Paved
Easy
Moderate
Difficult
Other

217

To reach Rampart Range Road you pass through beautiful Garden of the Gods Park.

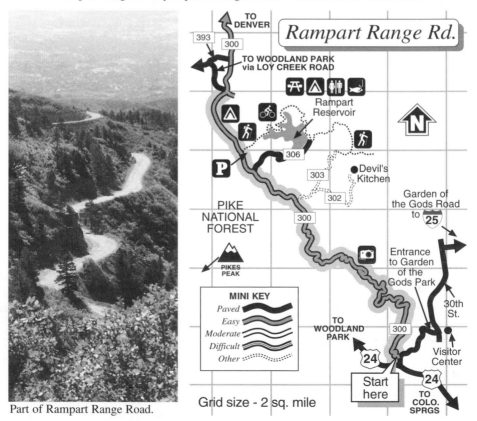

Part of Rampart Range Road.

Rampart Range Rd.

TO DENVER

393 300

TO WOODLAND PARK
via LOY CREEK ROAD

Rampart Reservoir

N

306

P

303

302

Devil's Kitchen

PIKE NATIONAL FOREST

300

Garden of the Gods Road to 25

Entrance to Garden of the Gods Park

30th St.

PIKES PEAK

MINI KEY
Paved
Easy
Moderate
Difficult
Other

TO WOODLAND PARK

300

Visitor Center

24

Start here

24

TO COLO. SPRGS

Grid size - 2 sq. mile

Rampart Range Road 60

Location: Only the southern end of Rampart Range Road is described here. It is located between Colorado Springs and Woodland Park.

Difficulty: Easy. High ground clearance recommended. Four-wheel drive might be needed in wet weather.

Features: The trail starts in Garden of the Gods Park and climbs to Rampart Reservoir where you find great hiking, mountain biking, camping, boating, and fishing. Views are breathtaking at every turn.

Time & Distance: About 21 miles from the start to the turn-off for Woodland Park. Allow at least 1 1/2 hours driving time one way.

To Get There: Exit I-25 at Garden of the Gods Road (Exit 146) and head west 2.2 miles to 30th Street. Turn left and drive 1.5 miles to the entrance to the park across from the Visitors Center. Turn right into the park and continue to make right turns following signs to Balanced Rock. Rampart Range Road 300 is just north of the parking area for Balanced Rock.

Trail Description: Set your odometer to zero as you start up Rampart Range Road. The main road is obvious all the way. The first couple of miles wind through the park on a rocky road with great views of Pikes Peak and the front range below. You pass a shooting range at 5.7 miles as the trail gradually becomes more forested. There are two great overlooks at 11.4 and 11.7 miles. An interesting and easy side road goes right at 14.8 miles. It splits into F.S. 302 and 303, both easy. At 16.9 miles paved road 306 to Rampart Reservoir goes to the right. This is a popular maintained area with many places to picnic and camp. At 18.4 miles a great hiking and mountain biking trail goes to the right. After passing a F.S. campground at 20 miles, you reach a four-way intersection at 20.7 miles.

Return Trip: Bear left at the four-way intersection and left again as paved roads take you into Woodland Park and Route 24 back to Colorado Springs. Continuing north on F.S. 300 would eventually take you to Denver.

Services: Full services in Colorado Springs and Woodland Park.

Maps: Pike National Forest, Trails Illustrated Pikes Peak, Canon City #137, Colorado Atlas and Gazetteer.

Looking down on Colorado Springs from near the top of Mt. Baldy.

Water crossings are shallow but add a little fun to the trip.

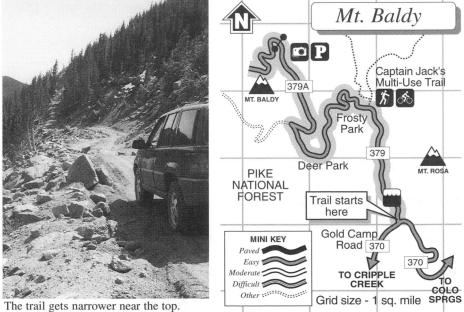

The trail gets narrower near the top.

Mt. Baldy

N

MT. BALDY

379A

Captain Jack's
Multi-Use Trail

Frosty
Park

379

MT. ROSA

Deer Park

PIKE
NATIONAL
FOREST

Trail starts
here

Gold Camp
Road 370

MINI KEY

Paved
Easy
Moderate
Difficult
Other

**TO CRIPPLE
CREEK**

370

**TO
COLO
SPRGS**

Grid size - 1 sq. mile

220

Location: Southwest of Colorado Springs.

Difficulty: Moderate. High ground clearance and four-wheel drive required.

Features: An out-of-the-way alternative to Pikes Peak offering similar views and more challenge.

Time & Distance: About 7 miles from the start to the top of Mt. Baldy. Allow at least an hour each way. Microwave towers mark the summit.

To Get There: From Colorado Springs, take Nevada Avenue south from I-25 to Lake Avenue. Head west on Lake to the Broadmoor Hotel. Swing to the right and then left around the back of the hotel. Bear left at Penrose Boulevard and within 0.5 miles turn right on Old Stage Road. This road climbs quickly through a residential area and provides some outstanding views. At about 7 miles Gold Camp Road joins Old Stage Road. From this intersection, go 5.7 miles and watch for the trail on the right. The trail is fenced on each side at the beginning as it passes through private property.

Trail Description: Set your odometer to zero at the start. This single-lane trail offers a variety of terrain, including moguls, rocks, and small stream crossings. At 1.7 miles the very popular Captain Jack's Multi-Use Trail departs on the right. At 2.3 you reach a sharp switchback to the left. Stay on the main part of the road. After passing through several meadows, watch for a sharp switchback up the hill to the right at 4.4 miles. The trail, marked as F.S. 379A, winds back to the east side of the mountain with great views of the front range. It is fairly narrow in places. Conditions can vary depending upon how recently the road was maintained. At 6.1 there is a wider area where you can pull over and park. Just around the corner is a large gate that is sometimes open. If it is open, you can go another mile or so to the top of the mountain. Bear to the left at a fork after the gate. The road is very narrow at the top. Do not proceed if snow is on the trail.

Return Trip: Return the way you came.

Services: Full services in Colorado Springs.

Maps: The Pike National Forest map is the only map which adequately shows this trail. It is only partially shown on the Trails Illustrated map #137.

Scenes like this are common along Phantom Canyon Road.

Shelf Road is narrower and less traveled than Phantom Canyon Road.

Phantom Canyon, Shelf Rd.

Location: Between Cripple Creek and Canon City.

Difficulty: Easy. The road surface of Phantom Canyon Road is well graded and suitable for passenger cars. However, vehicles longer than 25 feet, motorhomes, and trailers are not allowed. Shelf Road can be driven without four-wheel drive when dry, but because it is rougher and narrower than Phantom Canyon, you will feel more comfortable if four-wheel drive is available. Some places can get a little slippery in wet weather.

Features: This loop trail is part of the National Gold Belt Tour and offers some of the most beautiful scenery in Colorado. Shelf Road starts just a block south of Cripple Creek. The drive provides a nice getaway or an alternative to gambling in the casinos. Phantom Canyon is the easier of the two roads, but also has more tourist traffic. Generally Phantom Canyon is open all year except after a snowstorm.

Time & Distance: The entire loop is about 66 miles. Allow about 4 to 5 hours total driving time. From Cripple Creek to Canon City on the Shelf Road side is about 26 miles. Phantom Canyon Road is about 30 miles from Route 50 to Victor.

To Get There: To get to Cripple Creek take Route 24 west from Colorado Springs to Divide. Turn left at Divide and follow 67 all the way to Cripple Creek. Drive through the center of town to the bottom of the hill and turn left on Second Street, following signs to Victor. Drive 0.3 miles south and watch for County Road 88 on the right. If you prefer to drive Phantom Canyon Road only, continue following 67 to Victor. Phantom Canyon heads south east of Victor. The south end of Phantom Canyon Road starts from Route 67 about 32 miles west of Pueblo on U.S. 50.

Trail Description: Assuming you are driving the route as described here, set your odometer to zero at the start of the trail as shown on the map. **Shelf Road** is not too impressive at the beginning and is one reason why it is less traveled. The scenery improves quickly as the road follows Cripple Creek down a pretty valley. Many old mines dot the hillsides. Watch for a rock formation with a hole in the middle called Window Rock. After 9 miles the road becomes more narrow and steep. Nervous drivers may feel a little uncomfortable through this section. Look ahead as much as possible to avoid having to back up if passing is necessary. At 9.3 miles the road changes from Teller County 88 to Fremont County 9. The tough section ends at 13 miles as you reach a point where a road goes to the right. Bear left. Just after this point Sand Gulch Campground is on the right. You must pass through a gate to reach the campgrounds. Route 9 becomes paved at 15.3 miles. There is an overlook with a couple of picnic tables at 19.6. As you near Canon City bear left at 22.7 following Field Avenue. Turn left on Pear Street at a stop sign at 24.9 miles, then make an immediate right on North Reynolds which will take you to Route 50. Gold Belt Tour signs indicate that you should cross over 50 into the town of Florence. You may go this way or take a more direct route to Phantom Canyon by turning left at 50 and driving about 5 miles to Route 67.

Reset your odometer at the beginning of **Phantom Canyon** when you turn off Route 50. The first 4 miles are paved before the road turns to washboard gravel. Soon you enter the canyon marked by a prominent Gold Belt Tour sign. Several tunnels follow and at 12.4 miles you cross an old railroad bridge. (Note: This bridge is scheduled to be replaced soon. In addition, a couple of new public toilets will be built.) The most dramatic part of the canyon is very narrow. Use caution and drive slowly around the many blind curves. At 22.8 signs indicate the other end of the Gold Belt Tour. Route 67 changes to 86 when passing into Teller County. Route 861 joins 86 before reaching County Road 81 at Victor. Turn left for Route 67 back to Cripple Creek.

Other Activities: Both of these roads are suitable for mountain biking. Rock climbers will enjoy the challenge of the "The Banks" Climbing Area located 13 miles south of Cripple Creek. Picnic and camp at several places along the way. There are many tourist attractions in the area, including gambling in Cripple Creek.

Services: Full services in Cripple Creek and Canon City.

Maps: Trails Illustrated Pikes Peak, Canon City #137, Colorado Atlas and Gazetteer. Stop by your local Forest Service Office or Bureau of Land Management office and pick up a full-color flyer for this route entitled "The Gold Belt Tour - A Back Country Byway.

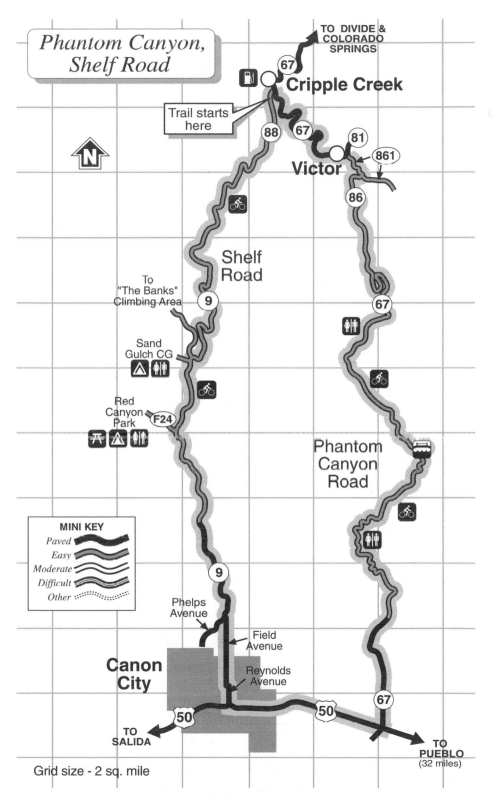

Phantom Canyon, Shelf Road

N

TO DIVIDE &
COLORADO SPRINGS

67

Cripple Creek

Trail starts here

88 67 81

861

Victor

86

Shelf Road

67

To "The Banks" Climbing Area

9

Sand Gulch CG

Red Canyon Park

F24

Phantom Canyon Road

MINI KEY

Paved
Easy
Moderate
Difficult
Other

9

Phelps Avenue

Field Avenue

Canon City

Reynolds Avenue

67

50

50

TO SALIDA

TO PUEBLO (32 miles)

Grid size - 2 sq. mile

225

AREA 7

63. Hayden Pass
64. Medano Pass
65. Blanca Peak

Sangre De Cristo
Mountain Range

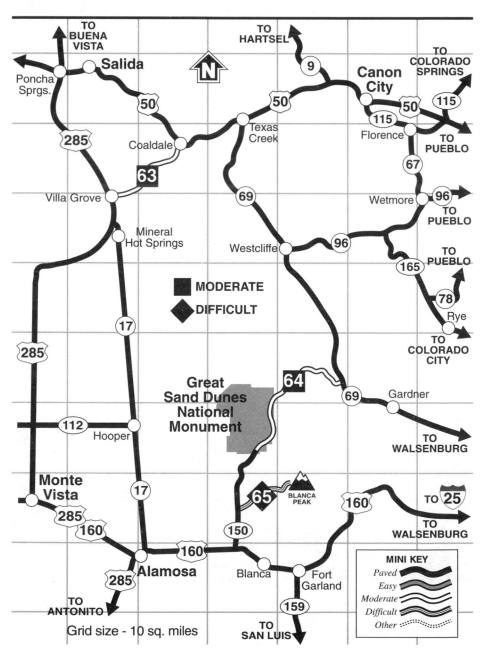

Grid size - 10 sq. miles

Sangre De Cristo Mountain Range

The Sangre De Cristo Mountain Range forms a majestic, 80-mile long sky-line between Salida and Fort Garland. The linear nature of this mountain range means that these trails do not connect. Hayden Pass (Trail #63) is entirely by itself. Medano Pass (Trail #64) and Blanca Peak (Trail #65) can be driven sequentially but not in one day. Driving distance to these trails from Denver and Colorado Springs is considerable, but the uniqueness of the trails is well worth the time. Hayden Pass is one of the best kept secrets in Colorado and provides just the right amount of challenge for modern sport utility vehicles. Medano Pass takes you through the back door of the Great Sand Dunes National Monument. You will not believe the towering mountains of sand that Mother Nature has deposited in middle of Colorado. The crown jewel of this area is Blanca Peak. It has some of the most challenging obstacles of any in America and draws hard-core four-wheelers from all over the world. The ultimate portfolio of four-wheel adventures is not complete without Blanca Peak.

The San Luis Valley is the backdrop for Blanca Peak (Trail #65).

227

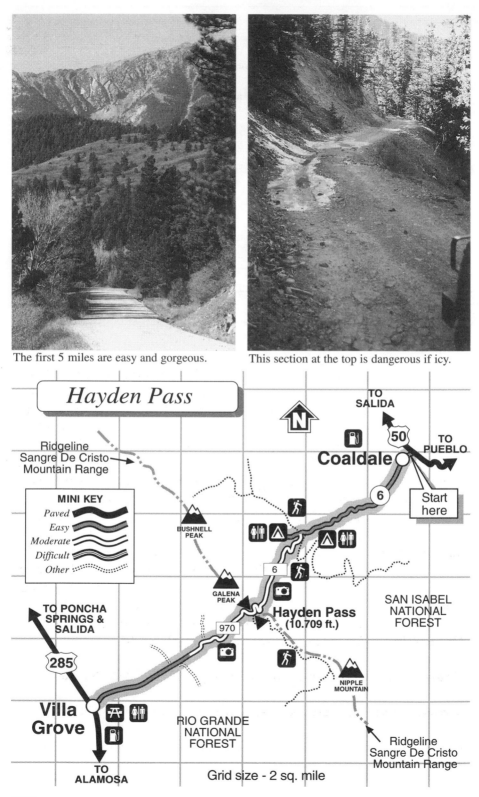

The first 5 miles are easy and gorgeous.

This section at the top is dangerous if icy.

Hayden Pass

TO SALIDA

TO PUEBLO

50

Coaldale

6

Start here

Ridgeline
Sangre De Cristo
Mountain Range

N

MINI KEY
Paved
Easy
Moderate
Difficult
Other

BUSHNELL
PEAK

GALENA
PEAK

6

Hayden Pass
(10.709 ft.)

SAN ISABEL
NATIONAL
FOREST

TO PONCHA
SPRINGS &
SALIDA

970

NIPPLE
MOUNTAIN

285

Villa Grove

RIO GRANDE
NATIONAL
FOREST

Ridgeline
Sangre De Cristo
Mountain Range

TO
ALAMOSA

Grid size - 2 sq. mile

Hayden Pass 63

Location: Between Coaldale and Villa Grove. Southeast of Salida.

Difficulty: Moderate. This rating applies to just the upper portion of the trail. The lower portions are easy. Travel only when dry and in the summer. During the spring and fall underground springs flow across the road, creating dangerous patches of ice on the narrowest part of the trail.

Features: A gorgeous drive with just enough challenge to make it fun. Two nice Forest Service campgrounds with hiking trails on the north side.

Time & Distance: About 16.5 miles from Coaldale to Villa Grove. Allow about two hours driving time one way.

To Get There: Take Route 50 west from Pueblo or south from Salida. Turn south at Coaldale.

Trail Description: Set your odometer to zero as you turn off Route 50. An easy road takes you to the Coaldale Campground at 3.6 miles, followed by the Hayden Campground at 5.1 miles. The four-wheel drive part of the trail goes up the hill to the left of the Hayden Campground. The trail is marked as F.S. Road 6. The trail is rocky and steep in spots so shift into low range at the start. Careful tire placement may be necessary in a few places. Use a spotter if necessary. As you climb, beautiful vistas appear to the north. At 8.8 miles the road becomes a fairly narrow ledge. Underground springs keep this part of the trail wet, and in the fall and spring it may be icy. This section is very dangerous if icy so turn around if any ice is present. *(Note: In late November of 1995, a Jeep slid off this portion of the trail and the driver was killed.)* You reach the top of the pass at 9.6 miles and the trail number changes to 970. The descent down the other side is easier with only an occasional stretch of loose shale. As you come out of the trees, the road swings to the right then drops to the valley below. Follow the main road to Villa Grove at 16.5 miles. There is a small rest area at U.S. 285.

Return Trip: Return the way you came or go right on 285 to Salida.

Services: Gas at Coaldale and Villa Grove. Full services in Salida.

Maps: San Isabel National Forest, Rio Grande National Forest, Colorado Atlas & Gazetteer.

Entering the the Great Sand Dunes National Monument from the north side.

Much of the trail is fairly easy.

Skiing the dunes. No snow required.

One of many water crossings. Some can be quite deep in the Spring.

Location: Between Westcliffe and the the Great Sand Dunes National Monument. Southwest of Pueblo.

Difficulty: Moderate. Most of the trail is easy except for a few rocky places that give it a moderate rating. It can be difficult to impassable during the spring because water crossings are deep. It is best to drive this trail later in the summer when it has had a chance to dry out.

Features: The trail crosses open pastures, streams, dense woods, and rocky hills, and ends with a roller coaster ride winding through the sandy lowlands of the Great Sand Dunes National Monument. Medano Pass forms a unique gateway through which wind currents carry and deposit their sandy payload to form the massive dunes of the Monument.

Time & Distance: About 20 miles from Route 69, to the Monument. Allow 2 to 3 hours depending upon conditions.

To Get There: From Pueblo take route 96 west to Westcliffe. Turn south on 69 and go 23.7 miles to road 559 on the right. From Colorado Springs take 115 south to Florence, 67 to Wetmore, 96 to Westcliffe, and 69 to route 559 as described above. To start on the south end of the trail take U.S. 160 west from Walsenburg and 150 north to the Great Sand Dunes National Monument.

Trail Description: After leaving paved route 69, follow dirt road 559 which winds its way through beautiful pasture land framed by the Sangre De Cristo Mountains. At 7 miles you reach the entrance to the San Isabel National Forest marked by a cattle guard and a white arrow sign. Reset your trip odometer. Bear left at 0.5 miles staying on 559. Notice places to camp along the way. At 1 mile you'll need four-wheel drive for a steep rocky section. Pick a path that keeps the wheels on the ground as much as possible. At 2.4 miles there is a gate with a sign to Medano Pass marked as F.S. 235.

The trail then passes through a beautiful scenic valley followed by some fun moguls and a few small mud holes. At 4 miles there is a clearing with a larger mud bog. You should have no trouble if you stay on the main part of the trail. After this section there are more stream crossings as you wind in and out of the woods. It gets narrow in places but still quite passable, although fallen trees could be a problem in the spring.

At 8.5 miles you reach the gated rear entrance to the park. Normally this gate is open but it is probably best to check with the National Park Service to make sure before embarking on your trip. You do not pay a fee when you enter through the back gate, but if you leave through the front gate, payment will be expected. As you approach the Monument, the road becomes more sandy. As the sand dunes come into view, you will be surprised by their size if you haven't seen them before. At 11.2 there is a picnic area directly below a large dune. This area is extremely popular for, believe it or not, sand skiing. For those hardy enough to climb to the top of these huge dunes, an exciting time awaits. I am told the sand is like skiing on heavy granulated wet snow.

Beyond this point the road becomes much more sandy and quite soft. It might be necessary to let some air out of your tires to avoid getting stuck. Otherwise, try to maintain a smooth even pace without stopping. This part of the trail is really fun as it twists back and forth amid a series of banked curves. At 13.4 miles you get back to pavement again inside the park. There is camping and more picnicking in this area. Make sure you stop at the Visitors Center which is to the right. It explains the natural conditions that formed the park. The front gate is a short distance south of the Visitors Center.

Return Trip: You can return the way you came or take Route 150 south to U.S. 160. Head east on 160 to I-25 at Walsenburg.

Services: There is gas, food, and air available just south of the main gate. Full services at Westcliffe, Alamosa, and Walsenburg. There are public restrooms with water at the Visitors Center.

Other Activities: A nice hiking trail leads to Medano Lake a little south of Medano Pass, and another trail over Mosca Pass departs from within the park opposite the picnic area closest to the Visitors Center. Mosca Pass was once a four-wheel drive trail but is now used only for hiking. Camping is allowed in most areas of the National Forest unless posted otherwise. You can also camp in the Sand Dunes Monument but you will need a permit.

Maps: San Isabel National Forest, Rio Grande National Forest, Colorado Atlas & Gazetteer.

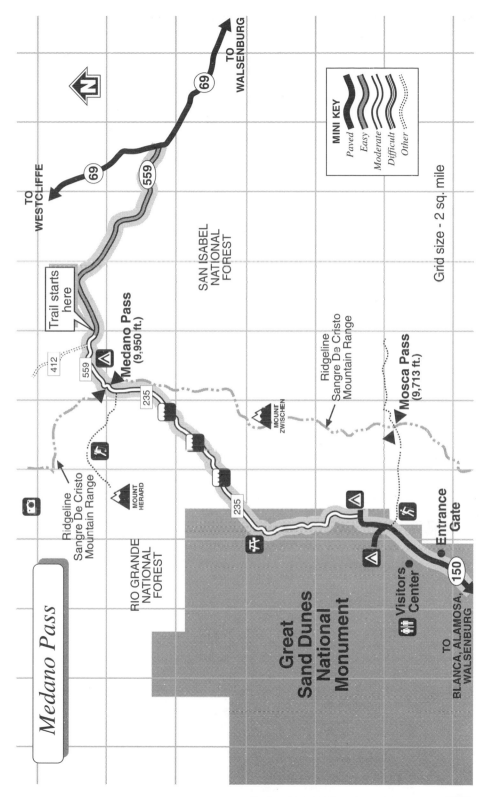

Medano Pass

TO WESTCLIFFE

TO WALSENBURG

69

69

559

Trail starts here

412

559

Medano Pass
(9,950 ft.)

235

MINI KEY
Paved
Easy
Moderate
Difficult
Other

Grid size - 2 sq. mile

SAN ISABEL NATIONAL FOREST

Ridgeline Sangre De Cristo Mountain Range

Mosca Pass
(9,713 ft.)

235

MOUNT ZWISCHEN

Ridgeline Sangre De Cristo Mountain Range

MOUNT HERARD

RIO GRANDE NATIONAL FOREST

Great Sand Dunes National Monument

Visitors Center

Entrance Gate

150

TO BLANCA, ALAMOSA, WALSENBURG

Jaws 1 usually requires several attempts to determine the correct line.

Jaws 2 is the most dangerous obstacle. Stay close to the uphill side to avoid a rollover.

Jaws 3 is the most difficult obstacle.

Como Lake near the end of the trail.

Location: West of Walsenburg. South of the Great Sand Dunes National Monument.

Difficulty: Difficult. The hardest trail in this book. There are numerous challenging obstacles requiring high ground clearance, differential lockers and/or a winch. This trail is for experienced drivers only and should never be driven alone.

Special Note: A battle has raged for years to keep this trail open for four-wheel use. The trail is very popular for hiking. Please be responsible by showing courtesy to all hikers and never straying from the trail. Use low impact driving techniques at all times. There is a controversial portion of the trail above Como Lake that is sometimes open and sometimes closed depending upon the latest ruling by the Forest Service. To avoid conflict which could possibly close the entire trail, I recommend you stay off the upper portion.

Features: This trail is nationally known as perhaps the best hard-core trail in Colorado. The trail has many challenging obstacles that test the most experienced drivers and best equipment. You are rewarded at the upper end of the trip with a serene high mountain lake that has great camping and fishing. Bring along some insect repellent.

Time & Distance: It is about 8 miles from paved highway 150 to Como Lake. You must start early to complete the round trip in one day. With a later start plan to camp overnight at the lake. Prepare for a cold night because the elevation at the lake is around 11,000 feet.

To Get There: Take Interstate 25 to Walsenburg and U.S. 160 west. Past the small town of Blanca, head north on route 150 for 3.3 miles and turn right on dirt road 975. A fun alternate route is to drive Medano Pass (Trail #64) into the Great Sand Dunes National Monument and take 150 south to 975.

Trail Description: Set your odometer to zero as you turn off paved road 150. There is plenty of space to park and camp along the side of the road at the beginning of 975, although camping conditions are not ideal. The landscape is quite barren and desert-like. You can park a trailer here if you've towed your rig. You cross several miles of flatland before you begin to climb a progressively rocky road. At 3.5 miles the climb becomes steeper as impressive views of the vast San Luis Valley can be seen to the west. The difficulty increases quickly as you climb up several narrow steep shelf roads. At 5.3 miles you pass through several water holes that can be deep after a period of heavy rain. Jaws 1 (a.k.a. "Finger Rock") is encountered at 5.9 miles. You may have to try several different times to find the right line for your vehicle.

You cross a shallow stream before reaching Jaws 2 (a.k.a. "Jeep Rock") at 6.5 miles. Hug the right side as tight as possible. The rock tends to slide and tilt you to the left. Many roll overs have occurred at this point, so attach a safety winch line if necessary. If you have a large group of vehicles, plan on spending an hour or two getting across this obstacle. There are several more tough spots before reaching Jaws 3 (a.k.a. "The Wall") at 6.9 miles. There is no easy way to get across this obstacle and vehicle damage is common. Fortunately, there is a bypass around the right side. After this obstacle you cross through a steep walled valley of talus before dropping down into a wooded section. Finally Como Lake appears at 7.6 miles. You can camp at various places around the lake. Much of the land around the lake is soft and muddy. Do not drive in these areas under any circumstances. Prior damage by irresponsible drivers is one of the main reasons this trail is in danger of being closed.

Return Trip: Return the way you came. Allow extra time since you may have to wait for any group coming uphill. The bottleneck usually occurs around Jaws 2. This obstacle requires even more caution going downhill.

Services: There is a gas station just south of the Great Sand Dunes National Monument. Full services in Blanca, Fort Garland, and Walsenburg.

Other Activities: This is a very popular hiking and backpacking area. You can hike beyond Como Lake all the way to Blanca Peak. Pack a fishing pole if you like to fish.

Maps: Rio Grande National Forest, Colorado Atlas and Gazetteer.

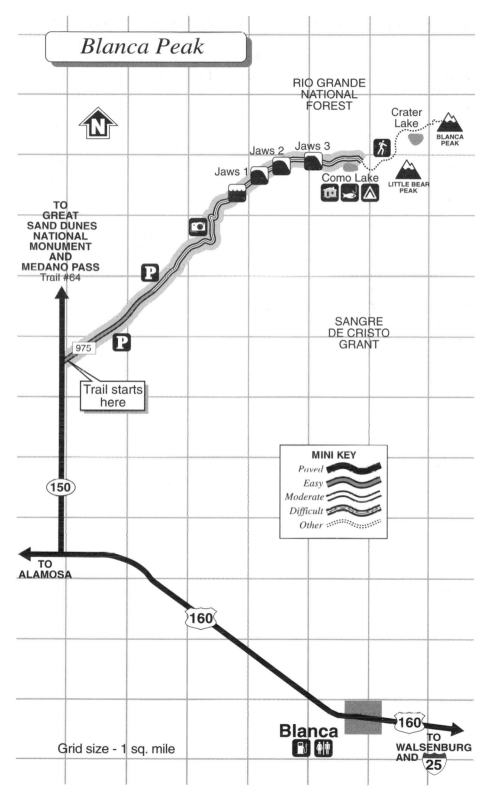

Blanca Peak

RIO GRANDE NATIONAL FOREST

SANGRE DE CRISTO GRANT

Crater Lake

BLANCA PEAK

LITTLE BEAR PEAK

Jaws 2   Jaws 3

Jaws 1

Como Lake

TO GREAT SAND DUNES NATIONAL MONUMENT AND MEDANO PASS
Trail #64

975

Trail starts here

150

TO ALAMOSA

160

MINI KEY

Paved
Easy
Moderate
Difficult
Other

Blanca

160

TO WALSENBURG AND 25

Grid size - 1 sq. mile

This falls at the wooden bridge on Schofield Pass can be reached over moderate terrain.

APPENDIX

Kebler Pass, Trail #21, Easy.

Glossary

Airing down - Letting air out of your tires to improve traction.

ARB lockers - A brand of differential locker that can be quickly activated when needed but turned off when not in use. (See differential locker.)

Articulation - The flexibility of your suspension system. Greater articulation means your wheels will go up and down more to better accommodate ground undulation.

BLM - Bureau of Land Management.

Boulder fields - Challenging stretches of rocky terrain.

C.G. - Campground.

Clevis - A U-shaped device with a pin at one end that is used to connect tow straps.

Come-along - A hand-operated ratchet that functions as a winch.

Corduroy road - Roadbed formed with split logs laying flat-side up.

Differential locker - Optional gearing installed inside your differential that equalizes power to wheels on both sides of an axle. Eliminates loss of power when climbing steep undulating hills. Not the same as locking-in your hubs.

F.S. - Forest Service.

Hard-core - The most challenging level of four-wheeling.

High centered - When your undercarriage gets stuck on a rock, mound, log, or ridge. Usually requires you to jack up your vehicle to get free.

High lift jack - A tool that allows you to quickly lift your vehicle high off the ground. Considered a necessity on hard-core trails. Also substitutes for a winch.

Lift - A vehicle modification that raises the suspension or body of a vehicle to provide greater ground clearance.

Locker - (See differential locker.)

Low range - A second range of gears that increases the power of your vehicle. Used for climbing steep grades, especially at higher altitude.

Marmot - A bushy-tailed, stocky rodent native to high mountain terrain. Makes a distinctive high-pitch chirping sound. Nicknamed " Whistle Pigs."

Moguls - Large bumps which form on steep hills.

Off-camber - The sideways lean of a vehicle away from a slope.

Scree - Loose fragmented rock formed by freezing and thawing above timberline.

Shelf road - A narrow road cut into a mountainside.

Skid plates - Plates that protect vulnerable parts of your undercarriage.

Snatch block - A pulley that opens so it can be slipped over your winch cable.

Spur road - A side road that is usually narrower and rougher than the main road.

SUV - Sport Utility Vehicle.

Switchback - A zig-zag road for climbing a steep grade.

Talus - (See Scree.)

Timberline - The point on a mountainside where trees stop growing. In Colorado about 11,000 ft.

Tow point, tow hook - A point on your vehicle that enables you to quickly and safely attach a tow strap. Considered a basic necessity for four wheeling.

Tow strap - A heavy-duty nylon strap used to pull vehicles when stuck.

Tree strap - A short tow strap that is used to wrap around trees and large rocks.

References & Reading

Adventures of the Pass Patrol, by Larry E. Heck, Pass Patrol, Inc., Aurora, CO. Guidebooks with maps, photos, and lighthearted stories of mostly hard-core trail adventures. Several volumes cover Colorado. (1987-1995)

Back Roads of the San Juan Mountains, by Backcountry Travelers, Inc., Durango, CO. Pocket sized guides of the Ouray area covering routes in great detail. Two versions cover the Alpine Loop and the Ophir/Imogene Loop.

Central Colorado 4-Wheeling, by Wayne W. Griffin, Who Press, Aspen, CO. Guidebook with maps and photos covering Aspen, Vail, Leadville, and Crested Butte. (1994)

(The) Colorado Pass Book, , by Don Koch, Pruett Publishing Company, Boulder, CO. Illustrated guide to Colorado passroads with in-depth historical analysis. Large, quality photographs. (Revised 1992)

Jeep Trails to Colorado Ghost Towns, by Robert L. Brown, Caxton Printers, Ltd. Caldwell, ID. Historical descriptions of Colorado ghost towns accessible by 4-wheel drive. Photos compare yesteryear to present. (Revised 1995)

Guide to Safe, Common Sense Off-Road Driving, by Mark A. Smith, Mark A. Smith Off-Roading, Inc., Georgetown, CA. A small 52 page illustrated booklet with off-road driving tips. (1991)

Mountain Mysteries-The Ouray Odyssey, by Marvin Gregory and P. David Smith, Wayfinder Press, Ridgway, CO. A detailed history of the Ouray area with photos and illustrations. (1992)

Scenic Driving Colorado, by Stewart Green, Falcon Press Publishing Co., Inc., Helena & Billings, MT. Scenic drives for passenger cars with maps and photos. (1994)

Tread Lightly! Guide to Responsible Four Wheeling, Published by Tread Lightly!, Inc. Ogden, UT. Illustrated guide featuring minimum impact four-wheel drive techniques and safety tips. (1997)

4 x 4 Trail Books, by the Colorado Association of 4 Wheel Drive Clubs, Inc. Wheatridge, CO. A series of four guidebooks with maps and descriptions covering primarily hard-core trails of Colorado. (1989-1996)

4-Wheel Freedom: The Art of Off-Road Driving, by Brad Delong, Paladin Press, Boulder, CO. An in-depth illustrated analysis of all aspects of four-wheeling. (1996)

Addresses & Phone Numbers

Bureau of Land Management Offices (Selected Locations):

Arkansas Headwaters Recreation Area
307 West Sackett
P.O. Box 126
Salida CO 81201
(719) 539-7289

Canon City District Office
3170 East Main Street
Canon City, CO 81212
(719) 269-8500

Colorado State Office
2850 Youngfield Street
Lakewood, CO 80215
(303) 239-3600

Glenwood Springs Resource Area
50629 Highways 6 & 24
P.O. Box 1009
Glenwood Springs, CO 81602
(970) 947-2800

Gunnison Resource Area
216 North Colorado
Gunnison, CO 81230
(970) 641-0471

Montrose District Office
2465 South Townsend
Montrose, CO 81401
(970) 240-5300

San Juan Resource Area
Federal Building
701 Camino del Rio
Durango, CO 81301
(970) 247-4082

San Luis Valley North Area
46525 Hwy 114
P.O. Box 67
Saguache, CO 81149
(719) 655-2547

San Luis Valley South Area
1921 State Street
Alamosa, CO 81101
(719) 589-4975

Chambers of Commerce:

Aspen	(970) 925-1940
Breckenridge	(970) 453-6018
Buena Vista	(719) 395-6612
Colorado Springs	(719) 635-1551
Crested Butte	(970) 349-6438
Cripple Creek	(719) 689-2169
Denver West	(303) 233-5555
Gunnison County	(970) 641-1501
Idaho Springs	(303)567-4382
Lake City	(970) 944-2577
Leadville	(719) 486-3900
Ouray County	(970) 325-4746
Paonia	(970) 527-3886
Pueblo	(719) 542-1704
Salida	(719) 539-2068
Silverton	(970) 387-5654
Summit County	(970) 668-5800
Telluride	(970) 728-3041
Vail	(970) 476-1000
Woodland Park	(719) 687-9885

Colorado State Parks:

Colorado State Parks
1313 Sherman Street
Room 618
Denver, CO 80203
(303) 866-3437

Four Wheel Drive Organizations & Support Groups:

BlueRibbon Coalition
1540 North Arthur
Pocatello, ID 83204
(208) 233-6570

Colorado Association of 4 Wheel Drive Clubs, Inc.
P.O.Box 1413
Wheat Ridge, CO 80034
(303) 343-0646

Tread Lightly!, Inc.
298 24th Street
Suite 325
Ogden, UT 84401
(801) 627-0077
or (800) 966-9900

United Four Wheel Drive Associations
4505 W. 700 S.
Shelbyville, IN 46176
1 (800) 448-3932

National Forest Service Ranger Districts (Selected Locations):

Aspen Ranger District
806 West Hallam
Aspen, CO 81611
(970) 925-3445

Clear Creek Ranger District
101 Chicago Creek, Box 3307
Idaho Springs, CO. 80452
(303) 567-2901

Dillon Ranger District
680 Blue River Parkway,
Box 620
Silverthorne, CO 80498
(970) 468-5400

Eagle Ranger District
125 West 5th Street, Box 720
Eagle, CO 81631
(970) 328- 6388

Holy Cross Ranger District
24747 US Highway 24,
Box 190
Minturn, CO 81645
(970) 827-5715

Leadville Ranger District
2015 Poplar
Leadville, CO 80461
(719) 486- 0749

Ouray Ranger District
2505 South Townsend
Montrose, CO 81401
(970) 240-5300

Paonia Ranger District
N. Rio Grande Avenue
P.O. Box 1030
Paonia, CO 81428
(970) 527-4131

Pikes Peak Ranger District
601 South Weber Street
Colorado Springs, CO 80903
(719) 636-1602

Pike/San Isabel National Forests
1920 Valley Drive
Pueblo, CO 81008
(719) 545-8737

Salida Ranger District
325 West Rainbow Blvd.
Salida, CO 81201
(719) 539-3591

San Carlos Ranger District
3170 East Main
Canon City, CO 81212
(719) 269-8500

**San Juan/Rio Grande
National Forests**
1803 West Highway 160
Monte Vista, CO 81144
(719) 852-5941

Sopris Ranger District
620 Main Street, Box 309
Carbondale, CO 81623
(970) 963-2266

South Park Ranger District
320 Highway 285, Box 219
Fairplay, CO 80440
(719) 836-2031

South Platte Ranger District
19316 Goddard Ranch Court
Morrison, CO 80465
(303) 275-5610

**Taylor River/Cebolla
Ranger District**
216 North Colorado
Gunnison, CO 81230
(970) 641-0471

National Parks (Selected Locations):

**Black Canyon of the Gunnison
National Monument**
102 Elk Creek
Gunnison, CO 81230
(970) 641-2337

**Curecanti National
Recreation Area**
102 Elk Creek
Gunnison, CO 81230
(970) 641-2337

**Florissant Fossil Beds
National Monument**
P.O. Box 185
Florissant, CO 80816

**Great Sand Dunes
National Monument**
11999 Highway 150
Mosca, CO 81146-9798
(719) 378-2312

Nationwide N.F. Camping Reservation Number:
1-800-280-2267

Index

About the Author

Charles A. Wells graduated from Ohio State University in 1969 with a degree in graphic design. After practicing design in Ohio, he moved to Colorado Springs in 1980 and now is a print production manager. He and his wife, Beverly, raised two children who have graduated from Colorado universities. Over the years, he and his family have enjoyed a wide array of recreational activities including hiking, biking, rafting, and skiing. This exposure to the Colorado backcountry led to his interest in four-wheeling in recent years. He became frustrated when he could not find a clear, simple backroad guide to Colorado; so he decided to write his own.

All of the trails in this book were driven by the author in the vehicles described below. He wrote the trail descriptions based on his own observations, shot all the photographs, and created all the maps. No sponsors were involved. The result of this hands-on approach is a valuable and unbiased reference for both novices and hard-core four-wheeling enthusiasts.

Author with Jeep Grand Cherokee at Engineer Pass. Equipped with automatic transmission, factory skid plates, tow points, all-terrain tires, and CB radio.

Jeep is a registered trademark of Chrysler Corporation.

Jeep Cherokee at Black Bear. Equipped with Tomken 5 1/2" lift, bumpers, rocker skids, tire carrier, and brush guard; 8,000 lb. Warn winch mounts front & rear; Dana 44 rear axle; 410 gears; ARBs front & rear; skid plates; stock 4-liter engine with 5-speed; K&N air filter; full interior roll cage; 32 x 11.50 BFG A/T tires; Optima battery; tow points; fold-in mirrors; and CB radio.

NOTES

NOTES

NOTES

NOTES